MW01055056

TSI

Assessment

SECRETS

Study Guide
Your Key to Exam Success

TSI Assessment Review for the
Texas Success Initiative Diagnostic
and Placement Tests

Published by
Mometrix Test Preparation
TSI Exam Secrets Test Prep Team

Written and edited by the TSI Exam Secrets Test Prep Staff

Printed in the United States of America

This paper meets the requirements of ANSI/NISO Z39.48-1992 (Permanence of Paper).

Mometrix offers volume discount pricing to institutions. For more information or a price quote, please contact our sales department at sales@mometrix.com or 888-248-1219.

ISBN 978-1-5167-0539-9

Dear Future Exam Success Story:

Congratulations on your purchase of our study guide. Our goal in writing our study guide was to cover the content on the test, as well as provide insight into typical test taking mistakes and how to overcome them.

Standardized tests are a key component of being successful, which only increases the importance of doing well in the high-pressure high-stakes environment of test day. How well you do on this test will have a significant impact on your future, and we have the research and practical advice to help you execute on test day.

The product you're reading now is designed to exploit weaknesses in the test itself, and help you avoid the most common errors test takers frequently make.

How to use this study guide

We don't want to waste your time. Our study guide is fast-paced and fluff-free. We suggest going through it a number of times, as repetition is an important part of learning new information and concepts.

First, read through the study guide completely to get a feel for the content and organization. Read the general success strategies first, and then proceed to the content sections. Each tip has been carefully selected for its effectiveness.

Second, read through the study guide again, and take notes in the margins and highlight those sections where you may have a particular weakness.

Finally, bring the manual with you on test day and study it before the exam begins.

Your success is our success

We would be delighted to hear about your success. Send us an email and tell us your story. Thanks for your business and we wish you continued success.

Sincerely,

Mometrix Test Preparation Team

Need more help? Check out our flashcards at: http://MometrixFlashcards.com/TSI

TABLE OF CONTENTS

Top 15 Test Taking Tips 1
Mathematics 2
    Elementary Algebra and Functions 2
    Intermediate Algebra and Functions 12
    Geometry and Measurement 16
    Data Analysis, Statistics, and Probability 26
Reading 34
    Literary Analysis 34
    Main Idea and Supporting Details 38
    Inference in a Text 41
    Author's Use of Language 43
Writing 48
    Essay Revision 48
    Agreement 51
    Sentence Structure 53
    Sentence Logic 55
Essay 58
    Final Note 60
Practice Test #1 62
    Practice Questions 62
    Math 62
    Reading 67
    Writing 73
    Essay 78
    Answers and Explanations 79
    Math 79
    Reading 81
    Writing 82
Practice Test #2 86
    Practice Questions 86
    Math 86
    Reading 91
    Writing 98
    Essay 103
    Answers and Explanations 104
    Math 104
    Reading 106
    Writing 108
Practice Test #3 111
    Practice Questions 111
    Math 111
    Reading 114
    Writing 121
    Essay 126
    Answers and Explanations 127
    Math 127
    Reading 129
    Writing 131
Practice Test #4 135

Practice Questions 135
Math 135
Reading 140
Writing 147
Essay 153
Answers and Explanations 154
Math 154
Reading 156
Writing 158
Practice Test #5 161
Practice Questions 161
Math 161
Reading 166
Writing 173
Essay 178
Answers and Explanations 179
Math 179
Reading 181
Writing 183
Success Strategies 187
How to Overcome Test Anxiety 192
Lack of Preparation 192
Physical Signals 193
Nervousness 193
Study Steps 195
Helpful Techniques 196
How to Overcome Your Fear of Math 201
Math Myths 203
Helpful Strategies 204
Pappas Method 207
Additional Bonus Material 209

Top 15 Test Taking Tips

1. Know the test directions, duration, topics, question types, how many questions
2. Setup a flexible study schedule at least 3-4 weeks before test day
3. Study during the time of day you are most alert, relaxed, and stress free
4. Maximize your learning style; visual learner use visual study aids, auditory learner use auditory study aids
5. Focus on your weakest knowledge base
6. Find a study partner to review with and help clarify questions
7. Practice, practice, practice
8. Get a good night's sleep; don't try to cram the night before the test
9. Eat a well balanced meal
10. Wear comfortable, loose fitting, layered clothing; prepare for it to be either cold or hot during the test
11. Eliminate the obviously wrong answer choices, then guess the first remaining choice
12. Pace yourself; don't rush, but keep working and move on if you get stuck
13. Maintain a positive attitude even if the test is going poorly
14. Keep your first answer unless you are positive it is wrong
15. Check your work, don't make a careless mistake

Mathematics

Elementary Algebra and Functions

Function and relation

When expressing functional relationships, the variables x and y are typically used. These values are often written as the coordinates, (x,y). The x-value is the independent variable and the y-value is the dependent variable. A relation is a set of data in which there is not a unique y-value for each x-value in the data set. This means that there can be two of the same x-values assigned to different y-values. A relation is simply a relationship between the x and y-values in each coordinate but does not apply to the relationship between the values of x and y in the data set. A function is a relation where one quantity depends on the other. For example, the amount of money that you make depends on the number of hours that you work. In a function, each x-value in the data set has one unique y-value because the y-value depends on the x-value.

Determining a function

You can determine whether an equation is a function by substituting different values into the equation for x. These values are called input values. All possible input values are referred to as the domain. The result of substituting these values into the equation is called the output, or range. You can display and organize these numbers in a data table. A data table contains the values for x and y, which you can also list as coordinates. In order for a function to exist, the table cannot contain any repeating x-values that correspond with different y-values. If each x-coordinate has a unique y-coordinate, the table contains a function. However, there can be repeating y-values that correspond with different x-values. An example of this is when the function contains an exponent. For example, if $x^2 = y$,$2^2 = 4$, and $(-2)^2 = 4$.

Equation using independent and dependent variables

To write an equation, you must first assign variables to the unknown values in the problem and then translate the words and phrases into expressions containing numbers and symbols. For example, if Ray earns $10 an hour, this can be represented by the expression $10x$, where x is equal to the number of hours that Ray works. The value of x represents the number of hours because it is the independent variable, or the amount that you can choose and can manipulate. To find out how much money he earns in y hours, you would write the equation, $10x = y$. The variable y is the dependent variable because it depends on x and cannot be manipulated. Once you have the equation for the function, you can choose any number of hours to find the corresponding amount that he earns. For example, if you want to know how much he would earn working 36 hours, you would substitute 36 in for x and multiply to find that he would earn $360.

Graphing a function

To graph a function, first create a table of values based on the equation modeled in the problem. Choose x-values (at least 2 for linear functions, more for quadratic) for the table and then substitute them into the equation to find the corresponding y-values. Use each x and y value as a coordinate pair and plot these points on the coordinate grid. Next, connect the points with a line. The graph of a function will show a relationship among the coordinates in that there are no two y-values assigned to each x-value. The vertical line test is used to determine whether a graph contains a function. This states that if you pass a vertical line anywhere along the graph, it will only pass through the graph at one point. If it passes through the graph at more than one point, it is not considered a function.

Graphs of linear and quadratic functions
Linear functions are in the form, $y = x$ and when graphed form a straight line. To graph a function, you need to find at least two points on the line. Choose values for x and substitute them into the equation. Since $y = x$, then $0 = 0$, $1 = 1$, $2 = 2$, etc. This means that the coordinates $(0, 0)$, $(1, 1)$, and $(2, 2)$ all lie on the line. Quadratic functions are in the form, $y = x^2$ and when graphed form a u-shaped parabola. Every x-value is squared, or multiplied by itself. After multiplying, you will find that the coordinates $(-2, 4)$, $(1, 1)$, and $(2, 4)$ all lie on the parabola. The graphs extend infinitely in both directions and contain an infinite number of points. These graphs are called the parent functions of linear and quadratic equations because they are the most basic in their family of functions; the equations do not contain any coefficients or constants.

Example
Consider the following situation: you drive 12 miles to school and maintain a constant speed until you hit traffic at 7:40 am. Once the traffic clears you resume your original speed until you get to school. Explain what the graph of this function would look like.

First, consider the variables that are involved in this situation. You are comparing the miles that you travel to school and the time that it takes you to get there. On the graph, the line that is formed by this relationship represents the speed that you travel. The graph should contain the correct labels and scales with the independent variable, the time, along the x-axis and the dependent variable, the distance, along the y-axis. If you maintain a constant speed, the graph would show a diagonal line increasing from zero. When you are stopped in traffic at 7:40 am, the distance is no longer increasing, however, the time is. Therefore, you would see the line continuing horizontally for a period of time. When the traffic clears, the line would again increase diagonally to represent the resumed speed. You can use the graph to analyze trends in the data in order to predict future events.

Writing a function rule using a table

If given a set of data, place the corresponding x and y-values into a table and analyze the relationship between them. Consider what you can do to each x-value to obtain the corresponding y-value. Try adding or subtracting different numbers to and from x and then try multiplying or dividing different numbers to and from x. If none of these operations give you the y-value, try combining the operations. Once you find a rule that works for one pair, make sure to try it with each additional set of ordered pairs in the table. If the same operation or combination of operations satisfies each set of coordinates, then the table contains a function. The rule is then used to write the equation of the function in "$y =$" form.

Using a function for future data

Suppose that the distance Greg travels in his car is represented by the function, $y = x - 5$, where x is equal to the time that it takes him to get to his destination and y is equal to his total distance in miles. How many miles would Greg travel in 90 minutes? Explain how you can use this function to find information about future data.

If you know the equation of a function, you can determine any value for x and y. Since x is the independent variable, it is the value that you can manipulate. The dependent variable is y because you cannot manipulate, or change, the result. You can choose any value for x to find the corresponding y-value. For example, if it takes Greg 90 minutes to get to his grandmother's house, you can substitute 90 for x to find the total distance. $90 - 5 = 85$, so Greg traveled 85 miles. Using functions and understanding the relationship between distance and time, Greg can determine when he needs to leave for school, work, trips, etc. in order to effectively schedule himself and arrive at the appropriate time.

Domain, range, continuous data, and discrete data

The domain of a function is the set of all of the possible x-values. These are the values that make the function true. The domain is expressed using inequality symbols and brackets. Often, the domain is all real numbers since these numbers satisfy many functions. The range of a function is the set of all possible y-values, or the result of the values in the domain. To find the range, you substitute the domain values into the equation and express the result within a set of brackets. Linear and quadratic functions contain continuous data. This means the data is represented in an interval and represents a range of data values. This type of data is displayed on the graph with a smooth line and all points on the line are a part of the solution set. Since there are an infinite number of points on a line, we know this represents continuous data. Discrete data values are specific, distinct numbers. This data can be counted and is displayed on the graph as points, or coordinates. The data represented in a scatter plot is an example of discrete data.

Example
Find $g(-3)$ if $g(x) = 2x^2 + x - 1$.

Substitute (-3) in for every value of x in the function:

$$g(-3) = 2(-3)^2 + (-3) - 1$$

Use the order of operations to simplify. First, simplify the exponents by squaring (-3):

$$g(-3) = 2(9) - 3 - 1$$

Multiply and divide from left to right:

$$g(-3) = 18 - 3 - 1$$

Add and subtract from left to right:

$$g(-3) = 14$$

- 4 -

Writing an equation with given coordinates

To write an equation given a function's coordinates, you must first place the ordered pairs into a table of values containing a column of x-values and a column of the corresponding y-values. Then analyze the relationship between each x and y value and identify a pattern.

<u>Example</u>
Write an equation given the coordinates: $(2, 4), (3, 5), (4, 6), (5, 7), and\ (6, 8)$.

Look at the first pair of numbers and determine what you can do to each x-value to get y-value as a result. The first pair is $(2, 4)$, so you could either add two or multiply by two to get a result of four. Choose one of the operations and apply it to the other ordered pairs in the table. The next pair is $(3, 5)$ and $3 + 2 = 5$, but $3 \times 2 \neq 5$. Once you find an operation that satisfies all of the pairs in the table, you can write an equation. Since adding by two is a consistent pattern, the equation that satisfies these coordinates is $y = x + 2$. Check your equation by substituting the remaining numbers from the table into the equation.

Solving equations

To solve an equation, first combine any "like" terms. "Like" terms are those that contain the same variables held to the same power or constants. Next, use inverse operations to isolate the variable on one side of the equation. Since both sides of an equation must remain equal, perform the same operation to both sides so that it remains balanced.

<u>Example</u>
Solve: $15 = -2x + 3$.

In this equation, since the opposite of addition is subtraction, first subtract 3 from both sides of the equation. This simplifies to $12 = -2x$. Next, the opposite, or inverse, of multiplication is division so divide both sides by -2. This results in $-6 = x$, or $x = -6$. When solving equations, always verify your answer by substituting your solution back in to the original equation.

Equation notation and function notation

Equations use numbers to show the equality of two expressions and use the variables x and y. Equation notation is written in "$y =$" form. Given an equation, you can find values for x and y by inputting a value for x and solving for y. These values are displayed as ordered pairs in a table of values. The ordered pairs can then be used as coordinates to graph the equation. An equation is a function if there is a unique relationship between x and y in that for every x-value, there is only one unique y-value. This can be determined from the graph using the vertical line test, in which a function exists if a vertical line can pass through the line at only one point. Function notation is written in the "$f(x)$" form. The notation y and $f(x)$ are essentially the same, one just refers to an equation and one refers to a function. Knowing that an equation is a function can give you more information about its graph. Functions use equations to represent relationships between quantities. All functions have equations but not all equations are functions.

Forms of linear equations

Linear equations can be written in three different forms, each used for a different purpose. The standard form of linear equations is $Ax + By = C$, where A, B and C are integers and A is a positive number. Any equation can be written in this form. This is helpful in solving and graphing systems of equations, where you must compare two or more equations. You can graph an equation in standard form by finding the intercepts. Determine the x-intercept by substituting zero in for y and vice versa. Next, the slope-intercept form of an equation is $y = mx + b$, where m is equal to the slope and b is equal to the y-intercept. You can graph an equation in this form by first plotting the y-intercept. If b is -2, you know that the y-intercept is equal to $(0, -2)$. From this point you can use the slope to create an additional point. If the slope is 4, or $\frac{4}{1}$, you would rise, or move up 4 units and run, or move over 1 unit from the y-intercept. Finally, the point-slope form of an equation is useful when you know the slope and a point on the line. It is written as $y - y_1 = m(x - x_1)$, where m is equal to the slope and (x_1, y_1) is a point on the line. You can graph an equation in point-slope form by plotting the given point and using the slope to plot additional points on the line.

Slope

The slope is the steepness or slant of a line. The steeper the line is, the larger the slope. It can be found on the graph by calculating the change in the y-values divided by the change in the x-values. The formula for slope is $m = \frac{(y_2 - y_1)}{(x_2 - x_1)}$, where (x_1, y_1) and (x_2, y_2) are any two points from the line. The slope of the line gives you an idea of how the data changes. If the line has a positive slope, you know that the data values steadily increase. If the line has a negative slope, the data values steadily decrease. A horizontal line indicates that there is a slope of 0. This is because the y-values do not change and 0 divided by anything is 0. A vertical line has no slope since the x-values do not change. You cannot divide a number by zero, so we say that this line has no slope. Understanding how to find the slope will allow you to write equations in slope-intercept and point-slope form.

Example
Find the slope of a line given the equation: $\frac{1}{2}y + 4 = x$.

Given an equation, you can find the slope by rewriting the equation in slope-intercept form. Slope-intercept form is $y = mx + b$, where m is equal to the slope and b is equal to the y-intercept. To rewrite the equation, use inverse operations to move the terms to the corresponding positions and determine the value of m. In the equation $\frac{1}{2}y + 4 = x$, to isolate y, you have to first undo any addition or subtraction. The opposite of addition is subtraction, so subtract 4 from both sides of the equation. This results in $\frac{1}{2}y = x - 4$. Next, y is multiplied by $\frac{1}{2}$ and to undo multiplication, divide both sides by $\frac{1}{2}$. Dividing by a fraction is the same as multiplying by its reciprocal, so multiply both sides by 2. Remember to use the distributive property to multiply 2 by the entire quantity $(x - 4)$. This results in, $y = 2x - 8$; therefore by the slope-intercept form, m or slope is equal to 2.

Intercepts

The x-intercept is the point on the graph where the line crosses the x-axis. The y-value along the x-axis at this point is 0. The y-intercept is the point of the graph where the line crosses the y-axis. The x-value along the y-axis at this point is 0. This means that to find the x-intercept, you can substitute 0 in for y and to find the y-intercept, you can substitute 0 in for x into the equation. The standard form of an equation makes it easy to find the intercepts using this rule. Once you find the x and y-intercepts, plot the two points and connect them to form a line. The x-intercepts of the graph are also called the roots of the function. The roots give you the number of solutions that an equation has. Since a linear function forms a line, it only crosses the x-axis at one point and therefore only has one solution.

<u>Example</u>
Find the x and y-intercepts of the line given the following table of values:

x	y
-2	-7
-1	-6
0	-5
1	-4
2	-3

The x-intercept is the point on the graph where y is equal to 0 and the y-intercept is the point on the graph where x is equal to 0. First, begin by looking at the x-values in the table. If you see an ordered pair where x is zero, then the corresponding y-value is the y-intercept. Since when $x = 0, y = -5$, the y-intercept is -5. There are no y-values that equal 0, so the next step is to write an equation. One method is to look for patterns among the ordered pairs. Looking at each x-value, you can see that subtracting 5 from x gives you the corresponding y-values, so $y = x - 5$. Substituting 0 in for y gives you $0 = x - 5$, which simplifies to $x = 5$. Therefore, the x-intercept is 5.

You could instead use the slope formula to calculate the change in y-values over the change in x-values. Here, $m = 1$, so you can then substitute this value and the y-intercept, $b = -5$, into the slope-intercept form of an equation, $y = mx + b$.

Additionally, you could use the point-slope form using a point from the table and the slope to write the equation.

Changing the slope and y-intercept

The slope is the steepness or slant of a line. If you change the value of the slope, it changes the steepness or slant of the line. A positive slope is one that increases from left to right. For example, a line with a slope of 5 increases very quickly, while a line with a slope of $\frac{2}{3}$ increases very slowly. A negative slope is one that decreases from left to right. For example, a line with a slope of $-\frac{1}{2}$ decreases slower than a line with a slope of -6. The y-intercept is the point that the line crosses the y-axis. Changing the y-intercept only raises or lowers the position of the line on the graph. A positive y-intercept falls above the origin and a negative y-intercept falls below the origin.

Graphing an equation

Graph an equation given the points: $(-2, -4)$ and $(-1, 6)$.

Label the ordered pairs, (x_1, y_1) and (x_2, y_2).
Using the equation, $m = \frac{(y_2 - y_1)}{(x_2 - x_1)}$, substitute the ordered pairs into the formula and simplify:
$$m = \frac{6 - (-4)}{-1 - (-2)}$$
Use the rules for subtracting integers to simplify:
$$m = \frac{6 + 4}{-1 + 2}$$
Use the rules for adding integers to simplify:
$$m = \frac{10}{1}$$
Divide to solve:
$m = 10$
Plot the points $(-2, -4)$ and $(-1, 6)$ on the coordinate grid.
Use the slope of 10 to rise ten units and run one unit in order to plot additional points on the graph.
Connect the points with a straight line.

Zeros of a function

Find the zeros of the function $f(x) = -2x + 5$.

The zeros of a function, also called the roots of the function, are the points where the function is equal to zero. On the graph, the zeros of a function are located at the points where the line crosses the x-axis, or the x-intercepts. Recall that at the x-intercept, $f(x)$ is equal to 0, so to find the roots of a function, calculate the x-intercept by substituting 0 in for $f(x)$. In the function $f(x) = -2x + 5 = 0$, isolate the term containing x and solve. $2x = 5$, or $x = 2.5$, so the root of the function is 2.5. Since there is only one root, the line crosses the x-axis at only one point.

Finding y-intercept and zeros

Find the y-intercept and zeros of the equation $-3x + 2y = 6$.

To find the y-intercept of an equation written in standard form, find the point where $x = 0$ by substituting 0 in for x, which gives: $0 + 2y = 6$. This is the same as $2y = 6$. Next, the opposite of multiplication is division, so divide by 2. This results in $y = 3$. To find the zeros of a function, you simply find the x-intercept. The x-intercept is the point where $y = 0$, so substitute 0 in for y which gives: $-3x + 0 = 6$. This is the same as $-3x = 6$. Again, using inverse operations, divide by -3 to isolate the variable. This results in $x = -2$. Therefore, the y-intercept of the function is $y = 3$ and the zero of the function is $x = -2$.

Translating situations into linear inequalities

Inequalities compare two expressions that are not equal. One expression can be greater than, less than, greater than or equal to, or less than or equal to the other expression. Inequality symbols are used to express these comparisons. To translate a situation into an inequality, you must analyze the words that correspond with these symbols. The terms less than or fewer refer to the symbol <. The terms greater than or more refer to the symbol >. The terms less than or equal to, at most, or no more than, refer to the symbol ≤. Finally, the terms greater than or equal to, at least, and no less than, refer to the symbol ≥. When translating, choose a variable to represent the unknown value and then change the words or phrases into symbols. Recall the terms and expressions used to identify addition (sum, increased by, more, total), subtraction (difference, decreased by, less), multiplication (product, of, times, factor) and division (quotient, out of, ratio). For example, if the sum of 2 and a number is at most 12, then you would write, $2 + b \leq 12$.

Solving linear inequalities

Solving linear inequalities is very similar to solving linear equations. You must isolate the variable on one side of the inequality by using the inverse, or opposite operations. To undo addition, you use subtraction and vice versa. To undo multiplication, you use division and vice versa. The only difference in solving linear inequalities occurs when you multiply or divide by a negative number. When this is the case, you must flip the inequality symbol. This means that less than becomes greater than, greater than becomes less than, etc. Another type of inequality is called a compound inequality. A compound inequality contains two inequalities separated by an "and" or an "or" statement. An "and" statement can also consist of a variable sandwiched in the middle of two inequality symbols. To solve this type of inequality, simply separate it into two inequalities applying the middle terms to each. Then, follow the steps to isolate the variable.

Graphing inequalities

Graph the inequality $10 > -2x + 4$.

In order to graph the inequality $10 > -2x + 4$, you must first solve for x. The opposite of addition is subtraction, so subtract 4 from both sides. This results in $6 > -2x$. Next, the opposite of multiplication is division, so divide both sides by -2. Don't forget to flip the inequality symbol since you are dividing by a negative number. This results in $-3 < x$. You can rewrite this as $x > -3$. To graph an inequality, you create a number line and put a circle around the value that is being compared to x. If you are graphing a greater than or less than inequality, as the one shown, the circle remains open. This represents all of the values excluding -3. If the inequality happens to be a greater than or equal to or less than or equal to, you draw a closed circle around the value. This would represent all of the values including the number. Finally, take a look at the values that the solution represents and shade the number line in the appropriate direction. You are graphing all of the values greater than -3 and since this is all of the numbers to the right of -3, shade this region on the number line.

Determining solutions to inequalities

Determine whether $(-2, 4)$ is a solution of the inequality $y \geq -2x + 3$.

To determine whether a coordinate is a solution of an inequality, you can either use the inequality or its graph. Using $(-2, 4)$ as (x, y), substitute the values into the inequality to see if it makes a true statement. This results in $4 \geq -2(-2) + 3$. Using the integer rules, simplify the right side of the inequality by multiplying and then adding. The result is $4 \geq 7$, which is a false statement. Therefore, the coordinate is not a solution of the inequality. You can also use the graph of an inequality to see if a coordinate is a part of the solution. The graph of an inequality is shaded over the section of the coordinate grid that is included in the solution. The graph of $y \geq -2x + 3$ includes the solid line $y = -2x + 3$ and is shaded to the right of the line, representing all of the points greater than and including the points on the line. This excludes the point $(-2, 4)$, so it is not a solution of the inequality.

Systems of equations

A system of equations is a set of 2 or more equations with the same variables. You can solve systems using the substitution method, the elimination method, matrices, or by graphing the systems. The solution of a system of equations is the value that both or all of the equations share. When looking at the graph of a system, the solution is the point that is shared by all of the equations. These systems are considered consistent because there is always only one solution. Systems can also be inconsistent (when the lines are parallel and there is no solution) or dependent (when the lines are the same and there is infinitely many solutions). Systems are often used to compare situations that involve cost. For example, suppose you are trying to cut costs on your monthly cell phone bill. Company A charges $30 a month for a data plan plus an additional $0.10 per minute to talk and company B charges $50 a month for a data plan and an additional $0.05 per minute to talk. You can write an equation for each situation and then use systems to find out how many minutes you would have to talk for the cost to be the same. This will allow you to determine which cell plan is the better deal for the average number of minutes that you talk per month.

Substitution

Solve the system $x + y = 8$ and $-3x - y = 6$ using the substitution method.

Solving systems using the substitution method involves solving one equation for a given variable and then substituting that value into the other equation. It does not matter which equation you choose to work with or which variable you isolate, the answer will be the same either way. Using mental math, you may notice that isolating a variable in the first equation requires only one step. If you choose to isolate the y, you would use the inverse operations and subtract x from both sides. This would result in $y = -x + 8$. Now, since you have solved one of the equations for y, you can substitute this value in for y in the other equation; $-3x - (-x + 8) = 6$. To solve for x, simplify using the integer rules. This results in $-3x + x - 8 = 6$, or $-2x - 8 = 6$. Next, add 8 on both sides and the result is $-2x = 14$. Finally divide by -2 to see that $x = -7$. Remember that the solution to a system of equations is the value of both variables that make sense in all equations. Therefore, you must substitute -7 back into one of the equations to find the value for y: $-3(-7) - y = 6$ simplifies to $y = 15$, so the solution is $(-7, 15)$. Always substitute you answer back into both equations to verify that it is correct.

Elimination method

Solve the system $x + y = 5$ and $-2x + 2y = 14$ using the elimination method.

The elimination method involves adding or subtracting two linear equations that are written in the same form in order to eliminate, or remove, one of the variables. First, make sure that the equations are in the same form. Here, both equations are written in standard form. Next, look at the two x-values and the two y-values. Adding these values together would not eliminate either variable, so think of a number that you could multiply on one equation that would result in the one variable cancelling the other if the equations are added together. Multiplying the first equation by 2 would result in $2x + 2y = 10$, and since $2x + (-2x)$ 0, the x-variable would be eliminated when adding the equations. Choose a method and multiply the entire equation by that value. Line the equations up vertically and add them together. The sum of the x-values is 0, so you are left with, $4y = 24$. Using the inverse operations to isolate the variable, the result is $y = 6$. Finally, use this y-value and substitute it back into one of the original equations to find the value of x. $x + (6) = 5$ simplifies to $x = -1$, so the solution is $(-1, 6)$. Remember to plug these values back into both equations to verify that your answer is correct.

Solving systems of equations and solving systems of inequalities

Solving systems of inequalities is very similar to solving systems of equations in that you are looking for a solution or a range of solutions that satisfy all of the equations in the system. Since solutions to inequalities are within a certain interval, it is best to solve this type of system by graphing. Follow the same steps to graph an inequality as you would an equation, but in addition, shade the portion of the graph that represents the solution. Recall that when graphing an inequality on the coordinate plane, you replace the inequality symbol with an equal sign and draw a solid line if the points are included (greater than or equal to or less than or equal to) or a dashed line if the points are not included (greater than or less than). Then replace the inequality symbol and shade the portion of the graph that is included in the solution. Choose a point that is not on the line and test it in the inequality to see if it is makes sense. In a system, you repeat this process for all of the equations and the solution is the region in which the graphs overlap. This is unlike solving a system of equations, in which the solution is a single point where the lines intersect.

Intermediate Algebra and Functions

Quadratic function

A quadratic function is a function in the form $y = ax^2 + bx + c$, where a does not equal 0. While a linear function forms a line, a quadratic function forms a parabola, which is a u-shaped figure that either opens upward or downward. A parabola that opens upward is said to be a positive quadratic function and a parabola that opens downward is said to be a negative quadratic function. The shape of a parabola can differ, depending on the values of a, b, and c. All parabolas contain a vertex, which is the highest possible point, the maximum, or the lowest possible point, the minimum. This is the point where the graph begins moving in the opposite direction. A quadratic function can have zero, one, or two solutions, and therefore, zero, one, or two x-intercepts. Recall that the x-intercepts are referred to as the zeros, or roots, of a function. A quadratic function will have only one y-intercept. Understanding the basic components of a quadratic function can give you an idea of the shape of its graph.

Simplifying polynomial expressions

Polynomials are a group of monomials added or subtracted together. Simplifying polynomials requires combining "like" terms. The "like" terms in a polynomial expression are those that have the same variable raised to the same power. It is often helpful to connect the "like" terms with arrows or lines in order to separate them from the other monomials. Once you have determined the "like" terms, you can re-arrange the polynomial by placing them together. Remember to include the sign that is in front of each term. Once the "like" terms are placed together, you can apply each operation and simplify. When adding and subtracting polynomials, only add and subtract the coefficient, or the number part; the variable and exponent stay the same.

To prove that polynomials are not closed under division, use a counterexample. Assume that polynomials are closed under division. This means the quotient $(x + 1) \div x = \frac{x+1}{x} = 1 + \frac{1}{x} = 1 + x^{-1}$ would have to be a polynomial. This expression, however, is not a polynomial, because the term x^{-1} contains a negative exponent (or would have to be written as the division by x). All terms of a polynomial must be of the form ax^n, where a is a real number and n is a non-negative integer. Although there are *some* quotients of polynomials that are polynomials, closure requires this to be true for *all* polynomials.

Position of parabola

A quadratic function is written in the form $y = ax^2 + bx + c$. Changing the leading coefficient, a, in the equation changes the direction of the parabola. If the value of a is positive, the graph opens upward. The vertex of this parabola is the minimum value of the graph. If the value of a is negative, the graph opens downward. The vertex of this parabola is the maximum value of the graph. The leading coefficient, a, also affects the width of the parabola. The closer a is to 0, the wider the parabola will be. The values of b and c both affect the position of the parabola on the graph. The effect from changing b depends on the sign of a. If a is negative, increasing the value of b moves the parabola to the right and decreasing the value of b moves it to the left. If a is positive, changes to b have the opposite effect. The value of c in the quadratic equation represents the y-intercept and therefore, moves the parabola up and down the y-axis. The larger the c-value, the higher the parabola is on the graph.

Finding roots

Find the roots of $y = x^2 + 6x - 16$ and explain why these values are important.

The roots of a quadratic equation are the solutions when $ax^2 + bx + c = 0$. To find the roots of a quadratic equation, first replace y with 0. If $0 = x^2 + 6x - 16$, then to find the values of x, you can factor the equation if possible. When factoring a quadratic equation where $a = 1$, find the factors of c that add up to b. That is the factors of -16 that add up to 6. The factors of -16 include, -4 and 4, -8 and 2 and -2 and 8. The factors that add up to equal 6 are -2 and 8. Write these factors as the product of two binomials, $0 = (x - 2)(x + 8)$. You can verify that these are the correct factors by using FOIL to multiply them together. Finally, since these binomials multiply together to equal zero, set them each equal to zero and solve for x. This results in $x - 2 = 0$, which simplifies to $x = 2$ and $x + 8 = 0$, which simplifies to $x = -8$. Therefore, the roots of the equation are 2 and -8. These values are important because they tell you where the graph of the equation crosses the x-axis. The points of intersection are $(2, 0)$ and $(-8, 0)$.

Solving quadratic equations

<u>Methods</u>
One way to find the solution or solutions of a quadratic equation is to use its graph. The solution(s) of a quadratic equation are the values of x when $y = 0$. On the graph, $y = 0$ is where the parabola crosses the x-axis, or the x-intercepts. This is also referred to as the roots, or zeros of a function. Given a graph, you can locate the x-intercepts to find the solutions. If there are no x-intercepts, the function has no solution. If the parabola crosses the x-axis at one point, there is one solution and if it crosses at two points, there are two solutions. Since the solutions exist where $y = 0$, you can also solve the equation by substituting 0 in for y. Then, try factoring the equation by finding the factors of ac that add up to equal b. You can use the guess and check method, the box method, or grouping. Once you find a pair that works, write them as the product of two binomials and set them equal to zero. Finally, solve for x to find the solutions. The last way to solve a quadratic equation is to use the quadratic formula. The quadratic formula is $x = \frac{-b \pm \sqrt{b^2 - 4ac}}{2a}$. Substitute the values of a, b, and c into the formula and solve for x. Remember that $\pm$ refers to two different solutions. Always check your solutions with the original equation to make sure they are valid.

<u>Example</u>
List the steps used in solving $y = 2x^2 + 8x + 4$.

First, substitute 0 in for y in the quadratic equation:
$$0 = 2x^2 + 8x + 4$$
Next, try to factor the quadratic equation. If $a \neq 1$, list the factors of ac, or 8:
$$(1, 8), (-1, -8), (2, 4), (-2, -4)$$
Look for the factors of ac that add up to b, or 8:

- 13 -

Since the equation cannot be factored, substitute the values of a, b, and c into the quadratic formula, $x = \frac{-b \pm \sqrt{b^2 - 4ac}}{2a}$:

$$x = \frac{-8 \pm \sqrt{8^2 - 4(2)(4)}}{2(2)}$$

Use the order of operations to simplify:

$$x = \frac{-8 \pm \sqrt{64 - 32}}{4}$$

$$x = \frac{-8 \pm \sqrt{32}}{4}$$

Reduce and simplify:

$$x = \frac{-8 \pm \sqrt{16 \times 2}}{4}$$

$$x = \frac{-8 \pm 4\sqrt{2}}{4}$$

$$x = 2 \pm \sqrt{2}$$

$$x = 2 + \sqrt{2} \text{ and } x = 2 - \sqrt{2}$$

Check both solutions with the original equation to make sure they are valid. Simplify the square roots and round to two decimal places.

$$x = 3.41 \text{ and } x = 0.59$$

Laws of exponents

Multiply $(2x^4)^2 (xy)^4 \cdot 4y^3$ using the laws of exponents.

According the order of operations, the first step in simplifying expressions to is to evaluate within the parenthesis. Moving from left to right, the first set of parenthesis contains a power raised to a power. The rules of exponents state that when a power is raised to a power, you multiply the exponents. Since $4 \times 2 = 8$, $(2x^4)^2$ can be written as $4x^8$. The second set of parenthesis raises a product to a power. The rules of exponents state that you raise every value within the parenthesis to the given power. Therefore, $(xy)^4$ can be written as x^4y^4. Combining these terms with the last term gives you, $4x^8 \cdot x^4y^4 \cdot 4y^3$. In this expression, there are powers with the same base. The rules of exponents state that you add powers with the same base, while multiplying the coefficients. You can group the expression as $(4x^8 \cdot x^4) \cdot (y^4 \cdot 4y^3)$ to organize the values with the same base. Then, using this rule add the exponents. The result is $4x^{12} \cdot 4y^7$, or $16y^{12}y^7$.

Using given roots to find quadratic equation

<u>Example</u>
Find a quadratic equation whose real roots are x = 2 and x = -1.

One way to find the roots of a quadratic equation is to factor the equation and use the zero product property, setting each factor of the equation equal to zero to find the corresponding root. We can use this technique in reverse to find an equation given its roots. Each root corresponds to a linear equation which in turn corresponds to a factor of the quadratic equation.

For example, the root $x = 2$ corresponds to the equation x – 2 = 0, and the root x = -1 corresponds to the equation x + 1 = 0.

These two equations correspond to the factors $(x - 2)$ and $(x + 1)$, from which we can derive the equation $(x - 2)(x + 1) = 0$, or x² – x – 2 = 0.

(Any integer multiple of this entire equation will also yield the same roots, as the integer will simply cancel out when the equation is factored. For example, 2x² – 2x – 4 = 0 factors as $2(x - 2)(x + 1) = 0$.)

Simplifying rational expressions

To simplify a rational expression, factor the numerator and denominator completely. Factors that are the same and appear in the numerator and denominator have a ratio of 1. The denominator, $1 - x^2$, is a difference of squares. It can be factored as $(1 - x)(1 + x)$. The factor $1 - x$ and the numerator $x - 1$ are opposites, and have a ratio of -1. Rewrite the numerator as $-1(1 - x)$. So, the rational expression can be simplified as follows:

$$\frac{x - 1}{1 - x^2} = \frac{-1(1 - x)}{(1 - x)(1 + x)} = \frac{-1}{1 + x}$$

(Note that since the original expression is defined for $x \neq \{-1, 1\}$, the simplified expression has the same restrictions.)

Geometry and Measurement

Point and line

A point is a specific location and is used to help understand and define all other concepts in geometry. A point is denoted by a single capital letter, such as point P.

A line is a straight continuous set of points and usually denoted by two points in that set. For instance, $\overleftrightarrow{AB}$ is the line which passes through points A and B.

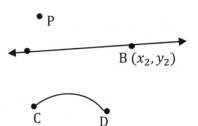

The distance along a line, or the distance between two points on a line, can be measured using a ruler. If the two points are located on the Cartesian plane, the distance can be found using the distance formula: $d = \sqrt{(x_2 - x_1)^2 + (y_2 - y_1)^2}$.

The distance around a circular arc, or the distance along a circle between two points, can be measured using a piece of string (to follow the shape of the circle) and then a ruler. The distance can also be found by finding the portion of the circle's circumference represented by the arc.

Angle, circle, perpendicular lines, parallel lines and line segment

Angle – The set of points which are part of two lines that intersect at a specific point. An angle is made up of two "half lines" called rays that begin at the shared point, called the vertex, and extend away from that point. An angle can be denoted simply by the angle's vertex ($\angle A$ or $\angle A$) or by three points: one from one ray, the point of intersection, and one from the second ray ($\angle BAC$ or $\angle BAC$).

Circle – A continuous set of points which are all equidistant from a separate point called the center. A circle usually shares the same label as its center: circle P with center at point P.

Perpendicular lines – Two lines which intersect at one specific point and create four 90° angles. Notation: $\overleftrightarrow{DE} \perp \overleftrightarrow{EF}$ when lines DE and EF intersect and form right angles at point E.

Parallel lines – Two lines which do not share any points and never intersect. Notation: $\overleftrightarrow{GH} \parallel \overleftrightarrow{IJ}$.

Line segment – The section of a line that is between two specific points on that line, usually denoted by two points: $\overline{KL}$.

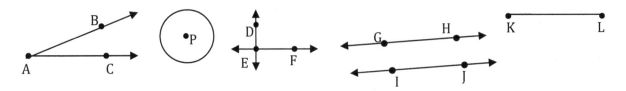

- 16 -

Rotation, center of rotation, and angle of rotation

A rotation is a transformation that turns a figure around a point called the center of rotation, which can lie anywhere in the plane. If a line is drawn from a point on a figure to the center of rotation, and another line is drawn from the center to the rotated image of that point, the angle between the two lines is the angle of rotation. The vertex of the angle of rotation is the center of rotation.

Reflection over a line and reflection in a point

A reflection of a figure over a line (a "flip") creates a congruent image that is the same distance from the line as the original figure but on the opposite side. The line of reflection is the perpendicular bisector of any line segment drawn from a point on the original figure to its reflected image (unless the point and its reflected image happen to be the same point, which happens when a figure is reflected over one of its own sides).

A reflection of a figure in a point is the same as the rotation of the figure 180° about that point. The image of the figure is congruent to the original figure. The point of reflection is the midpoint of a line segment which connects a point in the figure to its image (unless the point and its reflected image happen to be the same point, which happens when a figure is reflected in one of its own points).

<u>Example</u>
Use the coordinate plane of the given image below to reflect the image across the *y*-axis.

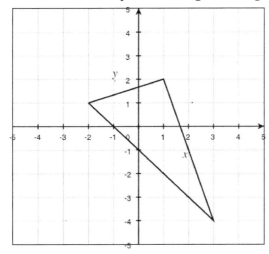

- 17 -

To reflect the image across the *y*-axis, replace each *x*-coordinate of the points that are the vertex of the triangle, *x*, with its negative, –*x*.

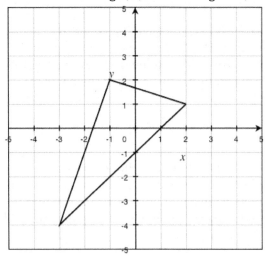

Translation

A translation is a transformation which slides a figure from one position in the plane to another position in the plane. The original figure and the translated figure have the same size, shape, and orientation.

Transforming a given figure using rotation, reflection, and translation

To rotate a given figure: 1. Identify the point of rotation. 2. Using tracing paper, geometry software, or by approximation, recreate the figure at a new location around the point of rotation.

To reflect a given figure: 1. Identify the line of reflection. 2. By folding the paper, using geometry software, or by approximation, recreate the image at a new location on the other side of the line of reflection.

To translate a given figure: 1. Identify the new location. 2. Using graph paper, geometry software, or by approximation, recreate the figure in the new location. If using graph paper, make a chart of the x- and y-values to keep track of the coordinates of all critical points.

Identifying what transformation was used when given a figure and its transformed image

To identify that a figure has been rotated, look for evidence that the figure is still face-up, but has changed its orientation.

To identify that a figure has been reflected across a line, look for evidence that the figure is now face-down.

To identify that a figure has been translated, look for evidence that a figure is still face-up and has not changed orientation; the only change is location.

To identify that a figure has been dilated, look for evidence that the figure has changed its size but not its orientation.

Dilation

A dilation is a transformation which proportionally stretches or shrinks a figure by a scale factor. The dilated image is the same shape and orientation as the original image but a different size. A polygon and its dilated image are similar.

<u>Example 1</u>
Use the coordinate plane to create a dilation of the given image below, where the dilation is the enlargement of the original image.

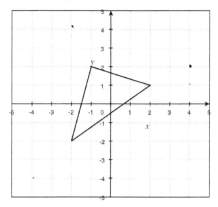

An enlargement can be found by multiplying each coordinate of the coordinate pairs located at the triangles vertices by a constant. If the figure is enlarged by a factor of 2, the new image would be:

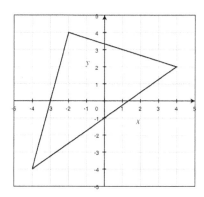

Using transparencies to represent transformations

After drawing a shape on a piece of transparency, the shape can be rotated by leaving the transparency on a flat surface and turning it clockwise or counterclockwise.

After drawing a shape on a piece of transparency, the shape can be translated by leaving the transparency on a flat surface and sliding it in any direction (left, right, up, down, or along a diagonal).

After drawing a shape on a piece of transparency, the shape can be reflected by turning the transparency over so that the side the shape is on the underside of the transparency, touching the table.

Perimeter

The perimeter of a rectangle is the sum of the lengths of its sides.

<u>Example</u>
Draw a rectangle with length: a and width: b. Describe the perimeter and write an equation to represent the perimeter of the rectangle.

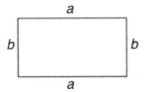

The perimeter of a rectangle is the sum of the length of the sides of the rectangle. The perimeter of the rectangle is: $a + b + a + b$, or $2a + 2b$.

Area

The area of a rectangle is the measurement of the inside of the rectangle. The area of a rectangle is found by the formula $A=lw$, where A is the area of the rectangle, l is the length (usually considered to be the longer side) and w is the width (usually considered to be the shorter side). The numbers for l and w are interchangeable.

<u>Example</u>
Draw a rectangle length x and width y. Describe the area of the rectangle and write an equation to represent the rectangle's area.

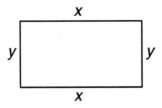

The area of the rectangle is: $x \cdot y$.

<u>Example 2</u>
Leslie decides to tile her bathroom floor with tiles that are rectangles. Each rectangle has a length of 10 inches and a width of 8 inches. Find the number of tiles needed for a floor with an area of 3600 in².

First, find the area of each tile. The area of a rectangle is: lw, where l is the length of the rectangle, and w is the width. The area of each tile is: 10 in · 8 in = 80 in². To find the number of tiles needed, divide the total area of the floor, 3600 in², by the area of each tile: 3600 in² ÷ 80 in² = 45. Leslie needs 45 tiles.

Volume

<u>Example</u>

Draw an object with the given volume:

1) $V = lwh$ in^3

2) $V = \frac{1}{3} lwh$ in^3

3) $V = \frac{4}{3} \pi r^3$ cm^3

1) This formula is used to find the volume of a rectangular prism of length, l, width, w, and height, h, all in inches.

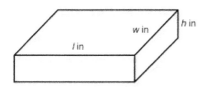

2) This formula is used to find the volume of a rectangular pyramid, whose base is a rectangle of length, l, and width, w. The pyramid has a height given by h, and all side lengths are in inches.

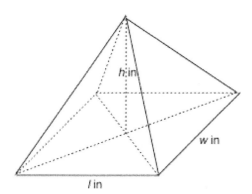

3) This formula is used to find the volume of a sphere with radius, r, in centimeters.

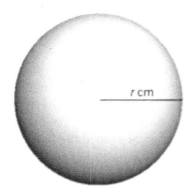

- 21 -

Surface area

<u>Example 1</u>
Find the surface area of the figure below. Each triangular face is congruent, and the base is a square.

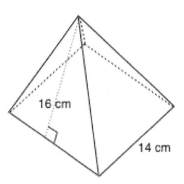

The surface area is the sum of the areas of the faces. The area of the base, which is given as a square, will be the side length squared:
$$a = s^2 = 14^2 = 196 \text{ cm}^2$$
The area of one of the triangular faces will be one half times the height and base of the triangle. The base of the triangle will be one of the sides of the square.
$$a = \frac{1}{2}bh = \frac{1}{2}(14)(16) = 112 \text{ cm}^2$$
There are four triangular faces, so the surface area will be four times the area of the triangular face plus the area of the square base.
$$SA = 4(\text{triangular face area}) + \text{square face area} = 4(112) + 196 = 448 + 196 = 644 \text{ cm}^2$$

<u>Example 2</u>
Sophia is covering a rectangular prism-shaped couch cushion with fabric. She will be covering all sides of the cushion. The cushion is 4 inches high, 20 inches wide, and 32 inches deep. Determine the area of the fabric needed to cover the cushion.

Drawing a diagram may be helpful. Label the dimensions as given in the problem.

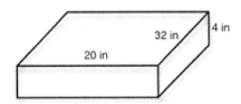

To find the area of fabric needed, find the surface area of the cushion. To find the surface area, sum the areas of each face of the rectangle prism. Opposite faces will have an equal area. The front/back faces of the prism have an area of: 20 in · 4 in = 80 in². The left/right side faces of the prism have an area of: 32 in · 4 in = 128 in². The top/bottom faces of the prism have an area of: 20 in · 32 in = 640 in². The total surface area of the prism, or area of the fabric needed to cover the cushion, is: 80 in² + 80 in² + 128 in² + 128 in² + 640 in² + 640 in² = 1696 in²

Pythagorean Theorem

<u>Example</u>

A ladder is needed to reach a window, 12 feet up, of a building. Use the diagram below to determine the length of the ladder, x, needed to reach the window if placed 5 feet from the base of a building.

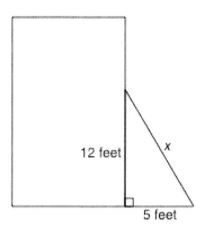

The length of the ladder, x, is the hypotenuse of a right triangle with legs: 12 and 5. There exists a Pythagorean triple for a right triangle: 13, 12, 5, where 13 is the length of the hypotenuse, and 12 and 5 are the lengths of the legs of the right triangle. The triangle formed by the ladder is a Pythagorean triple, with the length of the ladder being the length of the hypotenuse, 13. A 13-foot ladder is needed to reach the window 12 feet from the ground.

Proportional relationships to finding missing measurements

<u>Example 1</u>

To determine the height of a streetlamp, Dillon decides to use his shadow. He draws the diagram below, and fills in the measurements he knows. The larger outside triangle and the smaller inner triangle are similar. What is the height of the street lamp, s?

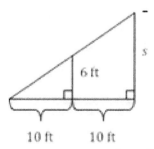

Using properties of similar triangles, Dillon can solve for s. To solve for s, set up a proportion:

$$\frac{6}{10} = \frac{s}{20}$$
$$120 = 10s$$
$$12 = s$$

The street lamp is 12 feet tall.

<u>Example 2</u>
The two rectangles below are similar.

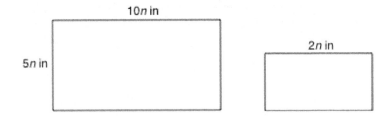

1. Describe the relationship between the perimeters of the two rectangles.
2. Describe the relationship between the areas of the two rectangles.

Since the two rectangles are similar, the width of the smaller rectangle can be determined. The relationship between the length of the larger and smaller rectangles is:
$$\frac{10n}{2n} = 5$$
The dimensions of the larger rectangle are five times each dimension of the smaller rectangle. The width of the smaller rectangle is:
$$5n \div 5 = n$$
1. The perimeter of the larger rectangle is: $(10n + 5n) \cdot 2 = 15n \cdot 2 = 30n$ in. The perimeter of the smaller rectangle is: $(2n + n) \cdot 2 = 3n \cdot 2 = 6n$ in. The perimeter of the larger rectangle is 5 times the perimeter of the smaller rectangle. The perimeter and side lengths of the similar rectangles have the same relationship.
2. The area of the larger rectangle is: $10n \cdot 5n = 50n^2$ in². The area of the smaller rectangle is: $2n \cdot n = 2n^2$ in². The area of the larger rectangle is 25 times the area of the smaller rectangle. The area of the larger rectangle is increased by the square of the relationship between the side lengths, or 5^2.

Proportional change of dimensions

<u>Example</u>
The area of a rectangle is 216 cm². Describe the area of a new rectangle if both dimensions are multiplied by a factor of $\frac{1}{3}$.

The area of a rectangle is a product of the length and width: $A = lw$. If both dimensions are multiplied by a factor of $\frac{1}{3}$, the new area would be: $A = \frac{1}{3}(l)\frac{1}{3}(w) = \frac{1}{9}lw$. The given area of the rectangle is 216 cm², and if both dimensions are multiplied by a factor of $\frac{1}{3}$, the new area will be multiplied by a factor of $\frac{1}{9}$:
$$\text{new } A = \frac{1}{9}(\text{original } A) = \frac{1}{9}(216) = 24 \text{ cm}^2$$
The new area is 24 cm².

Proportional changes and volume

<u>Example</u>
The two rectangular prisms below are similar.

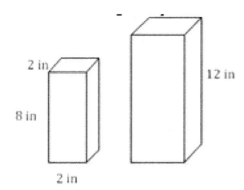

1. Describe the relationship between the dimensions of the two prisms.
2. Describe the relationship between the volumes of the two prisms.

1. Using the given heights, the relationship between the dimensions of the two prisms, as a proportion, is: $\frac{\text{height of smaller}}{\text{height of larger}} = \frac{8}{12} = \frac{2}{3}$.
2. The volume of the smaller prism is: (2)(2)(8) = 32 in³. To find the volume of the larger prism, first find the length and width of the larger prism. Because the length and width of the smaller prism are equal, the length and width of the larger prism are also equal. Use the proportion relating the dimensions to find one of the measurements, for example the length, of the larger prism:

$$\frac{2}{3} = \frac{2}{x}$$
$$2x = 6$$
$$x = 3$$

The length and width of the larger prism is 3 inches. Find the volume of the larger prism: (3)(3)(12) = 108 in³. The relationship between the two volumes, as a proportion, is:

$$\frac{\text{volume of smaller}}{\text{volume of larger}} = \frac{32}{108} = \frac{8}{27}$$

This relationship can also be determined by using the ratio of the dimensions. The ratio of the volumes of two three-dimensional shapes is the cube of the ratio of their dimensions:

$$\left(\frac{2}{3}\right)^3 = \frac{8}{27}$$

Data Analysis, Statistics, and Probability

Statistics

Statistics may be descriptive or inferential, in nature. Descriptive statistics does not involve inferences and includes measures of center and spread, frequencies, and percentages. Inferential statistics involves the process of making inferences about large populations based on the characteristics of random samples from the population. This field of statistics is useful because, for large populations, it may be impractical or impossible to measure the characteristics of each element of the population and determine the distributions of various properties exactly. By applying statistical methods, it's possible to make reasonable inferences about the distributions of a variable, or variables, throughout large populations by only examining a relatively small part of it. Of course, it's important that this be a "representative sample", that is, one in which the distribution of the variables of interest is similar to its distribution in the entire population. For this reason, it's desirable to create random samples, rather than choosing a set of similar samples.

Measures of central tendency

Mean
The mean is the average of the data points; that is, it is the sum of the data points divided by the number of data points. Mathematically, the mean of a set of data points $\{x_1, x_2, x_3, \ldots x_n\}$ can be written as $\bar{X} = \sum \frac{X}{N}$. For instance, for the data set (1, 3, 6, 8, 100, 800), the mean is $\frac{1+3+6+8+100+800}{6} = 153$.

The mean is most useful, when data is approximately normal and does not include extreme outliers. In the above example, the data shows much variation. Thus, the mean is not the best measure of central tendency to use, when interpreting the data. With this data set, the median will give a more complete picture of the distribution.

Median
The median is the value in the middle of the data set, in the sense that 50% of the data points lie above the median and 50% of the data points lie below. The median can be determined by simply putting the data points in order, and selecting the data point in the middle. If there is an even number of data points, then the median is the average of the middle two data points. For instance, for the data set {1, 3, 6, 8, 100, 800}, the median is $\frac{6+8}{2} = 7$.

For distributions with widely varying data points, especially those with large outliers, the median is a more appropriate measure of central tendency, and thus gives a better idea of a "typical" data point. Notice in the data set above, the mean is 153, while the median is 7.

Mode
The mode is the value that appears most often in the data set. For instance, for the data set {2, 6, 4, 9, 4, 5, 7, 6, 4, 1, 5, 6, 7, 5, 6}, the mode is 6: the number 6 appears four times in the data set, while the next most frequent values, 4 and 5, appear only three times each. It is possible for a data set to have more than one mode: in the data set {11, 14, 17, 16, 11, 17,

- 26 -

12, 14, 17, 14, 13}, 14 and 17 are both modes, appearing three times each. In the extreme case of a uniform distribution—a distribution in which all values appear with equal probability—all values in the data set are modes.

The mode is useful to get a general sense of the shape of the distribution; it shows where the peaks of the distribution are. More information is necessary to get a more detailed description of the full shape.

Relation to shape of measurement

The measurement of central tendency with the most clearly visible relationship to the shape is the mode. The mode defines the peak of the distribution, and a distribution with multiple modes has multiple peaks. The relationship of the shape to the other measurements of central tendency is more subtle. For a symmetrical distribution with a single peak, the mode, median, and mean all coincide. For a distribution skewed to the left or right, however, this is not generally the case. One rule of thumb often given is that the median is displaced from the mode in the same direction as the skew of the graph, and the mean in the same direction farther still.

First quartile

The first quartile of a data set is a value greater than or equal to one quarter of the data points (and less than the other three quarters). Various methods exist for defining the first quartile precisely; one of the simplest is to define the first quartile as the median of the first half of the ordered data (excluding the median if there are an odd number of data points). Applying this method, for example, to the data set {3, 1, 12, 7, 17, 4, 10, 8, 9, 20, 4}, we proceed as follows: Putting the data in order, we get {1, 3, 4, 4, 7, 8, 9, 10, 12, 17, 20}. The first half (excluding the median) is {1, 3, 4, 4, 7}, which has a median of 4. Therefore the first quartile of this data set is 4.

Third quartile

The third quartile of a data set is a value greater than or equal to three quarters of the data points (and less than the remaining quarter). Various methods exist for defining the third quartiles precisely; one of the simplest is to define the third quartile as the median of the second half of the ordered data (excluding the median if there are an odd number of data points). Applying this method, for example, to the data set {3, 1, 12, 7, 17, 4, 10, 8, 9, 20, 4}, we proceed as follows: Putting the data in order, we get {1, 3, 4, 4, 7, 8, 9, 10, 12, 17, 20}. The second half (excluding the median) is {9, 10, 12, 17, 20}, which has a median of 12. Therefore the third quartile of this data set is 12.

Interquartile range of a data set

The interquartile range of a data set is the difference between the third and first quartiles. That is, one quarter of the data fall below the interquartile range and one quarter of the data above it. Exactly half of the data points fall within the interquartile range, half of those above the median and half below. (This is, of course, why the quartile points are called "quartiles", because they divide the data into quarters: one quarter of the data points are below the first quartile, one quarter between the first and second quartile (the median), and so on.) The interquartile range is useful to get a rough idea of the spread of the data. The median by itself shows where the data are centered (or rather, shows one measure of central tendency); the interquartile range gives a better idea of how much the data points vary from this center.

Standard deviation

The standard deviation of a data set is a measurement of how much the data points vary from the mean. More precisely, it is equal to the square root of the average of the squares of the differences between each point and the mean: $s_x = \sqrt{\frac{\sum(X - \bar{X})^2}{N-1}}$.

The standard deviation is useful for determining the spread, or dispersion, of the data, or how far they vary from the mean. The smaller the standard deviation, the closer the values tend to be to the mean; the larger the standard deviation, the more they tend to be scattered far from the mean.

Outlier

An outlier is an extremely high or extremely low value in the data set. It may be the result of measurement error, in which case, the outlier is not a valid member of the data set. However, it may also be a valid member of the distribution. Unless a measurement error is identified, the experimenter cannot know for certain if an outlier is or is not a member of the distribution. There are arbitrary methods that can be employed to designate an extreme value as an outlier. One method designates an outlier (or possible outlier) to be any value less than $Q_1 - 1.5(IQR)$ or any value greater than $Q_3 + 1.5(IQR)$, where Q_1 and Q_3 are the first and third quartiles and IQR is the interquartile range. For instance, in the data set {42, 71, 22, 500, 33, 38, 62, 44, 58, 37, 61, 25}, the point 500 may be considered an outlier, since 500 is greater than 101.25 (61.5 + 1.5(26.5) = 101.25).

Effect on measurements of the center and spread of a data distribution
Regarding measurements of the center, outliers tend to have little or no effect on the mode, and in general little effect on the median, though their effects may be magnified for very small distributions. Means, however, are very sensitive to outliers; a single data point that lies far outside the range of the others may leave the mode and median almost unchanged while drastically altering the mean. For instance, the data set {2, 2, 5, 5, 5, 8, 11} has a mode and median of 5 and a mean of approximately 5.4; adding the outlying value 650 to the data set leaves the mode and median unchanged but increases the mean to 86.

Like the median, the interquartile range is little affected by outliers, though, again, the effect may be greater for small data sets. The standard deviation, like the mean, is much more sensitive to outliers, and may be significantly increased by a single outlier that lies far from the spread of the rest of the points.

Slope

In the case of a linear fit to a data set, of the form $y = mx + b$, the slope m corresponds to the rate of change of the dependent variable y with respect to the independent variable x. This can often be expressed in a form similar to "y per x". For instance, if the data represents the distance of an object from some point as a function of time, with the distance as y and the time as x, then the slope of the linear model represents the change in distance with respect to the corresponding change in time—i.e., the velocity. If the data represents the cost to produce various quantities of products, then the slope of the linear model is the change in the cost with respect to the quantity of products produced—i.e., the production cost per unit of product.

Intercept

In the case of a linear fit to a data set, of the form $y = mx + b$, the intercept b corresponds to the value of the dependent variable y when the independent variable x is equal to zero. This often can be expressed as the "initial value" of the variable, or as its offset. For instance, if the data represents the distance of an object from some point as a function of time, with the distance as y and the time as x, then the intercept of the linear model represents the object's distance at time zero—i.e., its initial distance. If the data represents the cost to produce various quantities of products, then the intercept of the linear model is the cost when no units are being produced—in other words, the overhead cost involved in the production.

Uniform probability model

A uniform probability model is a model in which the probabilities of all outcomes are equally likely. For example, the roll of a fair die can be simulated by such a model; it's equally likely that any face of the die come up on top. Likewise, the draw of a card from a well-shuffled deck can be represented by a uniform probability model; it's equally likely for any card to be drawn.

One useful feature of a uniform probability model is that probabilities can be determined by simply counting outcomes. The probability of an event A occurring is equal to the total number of outcomes in event A divided by the total number of outcomes in the sample set. For example, suppose we want to know the probability of drawing a face card from a well-shuffled deck of cards (without jokers). There are fifty-two cards in the deck, twelve of which are face cards. The probability of drawing a face card from the deck is therefore $\frac{12}{52} = \frac{3}{13}$.

When plotted, a uniform distribution is rather flat, in appearance. Uniform distribution results when plotting the sampling distribution of a large number of samples, thus illustrating the Central Limit Theorem.

Finding the conditional probability P(A|B)

Although one way of finding the conditional probability is to calculate $P(A|B) = \frac{P(A \cap B)}{P(B)}$, this is not the only way. For a uniform probability model, it's possible to find the conditional probability even without knowing the overall probability of any event, just knowing all the outcomes included in event B. To see this, consider that the probability of event B occurring is equal to the number of outcomes in event B, which we can call X_B, divided by the total number of outcomes in the sample space, X_{TOTAL}. Similarly, the probability of events A and B both occurring is equal to the number of outcomes in the intersection of A and B, $X_{A \cap B}$, divided by the total number of outcomes in the sample space, X_{TOTAL}. So the conditional probability $P(A|B) = \frac{P(A \cap B)}{P(B)} = \frac{X_{A \cap B}/X_{TOTAL}}{X_B/X_{TOTAL}} = \frac{X_{A \cap B}}{X_B}$. In other words, we can find the conditional probability $P(A|B)$ by simply dividing the number of outcomes that belong to both A and B by the number of outcomes that belong to B: $P(A|B)$ is the fraction of B's outcomes that also belong to A.

<u>Interpreting a conditional probability</u>
A conditional probability $P(A|B)$ is the probability that event A will occur given that event B occurs. For a uniform probability model, this is equal to the fraction of B's outcomes that also belong to A. For instance, suppose we are interested in knowing the number of students of each grade at a certain school who buy their lunch at the school and who take their lunch from home. We will call the event that a randomly chosen student is in the ninth grade event A, and the event that he buys his lunch at school event B. Since the students are randomly chosen with equal probability, this is a uniform probability model. The probability that a student buys his lunch at school, given that he is in the ninth grade, is $P(A|B)$, and is simply equal to the fraction of ninth-grade students who buy their lunches at the school.

<u>Independent events</u>
The conditional probability P(A|B) is the probability that event B will occur given that event A occurs. If the two events are independent, we do not expect that whether or not event A occurs should have any effect on whether or not event B occurs. In other words, we expect P(A|B)=P(A).
This can be proven using the usual equations for conditional probability and the joint probability of independent events. The conditional probability $P(A|B) = \frac{P(A \cap B)}{P(B)}$. But if A and B are independent, then $P(A \cap B) = P(A)P(B)$. So $P(A|B) = \frac{P(A)P(B)}{P(B)} = P(A)$.
By similar reasoning, if A and B are independent then P(B|A)=P(B).

Conditional probability

Given two events A and B, the conditional probability P(A|B)is the probability that event B will occur, given that event A has occurred. For instance, suppose you have a jar containing two red marbles and two blue marbles, and you draw two marbles at random. Note. The first drawn marble is not replaced. Consider event A being the event that the first marble drawn is red, and event B being the event that the second marble drawn is blue. With no conditions set, both P(A) and P(B) are equal to $\frac{1}{2}$. However, if we know that the first marble drawn was red—that is, that event A occurred—then that leaves one red marble and two blue marbles in the jar. In that case, the probability that the second marble is blue given that the first marble was red—that is, P(A|B)—is equal to $\frac{2}{3}$.

<u>Calculating the conditional probability P(A|B) in terms of the probabilities of events A and B and their union and/or intersection</u>
The conditional probability P(A|B) is the probability that event B will occur given that event A occurs. This cannot be calculated simply from P(A) and P(B); these probabilities alone do not give sufficient information to determine the conditional probability. It can, however, be determined given also $P(A \cap B)$, the probability that events A and B both occur.
Specifically, $P(A|B) = \frac{P(A \cap B)}{P(B)}$.
For instance, suppose you have a jar containing two red marbles and two blue marbles, and you draw two marbles at random. Consider event A being the event that the first marble drawn is red, and event B being the event that the second marble drawn is blue. P(A) is $\frac{1}{2}$,

and $P(A \cap B)$ is $\frac{1}{3}$. (The latter may not be obvious, but may be determined by finding the product of $\frac{1}{2}$ and $\frac{2}{3}$.) Therefore $P(A|B) = \frac{1/3}{1/2} = \frac{2}{3}$.

Estimating a conditional probability from a two-way frequency table
If we have a two-way frequency table, it is generally a straightforward matter to read off the probabilities of any two events A and B, as well as the joint probability of both events occurring, $P(A \cap B)$. We can then find the conditional probability P(A|B) by calculating $P(A|B) = \frac{P(A \cap B)}{P(B)}$.

For example, a certain store's recent T-shirt sales:

		Size			
		Small	Medium	Large	Total
Color	Blue	25	40	35	100
	White	27	25	22	74
	Black	8	23	15	26
	Total	60	88	72	220

Suppose we want to find the conditional probability that a customer buys a black shirt (event A), given that the shirt he buys is size small (event B). From the table, the probability P(A) that a customer buys a small shirt is $\frac{60}{220} = \frac{3}{11}$. The probability $P(A \cap B)$ that he buys a small, black shirt is $\frac{8}{220} = \frac{2}{55}$. The conditional probability P(A|B) that he buys a black shirt, given that he buys a small shirt, is therefore $P(A|B) = \frac{2/55}{3/11} = \frac{2}{15}$.

Conditional probability in everyday situations
Conditional probability often arises in everyday situations in, for example, estimating the risk or benefit of certain activities. The conditional probability of having a heart attack given that you exercise daily may be smaller than the overall probability of having a heart attack. The conditional probability of having lung cancer given that you are a smoker is larger than the overall probability of having lung cancer.
Note that changing the order of the conditional probability changes the meaning: the conditional probability of having lung cancer given that you are a smoker is a very different thing from the probability of being a smoker given that you have lung cancer. In an extreme case, suppose that a certain rare disease is caused only by eating a certain food, but even then is unlikely. Then the conditional probability of having that disease given that you eat the dangerous food is nonzero but low, but the conditional probability of having eaten that food given that you have the disease is 100%!

Independence

Determining independence from a two-way frequency table
If we have a two-way frequency table, it is generally a straightforward matter to read off the probabilities of any two events A and B, as well as the joint probability of both events occurring, $P(A \cap B)$. We can then check whether or not the events are independent by verifying whether $P(A)P(B) = P(A \cap B)$.

For example, consider the following table, showing a certain store's recent T-shirt sales, categorized by size and color:

		Size			
		Small	Medium	Large	Total
Color	Blue	25	40	35	100
	White	27	25	22	74
	Black	8	23	15	26
	Total	60	88	72	220

Suppose we want to check whether the event A that a customer buys a blue shirt is independent of the event B that a customer buys a medium shirt. From the table, $P(A) = \frac{100}{220} = \frac{5}{11}$ and $P(B) = \frac{88}{220} = \frac{4}{10}$. Also, $P(A \cap B) = \frac{40}{220} = \frac{2}{11}$. Since $\left(\frac{5}{11}\right)\left(\frac{4}{10}\right) = \frac{20}{220} = \frac{2}{11}$, $P(A)P(B) = P(A \cap B)$ and these two events are indeed independent.

Everyday situations
Even if we don't necessarily think of it in those terms, we often use independence of events in everyday situations. We know when playing a board game, for instance, that each roll of the die is independent, and is unaffected by previous rolls.
Sometimes, however, our intuition fails us and we tend to think of independent events as influencing each other; if we flip a coin and it comes up heads three times in a row, we may erroneously believe on some level that the next flip is more likely to come up tails because a tails is "overdue". Many gamblers make this mistake, seeing meaningful streaks in random results, and expecting certain results on the basis of previous events. Remembering what it means for events to be random helps avoid this error.

Addition rule

The addition rule for probabilities is $P(A \cup B) = P(A) + P(B) - P(A \cap B)$. In other words, the probability that either event A or event B will occur is equal to the sum of the probabilities of each event, minus the probability that they will both occur.
For example, suppose you want to find the probability that, when you roll two dice, either their numbers will match (event A) or they will add to eight (event B). $P(A) = \frac{6}{36} = \frac{1}{6}$, since there are six possible combinations of matching dice ((1,1), (2,2), (3,3), (4,4), (5,5), or (6,6)), and thirty-six combinations total. $P(B) = \frac{5}{36}$; there are five combinations that add to 8 ((2,6), (3,5), (4,4), (5,3), or (6,2)). $P(A \cap B) = \frac{1}{36}$; there is only one combination of matching dice that add to 8 (that is, (4,4)). So $P(A \cup B) = \frac{1}{6} + \frac{5}{36} - \frac{1}{36} = \frac{5}{18}$.

Interpreting the result in terms of a uniform probability model
The addition rule states that $P(A \cup B) = P(A) + P(B) - P(A \cap B)$. The result of the equation gives the probability that either event A or B will occur, which for a uniform probability distribution is equal to the fraction of outcomes in either A or B.
Suppose, for example, we are told that of the books on a certain shelf, $\frac{1}{3}$ are paperbacks, $\frac{1}{2}$ are fiction, and $\frac{1}{4}$ are paperback fiction books. We can call event A the event that a randomly chosen book is a paperback and event B the event that a randomly chosen book is fiction.

Since we are randomly choosing the books, this is a uniform probability model. From the given information, $P(A) = \frac{1}{3}$, $P(B) = \frac{1}{2}$, and $P(A \cap B)$—the probability that a randomly chosen book is both paperback and fiction—is equal to $\frac{1}{4}$. So $P(A \cup B) = \frac{1}{3} + \frac{1}{2} - \frac{1}{4} = \frac{7}{12}$. This indicates in this case that $\frac{7}{12}$ of the books are either paperback or fiction.

General multiplication rule

The general multiplication rule for probabilities states that $P(A \cap B) = P(A)P(B|A) = P(B)P(A|B)$. In other words, the probability that events A and B will both occur is equal to the probability that event A will occur times the probability that event B will occur on the condition that A occurs; or, equivalently, it is equal to the to the probability that event B will occur times the probability that event A will occur on the condition that B occurs.
For example, suppose we're told that a certain cat is in a certain yard half the time, and when it is in the yard there is a $\frac{1}{3}$ chance that a second cat will be with it. We will call the event of the first cat being in the yard A, and the event of the second cat being in the yard B. Then from the given information, P(A) = $\frac{1}{2}$ and $P(B|A) = \frac{1}{3}$. The probability that both cats are in the yard is then $P(A \cap B) = P(A)P(B|A) = \left(\frac{1}{2}\right)\left(\frac{1}{3}\right) = \frac{1}{6}$.

<u>Interpreting the result in terms of a uniform probability model</u>
The general multiplication rule states that $P(A \cap B) = P(A)P(B|A) = P(B)P(A|B)$. The result of this rule is the probability that events A and B will both occur, which for a uniform probability model is equal to the fraction of outcomes that are in both events A and B.
For example, suppose we are told that $\frac{1}{4}$ of the insects in a certain woman's insect collection are butterflies, and that $\frac{1}{5}$ of those butterflies are blue. We can call event A the event that a randomly chosen insect from the collection is a butterfly and event B the event that it is blue. So P(A) = $\frac{1}{4}$, and $P(B|A) = \frac{1}{5}$—the fraction of butterflies in the collection that are blue is equal to the probability that a randomly chosen insect in the collection is blue, given that it is a butterfly. Then by the multiplication rule, $P(A \cap B) = P(A)P(B|A) = \left(\frac{1}{4}\right)\left(\frac{1}{5}\right) = \frac{1}{20}$. So the probability that a randomly selected insect from the collection is both blue and a butterfly is $\frac{1}{20}$; $\frac{1}{20}$ of the insects are blue butterflies.

Reading

Literary Analysis

Setting and time frame

A literary text has both a setting and time frame. A setting is the place in which the story as a whole is set. The time frame is the period in which the story is set. This may be a historical period or that the story is set over the course of a single day. Both setting and time frame are relevant to a text's meaning because they help the reader place the story in time and space. An author uses setting and time frame to anchor a text, create a mood, and enhance its meaning; helping a reader understand why a character acts the way he does, or why certain events in the story are important. The setting impacts the plot and character motivations, while the time frame helps place the story in chronological context.

<u>Example</u>
Read the following excerpt from The Adventures of Huckleberry Finn by Mark Twain and analyze the relevance of setting to the text's meaning:

> We said there warn't no home like a raft, after all. Other places do seem so cramped up and smothery, but a raft don't. You feel mighty free and easy and comfortable on a raft.

This excerpt from *The Adventures of Huckleberry Finn* by Mark Twain reveals information about the setting of the book. By understanding that the main character, Huckleberry Finn, lives on a raft, the reader can place the story on a river, in this case, the Mississippi River in the South before the Civil War. The information about the setting also gives the reader clues about the character of Huck Finn: he clearly values independence and freedom and he likes the outdoors. The information about the setting in the quote helps the reader to better understand the rest of the text.

Theme

The theme of a passage is what the reader learns from the text or the passage. It is the lesson or moral contained in the passage. It also is a unifying idea that is used throughout the text; it can take the form of a common setting, idea, symbol, design, or recurring event. A passage can have two or more themes that convey its overall idea. The theme or themes of a passage are often based on universal themes. They can frequently be expressed using well-known sayings about life, society, or human nature, such as "Hard work pays off" or "Good triumphs over evil." Themes are not usually stated explicitly. The reader must figure them out by carefully reading the passage. Themes are often the reason why passages are written; they give a passage unity and meaning. Themes are created through plot development. The events of a story help shape the themes of a passage.

Explain why "Take care of what you care about" accurately describes the theme of the following excerpt.

> Luca collected baseball cards. But, Luca wasn't very careful with them. He left them around the house. His dog liked to chew. Luca and his friend Bart were looking at his collection. Then, they went outside. When Luca got home, he saw his dog chewing on his cards. They were ruined.

This excerpt tells the story of a boy who is careless with his baseball cards and leaves them lying around. His dog ends up chewing them and ruining them. The lesson is that if you care about something, you need to take care of it. This is the point of the story. The theme is the lesson that a story teaches. Some stories have more than one theme, but this is not really true of this excerpt. The reader needs to figure out the theme based on what happens in the story. Sometimes, as in the case of fables, the theme is stated directly in the text. However, this is not usually the case.

Conflict

Read the following paragraph and discuss the type of conflict present:
> Timothy was shocked out of sleep by the appearance of a bear just outside his tent. After panicking for a moment, he remembered some advice he had read in preparation for this trip: he should make noise so the bear would not be startled. As Timothy started to hum and sing, the bear wandered away.

There are three main types of conflict in literature: man versus man, man versus nature, and man versus self. This paragraph is an example of man versus nature. Timothy is in conflict with the bear. Even though no actual conflict, like an attack, exists, Timothy is pitted against the bear. Timothy uses his knowledge to "defeat" the bear and keep himself safe. The solution to the conflict is that Timothy makes noise, the bear wanders away, and Timothy is safe.

Conflict resolution

There are three main types of conflict in literature: man versus man, man versus nature, and man versus self. The way the conflict is resolved depends on the type of conflict. The plot of any book starts with the lead up to the conflict, then the conflict itself, then the solution, or resolution, to the conflict. In 'man versus man' conflicts, the conflict is often resolved by the two parties coming to some sort of agreement. In 'man versus nature' conflicts, the conflict is often resolved by man coming to some realization about some aspect of nature. In 'man versus self' conflicts, the conflict is often resolved by the character growing or coming to an understanding about part of himself.

Syntax and word choice

Authors use words and syntax, or sentence structure, to make their texts unique, convey their own writing style, and sometimes to make a point or emphasis. They know that word choice and syntax contribute to the reader's understanding of the text as well as to the tone and mood of a text.

Allusion

An allusion is an un-cited but recognizable reference to something else. Authors use language to make allusions to places, events, artwork, and other books in order to make their own text richer. For example, an author may allude to a very important text in order to make his own text seem more important. Martin Luther King, Jr. started his "I Have a Dream" speech by saying "Five score years ago..." This is a clear allusion to President Abraham Lincoln's "Gettysburg Address" and served to remind people of the significance of the event. An author may allude to a place to ground his text or make a cultural reference to make readers feel included. There are many reasons that authors make allusions.

Comic relief

Comic relief is the use of comedy by an author to break up a dramatic or tragic scene and infuse it with a bit of lightheartedness. In William Shakespeare's Hamlet, two gravediggers digging the grave for Ophelia share a joke while they work. The death and burial of Ophelia are tragic moments that directly follow each other. Shakespeare uses an instance of comedy to break up the tragedy and give his audience a bit of a break from the tragic drama. In general, authors use comic relief so that their work will not be overwhelmingly dark and depressing. Often, authors will use comedy to parallel what is happening in the tragic scenes.

Credibility of a text

When evaluating the credibility of a text, it is important to look at the author of the text. If the text is being put out by a person with a specific agenda (i.e., a political lobbyist) that text is going to be biased in a particular direction. The author's motivations for writing the text play a critical role in determining its credibility. Likewise, reports written about the Ozone layer by an environmental scientist and a hairdresser will have a different level of credibility. The extent of the author's knowledge of the topic and their motivation must be evaluated when assessing the credibility of a text.

Proofreading

Proofreading is an important part of the writing process. After finishing a first draft, one should always proofread to ensure the document is written as desired. When proofreading, one should do some editing as well as some revision. Editing includes things like checking for correct spelling, capitalization, comma use, and punctuation. Revision includes clarifying ideas, combining sentences, changing run-ons into two sentences, and looking carefully at word choice to make sure the flow of the piece is fluid and the thoughts are expressed as clearly as possible. If one does not proofread, they would invariably put out writing that was full of errors. As writing reflects upon the author, one needs to ensure that it is exactly how they want it to be.

Newspaper articles, short stories, and advertisements

When authors write, it is always with a purpose. There are four main purposes: to inform, to entertain, to describe, and to persuade. A newspaper article is most often a factual account of something that occurred, written to inform readers about the event. A short story is fiction; it may be sad, funny, or even uplifting; but regardless of the emotion it brings out, fiction is written to entertain. People read fiction to escape their lives and be entertained. Advertisements, whether in print, on television, or Internet ads, are written to convince the reader to do or buy something. The purpose of advertisements is to persuade the reader to do something.

Main Idea and Supporting Details

Determining the central idea of a passage

The central idea of a passage is what the passage is mostly about. It is the main point of the passage. Sometimes a passage states the main idea. In such passages, the main idea can be found in a topic sentence at the beginning of the passage or somewhere in the text. Sometimes the main idea is found in the conclusion of a passage. Oftentimes, however, the passage does not state the main idea outright. Instead, the reader needs to figure it out from the information or supporting details found in the passage. The main idea will become more and more evident as a person reads a passage. Most of the time, the main idea does not become evident until the reader has reached nearly the end of the passage. The central or main idea becomes evident as the reader encounters more details and information about the main idea. The details shape the main idea.

Discuss why the main idea of this excerpt is "The Irish have a long history."

> The Irish people of today descended from the three sons of Milesius, the king of Hispania, now known as Spain. They invaded Ireland a thousand years before Christ and intermarried with the local natives, known as the Tuatha De Danaan, who are said to have descended from the Irish goddess Danu.

The information in the excerpt deals the descendants of the Irish people. Furthermore, the passage tells how the three sons of the king of what is now Spain invaded Ireland and married the local natives. The details about the Irish are explicit, accurate facts and can be checked. The central idea emerges from these details. The details tell the early history of the Irish people. Supporting details shape or tell more about the main idea so the reader can tell what a passage is mostly about.

Example 1
Read the following sentences. Identify the main idea and supporting detail.

> The new art museum is set to open on September 1st of this year. Paintings from local artists will be displayed for purchase year-round.

A main idea is typically followed by a supporting detail, since a "supporting detail" indicates further information about the main idea. In the example, the reader first learns when the art museum will open, then what will be displayed at the museum. The second sentence gives further information about the art museum.

The main idea of a selection can often be found in the first one to two paragraphs of text. Supporting details come in subsequent paragraphs or further in the same paragraph. When looking for the main idea of a selection, recognize that the main idea will give the reader the main point of the entire story. This allows the reader to know what to expect while reading the rest of the selection.

<u>Example 2</u>
Read the excerpt below. Identify and discuss the main idea.

> Students who have jobs while attending high school tend not to have as much time to complete their homework as other students. They also do not have time for other activities. We should try to persuade our young people to concentrate on doing well in school, not to concentrate on making money. Having a job while you are a student is harmful.

The main idea of the excerpt is actually the last sentence: "Having a job while you are a student is harmful." This is what the excerpt is mostly about. The other sentences contain supporting information: students who have jobs don't have as much time for homework; students with jobs don't have time for as many activities. These are both supporting details that tell more about the main idea. The third sentence deals with a persuasive argument; it is another kind of detail. Only the last sentence tells what the excerpt is mostly about. Main ideas are sometimes found in a topic sentence at the start of a text or in the concluding sentence, which is the case in this excerpt.

Supporting Details

Supporting details provide evidence and backing for the main point. All texts contain details, but they are only classified as supporting details when they serve to reinforce some larger point. Supporting details are most commonly found in informative and persuasive texts. In some cases, they will be clearly indicated with words like for example or for instance, or they will be enumerated with words like first, second, and last. However, these special words are not a requirement. As a reader, it is important to consider whether the author's supporting details really back up his or her main point. Supporting details can be factual and correct but still not relevant to the author's point. Conversely, supporting details can seem pertinent but be ineffective because they are based on opinion or assertions that cannot be proven.

A good supporting detail would need to include information that supports or explains more about the main idea. A supporting detail might read: "She also loved to eat them," or "She also grew strawberries in her backyard." Supporting details provide additional information about the main idea that has not already been presented to the reader. A supporting detail further develops the topic of the story and provides an explanation of a part of the main idea.

In the example supporting details above, note that the topic is still focused on the subject of strawberries and action that the character takes in relation to that particular subject. A main idea will often appear in the first one to two paragraphs of a story. Supporting details appear later in a paragraph or in other paragraphs within the story.

Explicit information

Explicit information includes facts and statements that are found directly in a passage or a story. It is not information that is hinted at or information you need to make a conclusion about. Explicit information may be found in many forms; it can be contained in a quote as well as in a description. It can be found in dialogue and in actions. This information can sometimes be used to support an inference. The answers to questions about explicit information are found through careful reading of the text. Attention is given to pertinent facts or other information. In fiction, details about characters, events, and setting can be both explicit and implicit.

Read the following excerpt and identify the information that is explicit.

According to an ancient Greek legend, an inventor named Daedalus was imprisoned on an island by an angry king. His son, Icarus, was with him. The inventor came up with an escape plan. He created two pairs of wings from feathers and a wooden frame. He made one for himself and one for his son.

Explicit information is information found directly in the text. It is not inferred; it is not suggested. The explicit information in this excerpt is about the Greek myth that tells the story of the inventor Daedalus. The excerpt says that the inventor Daedalus and his son Icarus were imprisoned on an island by an angry king. It says that he had a plan of escape, and that he created two pairs of wings from feathers and a wooden frame. This information is found directly in the excerpt. It is not necessary to make any inferences or guesses to obtain this information.

Inference in a Text

Inference

An inference is a conclusion that a reader can make based on the facts and other information in a passage or a story. An inference is based both on what is found in a passage or a story and what is known from personal experience. For instance, a story may say that a character is frightened and that he can hear the sounds of wolves in the distance. Based on both what is in the text and personal knowledge, it might be a logical conclusion that the character is frightened because he hears the sound of wolves. A good inference is supported by the information in a passage. Inferences are different from explicit information, which is clearly stated in a passage. Inferences are not stated in a passage. A reader must put the information together to come up with a logical conclusion.

Read the excerpt and decide why Jana finally relaxed.

> Jana loved her job, but the work was very demanding. She had trouble relaxing. She called a friend, but she still thought about work. She ordered a pizza, but eating it did not help. Then her kitten jumped on her lap and began to purr. Jana leaned back and began to hum a little tune. She felt better.

You can draw the conclusion that Jana relaxes because her kitten jumped on her lap. The kitten purred, and Jana leaned back and hummed a tune. Then, she felt better. The excerpt does not explicitly say that this is the reason why she was able to relax. The text leaves the matter unclear. But, the reader can infer or make a "best guess" that this is the reason she is relaxing. This is a logical conclusion based on the information in the passage. It is the best conclusion a reader can make based on the information he or she has read. Inferences are based on the information in a passage, but they are not directly stated in the passage.

Comparison of two stories

When presented with two different stories, there will be similarities and differences between the two. A reader needs to make a list or other graphic organizer of the points presented in each story. Once the reader has written down the main point and supporting points for each story, the two sets of ideas can be compared. The reader can then present each idea and show how it is the same or different in the other story. This is called comparing and contrasting ideas. The reader can compare ideas by stating, for example: "In Story 1, the author believes that humankind will one day land on Mars, whereas in Story 2, the author believes that Mars is too far away for humans to ever step foot on." Note that the two viewpoints are different in each story that the reader is comparing. A reader may state that: "Both stories discussed the likelihood of humankind landing on Mars." This statement shows how the viewpoint presented in both stories is based on the same topic, rather than how each viewpoint is different. The reader will complete a comparison of two stories with a conclusion.

Drawing Conclusions

A common type of inference that a reader has to make is drawing a conclusion. The reader makes this conclusion based on the information provided within a text. Certain facts are included to help a reader come to a specific conclusion. For example, a story may open with a man trudging through the snow on a cold winter day, dragging a sled behind him. The reader can logically infer from the setting of the story that the man is wearing heavy winter clothes in order to stay warm. Information is implied based on the setting of a story, which is why setting is an important element of the text. If the same man in the example was trudging down a beach on a hot summer day, dragging a surf board behind him, the reader would assume that the man is not wearing heavy clothes. The reader makes inferences based on their own experiences and the information presented to them in the story.

Example 1
Read the following sentence and draw a conclusion based upon the information presented:

> "You know the reason Mother proposed not having any presents this Christmas was because it is going to be a hard winter for everyone; and she thinks we ought not to spend money for pleasure, when our men are suffering so in the army." (from *Little Women* by Louisa May Alcott, p. 3)

Based on the information in the sentence, the reader can conclude, or infer, that the men are away at war while the women are still at home. The pronoun 'our' gives a clue to the reader that the character is speaking about men she knows. In addition, the reader can assume that the character is speaking to a brother or sister, since the term Mother is used by the character while speaking to another person. The reader can also come to the conclusion that the characters celebrate Christmas, since it is mentioned in the context of the sentence. In the sentence, the Mother is presented as an unselfish character who is opinionated and thinks about the well-being of other people.

Author's Use of Language

Figurative use of a word

Authors use literary devices like figurative language to expand reality in a vivid way. An author can utilize figurative language to connect things in an exaggerated way, which results in a stronger, more vivid image. Examples of figurative language include simile, metaphor, personification, and hyperbole. Similes compare things using the comparing words *like* or *as*. "She is as brave as a lion" is an example of a simile. Metaphors compare things without using comparing words. An example of a metaphor is "She is a lion in the wild." Personification attributes human traits to an animal or non-living thing. "Time flew by" is an example of personification. Hyperbole is an exaggeration that is not believable. "He waited in line for years" is an example of this literary device.

Read the excerpt; identify the form of figurative language represented by the phrase "like a fresh April shower," and explain your answer.

> We had been sequestered inside the barn all afternoon. It was hot, really hot. When the sun finally set and I opened the door, the evening air swept over us like a fresh April shower, leaving us ready to enjoy the evening.

The phrase "like a fresh April shower" is an example of a simile. The phrase compares the air with a fresh April shower and uses the word "like," so it qualifies as a simile. Similes compare two things using the word "like" or "as." This phrase is not a metaphor. Although it compares two things, it uses the word "like"; metaphors do not use either "like" or "as" to compare two things. It is not an example of personification, because nothing is being given human traits. There is no sign of hyperbole here either; there is no sense of an exaggeration.

Author's Purpose

The author's purpose is going to be their reason for writing the paper or story. Some authors may write with the purpose of entertainment in mind. Most fiction novels would fall under this category. The author may also write with the purpose of trying to persuade or convince the reader. A Proposition and Support paper would be an example of this, where an author gives their opinion and then tries to convince the reader to see something from their point of view. An author can also write with the purpose of informing or teaching the reader. As the reader reads a paper they should always try to figure out the author's purpose for writing as this will help them to better understand the message that the author is trying to convey.

Impact of words on tone

Words can have a large impact on the tone of a passage. Tone is a result of the choice of language. For instance, when talking about or suggesting the mood of a person or a setting, it is vital to choose the right language to describe it. Is a person ecstatic, or is the person simply content? Is a room barren, or is it just empty? Similarly, using strong action verbs can create a tone that is forceful and remembered easily. The verb *buttress*, for instance, has a much stronger impact than the verb *strengthen*. Even though both words have basically the same meaning, the first one creates a more vivid image in the mind of the reader. It is important to use words that will be understood by the audience and will have the desired effect.

Understatement or a sense of irony

Many authors enjoy using a sense of irony or understatement as they write a story. Both techniques distance the writer from the characters and the events of a story. In either case, the reader must read between the lines to figure out what the author is actually getting at and what his or her point of view actually is. Understatement can be used as a humorous vehicle, allowing the author to comment on what is happening without being deeply emotionally invested in it. Irony allows the author to make a statement about what is really occurring without openly stating it. When reading a text, be sure to look for any underlying meaning that an author might be trying to convey. An initial reading of a text may not be enough to discern its true intended meaning. The way an author talks about what is happening often conveys that author's viewpoint of the events.

Determining the meaning of words or phrases as they are used in a text

When the reader does not understand a word or a phrase that is used in a passage or a story, it is important to examine the context clues around the word or phrase that provide hints about its meaning. Many words have more than one meaning, and it is only through an examination of the context that the reader can figure out the correct meaning. The word "crown" is a good example. This word has several meanings, including a coronet, the top of a head, the act of awarding something to someone, or even the act of hitting someone. Therefore, it is important to understand the context. In the sentence, "He sought to be crowned the winner of the competition," it is clear that the meaning is "to be awarded." Context must also be used to determine the meaning of phrases. In the sentence, "He wasn't going to stand for that anymore, so he told his boss off," the reader can use context to get a sense of the meaning of "going to stand for." In this case, the phrase means "not put up with."

Context clues

The best way to figure out the meaning of unknown words and expressions is to examine the surrounding context clues. Often many clues to the meaning of an expression or word in the sentences occur just before or after the unknown word or expression. Some words have more than one meaning, and only through the context of the text can these words be understood. For instance, the word "blunt" has several meanings, including "having a dull edge," "not being subtle," and "being slow to understand," so understanding the context is important. In the sentence, "He was a blunt talker, and I got his point quickly," it becomes clear that the meaning is "not being subtle." Phrases also must be understood through context. In the sentence, "She rolled up her sleeves and got to work," the reader can get the sense that "rolling up her sleeves" means to get ready for hard work.

Word choice and intended audience

Authors choose words carefully when they are writing. They choose words that precisely express what they want to get across. In addition, word choice impacts the style and tone of a piece of writing. Authors also think about their intended audience when they write. Authors might write the same story differently for different audiences. For example, if an author is writing a story for children, he or she might not include some more disturbing or provocative details that he or she would include when telling the story to adults. Word choice and intended audience impact the text by affecting content, style, and tone.

Rhetorical schemes

Authors use rhetorical schemes to emphasize, to draw analogies, and to engage the reader. A common technique is parallelism, in which several sentences are given the same grammatical structure in order to highlight the similarities between their content. For example, "Hector went to the store. He went to the bank. He went to the gym." By expressing this information in three very simple statements, the author suggests the dullness of these activities. Another rhetorical scheme is repetition, in which the author uses the same word several times quickly, either to call its meaning into question or to draw emphasis. Consider the sentence "They called him a slave, he thought of himself as a slave, and his prospects were no better than those of a slave." The repetition of the word *slave* mimics the plodding, hopeless nature of slavery, but also causes the reader to focus on the word and consider whether it is really appropriate here.

Organizational Patterns

When writing there are a variety of ways that an author can choose to organize their story. It is important for them to choose the pattern that best presents their information, as not all patterns will work for every piece of writing. For example, if an author wants to write a story about a series of events that happened one week they would organize their story in Chronological Order. However, if they were writing an informational text an author may want to use Order of Importance to organize the paper. Order of Importance would present their information from the most important point to the least important one.

Problem and Solution
Problem and Solution is an organizational pattern where the author will present some information as a problem and will then discuss a solution or attempted solution. In Problem and Solution there is generally one main problem, but that one problem may have several possible solutions. For example, let's say that Billy wants a new video game but does not have the money. There are several possible solutions to this. First he could just try asking his mom to buy it for him. If that does not work he could get a job mowing grass until he has enough money to buy it. A third solution would be if he is really patient he could wait until his birthday and ask for it then. Problem and Solution can sometimes be confused with Cause and Effect. However, the easy way to tell them apart is in Cause and Effect there is a cause or problem and then it discusses the effects but does not give a solution.

Proposition and Support
In Proposition and Support an author will state a proposition that is their opinion that they will debate in the paper. The topic is generally something that readers will feel uncertain about and may not already have an opinion on. The author will then give support for his argument. The support should include facts, statistics, logic and reasoning. The more hard evidence an author can give the reader the better it will help convince them to see things from the author's point of view.

Style, tone, and mood

An author can vary the feel of a text by changing the style, tone, and mood of each sentence. The style of a text refers to whether the author uses long, flowing sentences, short, choppy sentences, or something in-between. The text may be organized in short lines, short paragraphs, or long paragraphs. The tone of a paper helps to establish the mood of the text. Tone involves the attitude that the author displays in the paper. For example, the author may feel exuberant about a sunny day, but feel down on a gloomy day. The words that the author uses to describe the scene and situation in the story help to define its tone. The mood of a story may be uplifting, down, scared, or excited, again, depending upon the words the author uses. All of these elements: style, tone, and mood, can affect how the reader feels about the story.

Example 1
Describe the tone of the following sentence from "The Adventure of the Speckled Band" by Sir Arthur Conan Doyle:

> Then creeping up to me and making a trumpet of his hand, he whispered into my ear again so gently that it was all that I could do to distinguish the words.

The tone of the sentence is mysterious. The words "creeping" and "whispered into my ear" make the reader wonder why the character needs to be quiet in the story. The characters in the sentence seem to be waiting for something to happen, making the reader may feel that they need to hold their breath while waiting to see what happens to the characters in the story. The tone of the sentence is appropriately mysterious, since the story is written as a mystery. By creating suspense in the text, the author makes the reader want to see what happens next.

Example 2
Describe the style and mood of the following sentence from The Adventures of Tom Sawyer by Mark Twain:

> He surveyed the fence, and all gladness left him and a deep melancholy settled down upon his spirit.

The style of the sentence is fully descriptive of the character's feelings, painting a picture in the reader's mind of the character's thoughts. The author uses the word 'and' twice to signify the sinking spirits of the character in the sentence. The mood of the sentence mirrors the emotion of the character, as the character goes from level-headed to quite sad, from which the reader can deduce that the character does not want to do something, which has brought down his mood as a result. In this particular scenario, the character does not want to spend a long time whitewashing a fence while he had other plans on such a beautiful day. The style of the sentence is direct; it explains how the character feels in the story.

Text evidence

The term *text evidence* refers to information included in a text that supports the main point of the paper. A reader can draw conclusions or generalizations based upon information found in a text, in which the author will deliberately include key points that serve as

- 46 -

supporting details for the main point. For example, the main point of a paper may state: The average yearly rainfall in the city has risen by 2 inches per year since 1999. The paper would go on to include the amount of rainfall for each month or season and any contributing factors that may be causing an increase in yearly rainfall. Additional facts, or text evidence to support the point that yearly rainfall is rising in the city would help to prove that the author's main point is correct.

Example 1
Draw a conclusion based on the following sentence from The Adventures of Tom Sawyer by Mark Twain:

> He had discovered a great law of human action, without knowing it—
> namely, that in order to make a man or a boy covet a thing, it is only
> necessary to make the thing difficult to attain.

The reader can conclude from the sentence that the character did not set out to learn something, but through an action, the character learned that people will want what is hard to attain. The character learned a fact about human nature; that a person will value something more if they have to work hard for it than if it is simply given to them. The word *covet* means to desire, which the character learns can be manipulated by making an item or an outcome more difficult to grasp. In everyday life, this could apply toward taking a hard test and doing well. If someone studies for a hard test and does well, the person will value their score more than if the test was very easy and he or she did not study for the test.

Writing

Essay Revision

Revision

When one proofreads their writing, it is important to look for a number of things. One's text should be proofread at least twice, with a different focus each time: revision and editing. During the revision phase, the author will need to look for ways to improve the organization, content, clarity of ideas, word choice, writing style, and sentence structure and variety. This ensures that the paper is organized in a logical way and that the ideas flow. Are all the important points mentioned and substantiated with details? Is the writing style consistent and appropriate? Are the words specific and meaningful? Once the paper is revised, the author can then edit it for mechanical errors.

<u>Example</u>
Explain what is incorrect in the following sentence and discuss how to revise it to make it correct:

> My brother and I enjoys hiking and going on camping trips.

This sentence has an error in subject-verb agreement. In a correct sentence, the subject and verb need to agree in number. The given sentence has a plural subject (my brother and I) and a singular verb (enjoys). There are two ways to revise the sentence, depending on what the author really means. If it is intended to have a plural subject, it would be changed to:

> My brother and I <u>enjoy</u> hiking and going on camping trips.

If it was meant to have a singular subject, it would be changed to:

> <u>Each member</u> of my family <u>enjoys</u> hiking and going on camping trips.

Evaluate or critique one's own writing

It is important that one evaluate their own writing to know whether they are writing in a clear, logical, and readable way, or whether what they have just written would be hard for a reader to understand. Remember, authors write to get a point across. If a person's writing is not clear, they have not achieved in getting their point across. After a person finishes writing something, they should read it back. When doing this, they should ask if the content is clear, the grammar is correct, does the writing match the purpose and intended audience. In order to evaluate one's own writing, they would have to read it with the thought that they are simply a reader, not the writer.

Clear and coherent writing

Clear and coherent writing requires good initial planning. You need to determine what you are going to say, who you are saying it to, and how you want to say it, as well as the kind of tone you want to project. In the process of writing, organize your arguments and use a logical order to develop them. Use paragraph breaks to help organize your thoughts. Your sentences should be precise and to the point. Make sure your punctuation is correct. Your ideas should be supported by evidence, and opposing ideas should be mentioned as well. When you get to your conclusion, avoid being repetitious; concentrate on summarizing. Proofread what you have written to check for any errors; reading the text aloud is often helpful.

Creating cohesion

Appropriate transition words help clarify the relationships between ideas and concepts and create a more cohesive passage. Good writers know that such words and phrases serve to clarify the relationships between ideas and concepts. Words or phrases that show causality between ideas include *consequently, therefore,* and *as a result of. However, on the other hand, in contrast, but,* or *similarly* indicate a compare and contrast relationship. When examples of different concepts are used, words such *as namely, for example,* or *for instance* act as transition words. When it is necessary to show the order of importance of ideas or concepts, transition words such as *at first, primarily, secondly, former,* or *latter* can be used.

How could the following sentences be written with a better transition between the ideas?

They didn't know what they were doing. The boat often ran aground.

Rewriting the two sentences requires understanding the sentences' relationships with each other. In this passage, causality is suggested. The boat ran aground because they didn't know what they were doing. To combine the sentences, you need to use an appropriate transition word. This case has several options. The phrase "as a result" works well. It shows the causality between the two thoughts: "They didn't know what they were doing; as a result, the boat often ran aground." Other causality words include *because, consequently,* or *therefore.* The two sentences could be joined with any of those words, and the combination would make more sense than the separate sentences.

Using precise language

Writers of informational or explanatory texts must use precise language and domain-specific vocabulary in order to accurately communicate their ideas. General vocabulary words will not assert the necessary points. The reader will not follow the main idea of the passage if it lacks details supplied by carefully chosen, precise, and domain-specific language. For instance, using the term *renal* in a in a medical text is more technical than the term *kidney.* While researching a subject, you should include technical vocabulary to use during the writing of the text. Oftentimes it may be necessary to define domain-specific words for the reader.

Supporting evidence from text

When discussing a text, it is important to use elements of the text to strengthen one's position. If one needs to clarify something they read, they should go back to the text, reread it, and use the text to make sure they have a firm understanding of the point the author is trying to make. Similarly, when one is interpreting a piece of text, you're the interpretation needs to be based upon the text itself. Using supporting evidence from the text strengthens the interpretation because it is made clear that the original text was thoroughly read and that the interpretation was based on the details and facts within it. Elements of text that can be used in a response include: facts, details, statistics, and direct quotations from the text.

Agreement

Subject-verb agreement

Subject-verb agreement means that the subject and verb in a sentence have to agree in number. A singular subject needs a singular verb, just as a plural subject needs a plural verb. Errors occur when people incorrectly match the number of the subject and the verb. Here is an example of an incorrect sentence: The dogs of the neighborhood was barking loudly. The sentence is incorrect because the subject, *dogs*, is plural. The sentence is referring to more than one dog. The verb, *was*, is singular. The subject and verb do not match. Here are two correct versions of the sentence, depending on the meaning the author wants to convey:

The <u>dog</u> of the neighborhood <u>was</u> barking loudly.
The <u>dogs</u> of the neighborhood <u>were</u> barking loudly.

<u>Example</u>
Revise the following sentence:
> My mother and I likes to go for a walk around our neighborhood every night after dinner.

This sentence has an error in subject-verb agreement. The subject of the sentence is *my mother and I*. This is a plural subject because two people are doing the action. The problem is that a singular verb (*likes*) is used with the plural subject. The subject and verb in a sentence need to agree in number for it to make grammatical sense. The sentence needs to be revised to correct the number of the verb form. The correct sentence should read:
> My mother and I like to go for a walk around our neighborhood every night after dinner.

Pronoun-antecedent agreement

Pronoun-antecedent agreement means that the pronoun and the antecedent (the word that refers back to the pronoun) need to match in number and gender. A singular pronoun needs a singular antecedent, just as a plural pronoun needs a plural antecedent. Likewise, masculine pronouns need masculine antecedents, and feminine pronouns need feminine antecedents.

<u>Example 1</u>
Here is an example of a sentence with a mistake in pronoun-antecedent agreement: The bike rack is there for everyone to lock up their bikes. This is a very common error and one that people make in speaking and in writing all the time. In the sentence, the pronoun is *everyone*. This is a singular pronoun. In the sentence, the antecedent is *their*, which is plural. The sentence should have correct pronoun-antecedent agreement. Here is the correct revision of the sentence:

The bike rack is there for everyone to lock up his bike.

<u>Example 2</u>
Explain what is incorrect in the following sentence and discuss how to revise it to make it correct:

If a person wants to ride a bicycle safely, they should wear a helmet.

This sentence has an error in pronoun-antecedent agreement. This means that the pronoun and its antecedent do not match in either number or gender. In this case, *person* is the pronoun. It is a singular pronoun, but the antecedent *they*, which is used in the sentence, is a plural antecedent. This does not work because there is no number match. To correct the error, the antecedent must be made singular. Here is a correct version of the sentence:
If a person wants to ride a bicycle safely, <u>he</u> should wear a helmet.

Verb tenses

Verb tenses are ways in which verbs show that an action takes place. Verbs change according to when an action occurs. An action can take place in the present tense, which means the action is happening right now. An action can take place in the past tense, which means the action has already happened and is in the past. An action can take place in the future, which means the action has not yet happened but will do so. A progressive tense shows that the action is ongoing and continuing to go on in the present.

Verbs change form to agree with the subject of the action and to indicate the time or tense of the action. Verb tenses can be categorized as simple or perfect. Each of these tenses has a continuous form. *Simple present tense* expresses habitual or repeated actions, general truths, future actions, literary or historic present, and states or qualities of being. In statements, do/does expresses emphasis. See examples below:

Susie exercises on Thursdays and Fridays. habitual action
Fred is a doctor. linking verb--state of being
Simple past tense expresses finished actions. Did in statements expresses emphasis. See examples below.
World War II ended in 1945. finished action
Benedict Arnold began as a loyal American, but later he did betray his country. emphasis
Future tense expresses actions or conditions occurring in the future. Simple present tense with an adverb of time can indicate future.
She will see it next week. future tense
The insurance coverage ends next month. simple present

Sentence Structure

Parallel structure

Parallel structure means keeping the structure of one's writing the same throughout a sentence. All nouns, verbs, and phrases should have the same structure. Many people often make mistakes, particularly with parallel verbs and verb phrases. If one is writing with a series of verbs, they must each have the same structure and tense (i.e., they all end in -ing). In the following sentence, the verbs are parallel: Penny is laughing while she is chewing. Both *laughing* and *chewing* are progressive present tense verbs. Parallelism also applies to phrases. An example of this is: I have to *go* to the store, *stop* by the bank, and *ride* my bicycle home. If the sentence were written without parallel structure for the verb phrases, the sentence would seem awkward (e.g., I have to *go* to the store, *stop* by the bank, and *riding* my bicycle home.).

Example
> When we went on our hike, we had fun climbing the mountain, eating a
> picnic lunch, and we stopped at the top to admire the view.

The sentence on the front of the card does not have parallel structure with the items in the comma series. The phrases *climbing the mountain*, *eating a picnic lunch*, and *we stopped at the top to admire the view* should all be parallel in verb structure, but they are not. In order to revise the sentence, the phrases in the comma series need to be made parallel. One way to correctly revise the sentence is:
> When we went on our hike, we had fun climbing the mountain, eating a
> picnic lunch, and admiring the view from the top.

Here is another correct revision:
When we went on our hike, we climbed the mountain, ate a picnic lunch, and stopped at the top to admire the view.

Comma Use

1. Commas may be used to separate the items in a sequence (three or more things). For example, "She went to the store, dropped off the clothes at the dry cleaners, and stopped by the post office."
2. Use a comma along with a conjunction (and, but, for, nor, yet, or, so) to connect two independent clauses. For example, "She wanted to go to the store, but she did not have a car."
3. Use a comma to set off introductory elements. For example, "Driving to the grocery store, she suddenly realized that she forgot her purse."
4. Use a comma to set off parenthetical elements. For example, "The Statue of Liberty, which stands in New York Harbor, was a gift to the United States."

Comma Splice

A comma splice is the use of a comma between two independent clauses. A comma splice can typically be corrected by changing the comma to a period and therefore making the two clauses into two separate sentences, by changing the comma to a semicolon, or by making one clause dependent by inserting a dependent marker word in front of it.

Incorrect: She eats an apple every day, it tastes delicious.

Correct: She eats an apple every day. It tastes delicious.

(or) She eats an apple every day; it tastes delicious.

(or) She eats an apple every day, and it tastes delicious.

(or) She eats an apple every day because it tastes delicious.

(or) Because it tastes delicious, she eats an apple every day.

Run-on

A run-on sentence is a sentence that should be written as two or more sentences. It contains too much information for a single sentence. When reading a run-on sentence, a reader would be out of breath, or very confused. When revising their writing, the author needs to read carefully to be sure to catch any run-ons and revise them. Usually, the easiest way to revise a run-on sentence is to split it up into two or more complete sentences. Figure out where to put the period to make the first part a complete sentence, then, read the second part. You may have to tweak it a bit to make the second part a complete sentence as well.

Example

Revise the following run-on sentence and make it two complete sentences without changing the meaning:

> I get so frustrated when my internet connection fails I just need to take a deep breath, unplug the device and plug it back in again.

This sentence is a run-on sentence that needs to be split into two complete sentences. The way to revise a run-on sentence is to figure out where to put a period to make the first part of the run-on a complete sentence. Then, you can look at the second part of the run-on and identify if it is a complete sentence by itself or if you need to revise it to make it a complete sentence. In the case of the given sentence, the run-on can be split cleanly into two complete sentences that do not alter the meaning. The correct revision is:

> I get so frustrated when my internet connection fails. I just need to take a deep breath, unplug the device and plug it back in again.

Fragment

A *fragment* is an incomplete sentence or thought that cannot stand on its own. Fragments are missing either nouns or verbs and are very confusing to the reader because the thought is not complete. When revising their writing, the author needs to read carefully to be sure to catch any fragments and revise them, making sure to read each word on the page and only the words on the page. The author will want to identify whether the fragment is missing a noun or verb and replace it. Sometimes, a fragment is the beginning part of the next sentence. In this case, you can combine it with the following sentence in order to make one complete thought.

Sentence Logic

Transitional words and phrases

A good writer will use transitional words and phrases to guide the reader through the text. You are no doubt familiar with the common transitions, though you may never have considered how they operate. Some transitional phrases (*after, before, during, in the middle of*) give information about time. Some indicate that an example is about to be given (*for example, in fact, for instance*). Writers use them to compare (*also, likewise*) and contrast (*however, but, yet*). Transitional words and phrases can suggest addition (*and, also, furthermore, moreover*) and logical relationships (*if, then, therefore, as a result, since*). Finally, transitional words and phrases can demarcate the steps in a process (*first, second, last*). You should incorporate transitional words and phrases where they will orient your reader and illuminate the structure of your composition.

Function of phrases

A phrase is a group of words in a sentence which can act as a single part of speech. There are noun phrases and verb phrases. The additional words make the meaning more specific, so there are also prepositional phrases, appositive phrases, and absolute phrases. Phrases are not complete sentences because they lack either a predicate or a subject. Phrases are parts of sentences, and sentences are frequently made up of one or more phrases. An example of a phrase is "the white horse" or "went very quickly." As you can see, neither phrase is a complete sentence. The first phrase lacks a predicate and the second phrase lacks a subject.

Clause

A clause is a word group that has a subject and a predicate and is used by itself or as part of a sentence. Unlike a phrase, a clause can be independent or stand by itself. It can also be dependent, which means it doesn't stand on its own and depends on an independent clause. Dependent clauses begin with a relative pronoun such as: that, who, whom, whose, which, where, when, or why; or a subordinating conjunction, such as: after, because, if, since, unless, to name a few. Dependent clauses can act as nouns, adjectives, and adverbs. *"If we knew what it was we were doing, it would not be called research, would it?"* (Albert Einstein). In this sentence, "If we knew what it was we were doing" is a dependent clause acting as a noun.

Simple vs. compound sentence

A simple sentence has one main clause with one subject and one predicate and no dependent clauses, while a compound sentence has two or more clauses, often joined by a comma and a conjunction, and sometimes by a semicolon. The addition of various phrases can sometimes make a simple sentence appear compound, but if the sentence has only one main clause, it is a simple sentence: For example: *Children around the world love soccer.* (Simple) *Children around the world love soccer, and it is the world's most popular sport.* (Compound)

Complex vs. compound-complex sentence

Adding dependent clauses to simple and compound sentences produces complex and compound-complex sentences. A complex sentence has one main clause and at least one dependent clause. A compound-complex sentence will have more than one main clause and at least one dependent clause.

"The path to my fixed purpose is laid on iron rails, on which my soul is grooved to run.'" (*Moby Dick,* Herman Melville) (Complex) *Although I love going to the movies, I haven't had very much time recently, and I don't know who to ask out.* (Compound-complex) It has two main clauses (I *haven't had much time,* I *don't know who to ask out)* and a dependent clause *(Although I love going to the movies).*

Identify what kind of sentence the following is and explain why this is true.

> George and his sister Veronica landed at the airport about 4:30 and left on the shuttle bus before we got there.

Many times looks can deceive. This is a simple sentence. There is one main clause. If it were a compound sentence, there would have to be two or more main clauses. It might be confusing because the simple subject and the simple predicate are expanded. It has a compound subject (*George and his sister Veronica*), compound verb *(landed and left),* adverbial phrase (*about 4:30*), and two prepositional phrases *(on the shuttle bus* and *before we got there*); therefore, despite the fact that it is a lengthy sentence, it is still just a simple sentence.

Describe how to rewrite the sentences below to include two dependent clauses.

> I graduated from high school. I was given a hunting knife. My grandfather once owned it.

The sentences are all short and are all about the same topic. They can be put together to make a more interesting sentence that will contain the same information by using clauses. Here is one way a writer could change the sentences to improve the expression of the sentence.

> After I graduated from high school, I was given a hunting knife that my grandfather once owned.

This revised sentence makes use of the dependent clause *After I graduated from high school* and the dependent clause *that my grandfather once owned* to make the passage more interesting to read.

Placing phrases and clauses within a sentence

Modifying phrases or clauses should be placed as closely as possible to the words they modify to ensure that the meaning of the sentence is clear. A misplaced modifier makes the meaning of a sentence murky. For instance, the meaning of *Walt barely missed the dog speeding down the street* becomes evident when the phrase is moved: *Speeding down the street, Walt barely missed the dog.* A dangling modifier doesn't have a word that it is modifying, so a word must be put into the sentence in order to complete its meaning. *Having arrived late for assembly, a written excuse was needed.* This sentence makes it sound as though the written excuse was late for assembly, so something needs to be added to the sentence. The meaning is clear when the name Jessica is added. *Having arrived late for assembly, Jessica needed a written excuse.* Here the phrase modifies Jessica.

Rewrite the following sentence so that it makes sense.

> A poem which received little acclaim when he was alive, today readers all over the world enjoy reading Walt Whitman's Leaves of Grass.

In this sentence it is not clear what the clause *A poem which received little acclaim when he was alive* is actually modifying because *poem* is too far away from the title of the poem, *Leaves of Grass.* The reader is forced to pause and think about what the sentence means, so the writing is unclear. Rewritten as *Readers all over the world today enjoy Walt Whitman's Leaves of Grass, a poem which received little acclaim when he was alive* places the modifier correctly so that the reader can immediately grasp the author's meaning. It is important when writing to check for dangling modifiers.

Essay

A topic of current interest or one that is seen to be controversial will be presented to you and you will be required to write a multi-paragraph persuasive essay (350-500 words) giving your opinion on the issue. There is not a "correct" answer for the essay. You must evaluate the issue, organize your ideas, and develop them into a cohesive and coherent response.

You will be measured on how well you are able to utilize standard written English, organize and explain your thoughts, and support those thoughts with reasons and examples. You must state your main idea clearly and provide specific supporting arguments for the position you take.

Brainstorm

Spend the first few minutes brainstorming out ideas. Write down any ideas you might have on the topic. The purpose is to extract from the recesses of your memory any relevant information. In this stage, anything goes down. Write down any idea, regardless of how good it may initially seem.

Strength through Diversity

The best essays will contain diversity of examples and reasoning. As you brainstorm consider different perspectives. Not only are there two sides to every issue, but there are also countless perspectives that can be considered. On any issue, different groups are impacted, with many reaching the same conclusion or position, but through vastly different paths. Try to "see" the issue through as many different eyes as you can. Look at it from every angle and from every vantage point. The more diverse the reasoning used, the more balanced the essay will become and the better the score.

Example:
The issue of free trade is not just two sided. It impacts politicians, domestic (US) manufacturers, foreign manufacturers, the US economy, the world economy, strategic alliances, retailers, wholesalers, consumers, unions, workers, and the exchange of more than just goods, but also of ideas, beliefs, and cultures. The more of these angles that you can approach the issue from, the more solid your reasoning and the stronger your position.

Furthermore, don't just use information as to how the issue impacts other people. Draw liberally from your own experience and your own observations. Explain a personal experience that you have had and your own emotions from that moment. Anything that you've seen in your community or observed in society can be expanded upon to further round out your position on the issue.

Pick a Main Idea

Once you have finished with your creative flow, stop and review it. Which idea were you able to come up with the most supporting information? It's extremely important that you pick an angle that will allow you to have a thorough and comprehensive coverage of the topic. This is not about your personal convictions, but about writing a concise rational discussion of an idea.

Weed the Garden

Every garden of ideas gets weeds in it. The ideas that you brainstormed over are going to be random pieces of information of mixed value. Go through it methodically and pick out the ones that are the best. The best ideas are strong points that it will be easy to write a few sentences or a paragraph about.

Create a Logical Flow

Now that you know which ideas you are going to use and focus upon, organize them. Put your writing points in a logical order. You have your main ideas that you will focus on, and must align them in a sequence that will flow in a smooth, sensible path from point to point, so that the reader will go smoothly from one idea to the next in a logical path. Readers must have a sense of continuity as they read your essay. You don't want to have an essay that rambles back and forth.

Start Your Engines

You have a logical flow of main ideas with which to start writing. Begin expanding on the issues in the sequence that you have set for yourself. Pace yourself. Don't spend too much time on any one of the ideas that you are expanding upon. You want to have time for all of them.

Once you finish expanding on each idea, go back to your brainstorming session up above, where you wrote out your ideas. Go ahead and erase the ideas as you write about them. This will let you see what you need to write about next, and also allow you to pace yourself and see what you have left to cover.

First Paragraph
Your first paragraph should have several easily identifiable features.

First, it should have a quick description or paraphrasing of the topic. Use your own words to briefly explain what the topic is about.

Second, you should explain your opinion of the topic and give an explanation of why you feel that way. What is your decision or conclusion on the topic?

Third, you should list your "writing points". What are the main ideas that you came up with earlier? This is your opportunity to outline the rest of your essay. Have a sentence explaining each idea that you will go intend further depth in additional paragraphs. If someone was to only read this paragraph, they should be able to get an "executive summary" of the entire essay.

Body Paragraph
Each of your successive paragraphs should expand upon one of the points listed in the main paragraph. Use your personal experience and knowledge to support each of your points. Examples should back up everything.

Conclusion Paragraph

Once you have finished expanding upon each of your main points, wrap it up. Summarize what you have said and covered in a conclusion paragraph. Explain once more your opinion of the topic and quickly review why you feel that way. At this stage, you have already backed up your statements, so there is no need to do that again. All you are doing is refreshing in the mind of the reader the main points that you have made.

Don't Panic

Panicking will not put down any more words down for you. Therefore, it isn't helpful. When you first see the topic, if your mind goes as blank as the page on which you have to write out your essay, take a deep breath. Force yourself to mechanically go through the steps listed above.

Secondly, don't get clock fever. It's easy to be overwhelmed when you're looking at a page that doesn't seem to have much text, there is a lot of blank space further down, your mind is full of random thoughts and feeling confused, and the clock is ticking down faster than you would like. You brainstormed first so that you don't have to keep coming up with ideas. If you're running out of time and you have a lot of ideas that you haven't expanded upon, don't be afraid to make some cuts. Start picking the best ideas that you have left and expand on those few. Don't feel like you have to write down and expand all of your ideas.

Check Your Work

It is more important to have a shorter essay that is well written and well organized, than a longer essay that is poorly written and poorly organized. Don't keep writing about a subject just to add words and sentences, and certainly don't start repeating yourself. Expand on the ideas that you identified in the brainstorming session and make sure that you remember to go back and check your work. Reread and make sure that everything you've written makes sense and flows. Clean up any spelling or grammar mistakes that you might have made. Also, go ahead and erase any brainstorming ideas that you weren't able to expand upon and clean up any other extraneous information that you might have written that doesn't fit into your essay.

As you proofread, make sure there aren't any fragments or run-ons. Check for sentences that are too short or too long. If the sentence is too short, look to see if you have an identifiable subject and verb. If it is too long, break it up into two separate sentences. Watch out for any "big" words you may have used. It's good to use difficult vocabulary words, but only if you are positive that you are using them correctly. Your essay has to be correct, it doesn't have to be fancy. You're not trying to impress anyone with your vocabulary, just your ability to develop and express ideas.

Final Note

Depending on your test taking preferences and personality, the essay writing will probably be your hardest or your easiest section. You are required to go through the entire process of writing a position paper very quickly, which can be quite a challenge.

Focus upon each of the steps listed above. Go through the process of creative flow first, generating ideas and thoughts about the topic. Then organize those ideas into a smooth logical flow. Pick out the ones that are best from the list you have created. Decide which main idea or angle of the topic you will discuss.

Create a recognizable structure in your essay, with an introductory paragraph explaining what you have decided upon, and what your main points will be. Use the body paragraphs to expand on those main points and have a conclusion that wraps up the issue or topic.

Take a few moments to go back and review what you have written. Clean up any minor mistakes that you might have had and give it those last few critical touches that can make a huge difference. Finally, be proud and confident of what you have written!

Practice Test #1

Practice Questions

Math

1. If $x + y > 0$ when $x > y$, which of the following cannot be true?
   A. $x = 3$ and $y = 0$
   B. $x = -3$ and $y = 0$
   C. $x = -4$ and $y = -3$
   D. $x = 3$ and $y = -3$

Question 2 is based on the following table.

Hours	1	2	3
Cost	$3.60	$7.20	$10.80

2. The table shows the cost of renting a bicycle for 1, 2 or 3 hours. Which of the following equations best represents the data, if C represents the cost and h represents the time of the rental?
   A. $C = 3.60h$
   B. $C = h + 3.60$
   C. $C = 3.60h + 10.80$
   D. $C = 10.80/h$

3. Rafael has a business selling computers. He buys computers from the manufacturer for $450 each and sells them for $800. Each month, he must also pay fixed costs of $3000 for rent and utilities at his store. If he sells n computers in a month, which of the following equations can be used to calculate his profit?
   A. $P = n(800 - 450 - 3000)$
   B. $P = 3000\,n(800 - 450)$
   C. $P = n(800 - 450) - 3000$
   D. $P = n(800 - 450) + 3000$

4. If $(-1/3)x + 7 = 4$, what is the value for $(1/3)x + 3$?
   A. 3
   B. 6
   C. 9
   D. 12

5. Jack and Kevin play in a basketball game. If the ratio of points scored by Jack to points scored by Kevin is 4 to 3, which of the following could NOT be the total number of points scored by the two boys?
   A. 14
   B. 16
   C. 28
   D. 35

- 62 -

6. How many 3-inch segments can a 4.5-yard line be divided into?
    A. 45
    B. 54
    C. 64
    D. 84

7. Which of the following expressions is equivalent to $(a + b)(a - b)$?
    A. $a^2 - b^2$
    B. $(a + b)^2$
    C. $(a - b)^2$
    D. $ab(a - b)$

8. If $2^4 = 4^x$, then x =
    A. 2
    B. 4
    C. 6
    D. 8

9. $(2x^2 + 3x + 2) - (x^2 + 2x - 3) =$
    A. $x^2 + x + 5$
    B. $x^2 + x - 1$
    C. $x^2 + 5x + 5$
    D. $x^2 + 5x - 1$

10. Which of the following is equivalent to $\left(\sqrt[3]{x^4}\right)^5$?
    A. $x^{\frac{12}{5}}$
    B. $x^{\frac{15}{4}}$
    C. $x^{\frac{20}{3}}$
    D. x^{60}

Question 11 is based on the following figure.

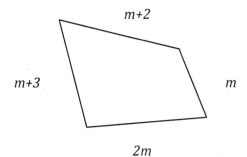

$m+2$

$m+3$

m

$2m$

- 63 -

11. The figure shows an irregular quadrilateral and the lengths of its individual sides. Which of the following equations best represents the perimeter of the quadrilateral?

    A. $2m^4 + 5$

    B. $4m + 5$

    C. $5m + 5$

    D. $4m^2 + 5$

12. Which of the following could be a graph of the function $y = \dfrac{1}{x}$?

A.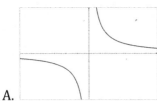

B.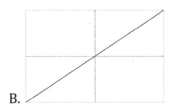

C.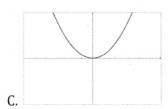

D.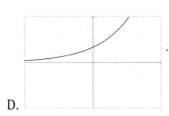

13. Which of the following statements is true?
    A. Perpendicular lines have opposite slopes
    B. Perpendicular lines have the same slopes
    C. Perpendicular lines have reciprocal slopes
    D. Perpendicular lines have opposite reciprocal slopes

Question 14 is based upon the following figure:

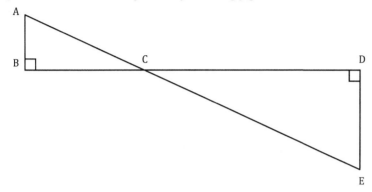

14. In the figure above, segment BC is 4 units long, segment CD is 8 units long, and segment DE is 6 units long. What is the length of segment AC?
    A. a5 units
    B. 3 units
    C. 2.5 units
    D. 4 units

15. If a rectangle's length and width are doubled, by what percentage does its area increase?
    A. 80
    B. 160
    C. 240
    D.300

16. Which of the following are complementary angles?
    A. 71° and 19°
    B. 90° and 90°
    C. 90° and 45°
    D. 15° and 30°

17. Given the double bar graph shown below, which of the following statements is true?

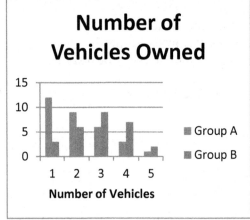

A. Group A is negatively skewed, while Group B is approximately normal.
B. Group A is positively skewed, while Group B is approximately normal.
C. Group A is approximately normal, while Group B is negatively skewed.
D. Group A is approximately normal, while Group B is positively skewed.

18. Which of the following correlation coefficients represents the weakest correlation?
A. 0.3
B. −0.1
C. 0.4
D. −0.9

19. Elizabeth rolls a standard die, labeled 1 to 6, 100 times. Which of the following experimental outcomes is *not* likely?
A. 67 rolls will show a number greater than 2.
B. 50 rolls will show an even number.
C. 75 rolls will show a number less than 4.
D. 33 rolls will show a number less than 3.

20. A bag contains 8 red marbles, 3 blue marbles, and 4 green marbles. What is the probability Carlos draws a red marble, does not replace it, and then draws another red marble?
A. $\frac{4}{15}$
B. $\frac{32}{105}$
C. $\frac{64}{225}$
D. $\frac{2}{15}$

Reading

Directions for questions 1 - 6

Read the statement or passage and then choose the best answer to the question. Answer the question based on what is stated or implied in the statement or passage.

1. The Amazon Rainforest is one of the most important ecosystems in the world. However, it is slowly being destroyed. Areas of the rainforest are being cleared for farms and roads, and much of the wood is also being harvested and sold. There are several compelling reasons to protect this area. First, a significant number of pharmaceuticals are made from plants that have been discovered in the rainforest, and it's quite possible there are still important plants that have not yet been discovered. Secondly, the rainforest provides a significant portion of the world's oxygen and also absorbs great amounts of carbon dioxide. Without rainforests, global warming could accelerate.

The main purpose of the passage is

    A. to present the major reasons why the Amazon Rainforest is being destroyed.

    B. to explain why the Amazon Rainforest should be protected.

    C. to argue that rainforest destruction is a major cause of global warming.

    D. to discuss how the rainforest has helped in the development of medications.

2. Howard Gardner was a psychologist best known for developing the theory of multiple intelligences. Basically, the theory states that the idea of general intelligence or overall intelligence is somewhat inaccurate. This is because people often show intelligence in different areas. He argued that there are actually different types of intelligence. One type of intelligence that Gardner identified was interpersonal intelligence. People who possess this type of intelligence relate and interact well with others. Intrapersonal intelligence, on the other hand, implies that people are in touch with their own feelings. They enjoy thinking about theories and developing their own thoughts and ideas. People who have linguistic intelligence learn best by taking notes and reading textbooks. These people usually excel in traditional academic environments, as many academic subjects stress these types of activities. The other types of intelligence are kinesthetic, musical, spatial, and logical/mathematical.

We can conclude from the passage that

    A. Gardner believed that linguistic intelligence was the most desirable type to have.

    B. most people who have a high level of intrapersonal intelligence do well in school.

    C. people who have a high level of interpersonal intelligence work well in groups.

    D. people who have mathematical intelligence would do the best on a standard IQ test.

3. The Internet has made life a whole lot easier for many people, but being online also brings with it very real risks. Hackers can steal personal and financial information. There are several precautions that computer users can take to minimize the level of risk that is involved with being online. One of the most obvious safety precautions is to purchase a good anti-virus and anti-spyware program. Passwords are also a very important part of online security, and several tips can help users create more secure passwords. First, they should be something that can easily be remembered, but they shouldn't be something others can guess easily. Your first or last name, phone number, or the name of your street are all bad choices, as people could learn this information quite easily. Longer passwords are more secure, and those that use a mixture of upper and lower case letters and a combination of letters and numbers are more secure than those that don't. Finally, passwords should be changed often. This can make remembering them more difficult, but the extra effort is worth the added security.

The main purpose of this passage is to
    A. discuss the major risks associated with Internet use.
    B. talk about the importance of anti-virus programs.
    C. outline important considerations for passwords.
    D. discuss why certain types of passwords shouldn't be used.

4. When people are conducting research, particularly historical research, they usually rely on primary and secondary sources. Primary sources are the more direct type of information. They are accounts of an event that are produced by individuals who were actually present. Some examples of primary sources include a person's diary entry about an event, an interview with an eyewitness, a newspaper article, or a transcribed conversation. Secondary sources are pieces of information that are constructed through the use of other, primary sources. Often, the person who creates the secondary source was not actually present at the event. Secondary sources could include books, research papers, and magazine articles.

From the passage it can be assumed that
    A. primary sources are easier to find than secondary sources.
    B. primary sources provide more accurate information than secondary sources.
    C. secondary sources give more accurate information than primary sources.
    D. secondary sources are always used when books or articles are being written.

5. Many people fail to realize just how crucial getting a good night's sleep actually is. It is usually suggested that adults get about seven hours of sleep every night, and younger children should get even more. Sleep has several benefits. First, it is believed to improve memory. This is one reason why it is always preferable to sleep the night before a test rather than stay up for the entire night to review the information. On a related note, sleep also improves concentration and mental alertness. Those who get sufficient sleep are able to concentrate on work tasks better and also react faster when they are driving a car, for example. Finally, people who get enough sleep have better immunity against illness. The reason for this is not fully understood, but researchers believe that an increase in the production of growth hormone and melatonin plays a role.

The main purpose of this passage is
    A. to talk about the benefits of sleep.
    B. to discuss how much sleep people should get.
    C. to identify which hormones can boost immunity.
    D. to present strategies for improving memory and concentration.

6. Feudalism was a type of social system that existed in parts of Europe during the Middle Ages. Essentially, there were several different classes within a feudal society. The king controlled all of the land in his jurisdiction. He divided this land among a few barons. The barons then divided up the land they were given and distributed it to knights. It was then split up again and distributed to serfs, who were the lowest members of feudal society. They were permitted to farm a small section of land, but they had to give a portion of their food to the knights in exchange for this privilege. They also had to give free labor to the knights who allowed them to use their land. Serfs had very few rights; they weren't even allowed to leave their land without permission from the knight who controlled the land. The system of feudalism ended when money began to be used as currency instead of land.

It can be concluded that
  A. serfs were in a better position when the economy changed to a money-based one.
  B. there were more knights in a typical feudal society than barons.
  C. the knights did not have to do anything for the barons in exchange for land.
  D. most feudal societies in Europe were ruled by more than one king.

Questions 7 - 13 are based upon the following passage:

In the United States, where we have more land than people, it is not at all difficult for persons in good health to make money. In this comparatively new field there are so many avenues of success open, so many vocations which are not crowded, that any person of either sex who is willing, at least for the time being, to engage in any respectable occupation that offers, may find lucrative employment.

Those who really desire to attain an independence, have only to set their minds upon it, and adopt the proper means, as they do in regard to any other object which they wish to accomplish, and the thing is easily done. But however easy it may be found to make money, I have no doubt many of my hearers will agree it is the most difficult thing in the world to keep it. The road to wealth is, as Dr. Franklin truly says, "as plain as the road to the mill." It consists simply in expending less than we earn; that seems to be a very simple problem. Mr. Micawber, one of those happy creations of the genial Dickens, puts the case in a strong light when he says that to have annual income of twenty pounds per annum, and spend twenty pounds and sixpence, is to be the most miserable of men; whereas, to have an income of only twenty pounds, and spend but nineteen pounds and sixpence is to be the happiest of mortals.

Many of my readers may say, "we understand this: this is economy, and we know economy is wealth; we know we can't eat our cake and keep it also." Yet I beg to say that perhaps more cases of failure arise from mistakes on this point than almost any other. The fact is, many people think they understand economy when they really do not.

7. Which of the following statements best expresses the main idea of the passage?
  A. Getting a job is easier now than it ever has been before.
  B. Earning money is much less difficult than managing it properly.
  C. Dr. Franklin advocated getting a job in a mill.
  D. Spending money is the greatest temptation in the world.

8. What would this author's attitude likely be to a person unable to find employment?
    A. descriptive
    B. conciliatory
    C. ingenuous
    D. incredulous

9. According to the author, what is more difficult than making money?
    A. managing money
    B. traveling to a mill
    C. reading Dickens
    D. understanding the economy

10. Who is the most likely audience for this passage?
    A. economists
    B. general readers
    C. teachers
    D. philanthropists

11. What is the best definition of *economy* as it is used in this passage?
    A. exchange of money, goods, and services
    B. delegation of household affairs
    C. efficient money management
    D. less expensive

12. Which word best describes the author's attitude towards those who believe they understand money?
    A. supportive
    B. incriminating
    C. excessive
    D. patronizing

13. This passage is most likely taken from a(n) _____.
    A. self-help manual
    B. autobiography
    C. epistle
    D. novel

Questions 14 - 20 are based upon the following passage:

We all know the drill: the consequences of urban sprawl, American's long work hours, and devotion to television and the internet are doing nothing good for American communities.

A new study by sociologists at Duke University and the University of Arizona adds more grist to this mill, noting that Americans in 2004 had smaller networks of people with whom they talk about matters important to them than they did in 1985. (*Social Isolation in America: Changes in Core Discussion Networks Over Two Decades*, American Sociological Review, June 2006.) In 1985, Americans had three confidants, in 2004, we averaged two. The number of Americans who had no one with whom to talk about

- 70 -

important matters almost doubled in 2004 to over 25%. Increasingly, most confidants are family: in 2004, 80% of people talked only to family about important matters and about 9% people depended totally on their spouse. This decrease in confidants is part (a result) of the same trend that's leaving fewer people knowing their neighbors or participating in social clubs or public affairs than in the past (phenomena noted in the book <u>Better Together: Restoring the American Community</u> by Robert Putnam and Lewis Feldstein). We know a lot of people, but not necessarily very well.

Left to our own devices and cultural trends then, we seem to be moving in an unpleasant direction. Communities are formed ad hoc, around specific shared individual interests. This wouldn't be bad, of course, except that those communities seem to exist only within the constraints of those shared interests, and don't develop into close and meaningful relationships. The transient and specific nature of many of our relationships today can keep us socially busy without building the lasting relationships and communities that we want.

So what do we do about it if we want to change things? Harvard University's School of Government put together 150 ways to increase what they call "social capital" (the value of our social networks). Among their suggestions are: support local merchants; audition for community theater or volunteer to usher; participate in political campaigns; start or join a carpool; eat breakfast at a local gathering spot on Saturdays; and stop and make sure the person on the side of the highway is OK.

14. According to the author, which of the following was true in 2004:
   A. The average American had three confidants and 9% of people depended totally on their spouse for discussion of important matters.
   B. The average American had two confidants, and 80% of people discussed important matters only with their spouses.
   C. The average American had two confidants, and 9% of people discussed important matters only with family members.
   D. The average American had two confidants, and 80% of people discussed important matters only with family members.

15. The author argues that the transient nature of many of today's relationships is problematic because:
   A. we don't share specific interests
   B. we don't know many people
   C. it prevents us building lasting relationships and communities
   D. we have too much social capital

16. Which of the following are some of the causes to which the author attributes problems in American communities:
   A. too much homework and devotion to television
   B. urban sprawl and long work hours
   C. long work hours and too much homework
   D. urban sprawl and decline of sports team membership

17. Which of the following is not something the author states was suggested by Harvard University as a way to increase social capital:
    A. eat breakfast at a local gathering spot
    B. join a bowling team
    C. support local merchants
    D. join a carpool

18. In what year was the Duke University study cited by the author published?
    A. 2006
    B. 2000
    C. 1985
    D. 2002

19. How many ways did Harvard University's School of Government suggest to increase social capital?
    A. 25
    B. 80
    C. 100
    D. 150

20. According to the author, "social capital" means which of the following:
    A. the value of our social networks
    B. the number of confidants with whom we share information
    C. the value we place on friendships outside family members
    D. the number of activities in which we engage

Questions 21 - 24 are based on the following passage.
    In the American Southwest of the late 1800s, the introduction of barbed wire fencing led to fierce disputes between ranchers and farmers, both eager to protect their rights and their livelihood. The farmers were the clear winners of the two groups, and the barbed wire fences stayed and proliferated. Barbed wire proved to be ideal for use in western conditions; it was cheaper and easier to use than the alternatives of wood fences, stone walls or hedges. Within a few decades all the previously open range land became fenced-in private property. This change was so dramatic to the western culture that some consider the introduction of barbed wire fencing to be the event that ended the Old West period of our history.

21. According to the author, which group supported the use of barbed wire fences?
    A. the ranchers
    B. the farmers
    C. both the ranchers and the farmers
    D. neither the ranchers nor the farmers

22. According to the author, what do some believe the introduction of barbed wire ended?
    A. the disputes between the farmers and the ranchers
    B. the controversy over whether wood fences or stone walls were better
    C. the Old West period of our history
    D. the livelihood of the farmers

23. Which of the following did the author <u>not</u> imply would have been found in the Old West prior to the introduction of barbed wire fencing?
    A. no fencing in some places
    B. wood fences
    C. hedges
    D. brick walls

24. According to the author, when did the introduction of barbed wire fencing occur?
    A. the late 16th century
    B. the late 17th century
    C. the late 18th century
    D. the late 19th century

Writing

Johnna's American history teacher has assigned a research essay on a figure from the American Revolution. Johnna decided to write about Paul Revere and would like your help revising and improving the essay. After you read her essay, answer questions 1 - 10.

(1) In the early 1760s, Paul Revere, ran a busy metalworking shop. (2) People from all over Boston came to buy the silver and gold cups, medals, and cutlery he made. (3) Everything changed in 1765. (4) Many colonists ran low on money and stopped shopping at Paul's shop.

(5) Things got worse when the british passed the Stamp Act. (6) The Stamp Act created a tax to help the British earn money. (7) Colonists like Paul Revere hated the Stamp Act because it would make things more expensive. (8) Under the Stamp Act, colonists needed to pay for everything that was printed, such as newspapers, magazines, and business contracts. (9) After a colonist paid the tax, the tax collector put a stamp on the paper to show that the tax had been paid. (10) The Stamp Act made it very expensive for Paul to run his business. (11) For example, if he wanted a new apprentice for his silver shop, he needed to buy a Stamp for the signed contract.

(12) Paul wasn't just angry about buying stamps. (13) He also felt that the British shouldn't be allowed to tax the colonies. (14) There was no American colonists in the British parliament, which passed the tax. (15) Paul and the other colonists didn't want taxation without representation. (16) They wanted to be able to choose their own taxes.

(17) The colonists refused to buy stamps. (18) They were determined to get the Stamp Act repealed.

(19) Paul joined a group called the Sons of Liberty. (20) They wore silver medals on their coats that said "Sons of Liberty." (21) Paul may have helped make the medals in his silver shop.

(22) The Sons of Liberty staged demonstrations at the Liberty Tree, a huge elm tree, that stood in Boston. (23) Paul drew cartoons and wrote poems about liberty. (24) He published them in the local newspaper, *The Boston Gazette.*

(25) After a year of hard work fighting the Stamp Act Paul and the Sons of Liberty received the happy news. (26) The Stamp Act had been repealed!

(27) People celebrated all over Boston; they lit bonfires, set off fireworks, and decorated houses and ships with flags and streamers. (28) Paul attended the biggest celebration, which took place at the Liberty Tree. (29) The people hung 280 lanterns on the tree's branches lighting up the night sky.

(30) Some members of the Sons of Liberty constructed a paper obelisk. (31) An obelisk is the same shape as the Washington Monument. (32) They decorated the obelisk with pictures and verses about the struggle to repeal the Stamp Act and hung it from the Liberty Tree.

(33) Paul may have helped construct the obelisk, even if he wasn't involved in the direct construction, he probably knew about and supported it. (34) After the celebration, he made a copper engraving showing the pictures and verses on the obelisk's four sides. (35) His engraving records the celebration under the Liberty Tree. (36) Even though Paul Revere may be better known for his silver work and famous ride, his engravings, like the engraving of the obelisk, help us see the American Revolution through his eyes.

1. What change should be made to sentence 1?
   A. Change *1760s* to *1760's*
   B. Delete the comma after *1760s*
   C. Delete the comma after *Revere*
   D. Add a comma after *busy*

2. What change should be made to sentence 5?
   A. Change *got* to *get*
   B. Change *worse* to *worst*
   C. Change *british* to *British*
   D. Change *Stamp Act* to *stamp act*

3. What change should be made to sentence 11?
   A. Delete the comma after *example*
   B. Delete the comma after *shop*
   C. Change *Stamp* to *stamp*
   D. Change *signed contract* to *Signed Contract*

4. What change should be made to sentence 14?
   A. Change *was* to *were*
   B. Change *parliament* to *parlaiment*
   C. Delete the comma after *parliament*
   D. Change *which* to *that*

5. What is the most effective way to combine sentences 17 and 18?
   A. The colonists refused to buy stamps and they were determined to get the Stamp Act repealed.
   B. The colonists refused to buy stamps, and they were determined to get the Stamp Act repealed.
   C. The colonists refused to buy stamps, and were determined to get the Stamp Act repealed.
   D. The colonists refused to buy stamps, were determined to get the Stamp Act repealed.

6. What change should be made to sentence 22?
   A. Change *demonstrations* to *demonstration*
   B Insert *and* after the comma
   C. Delete the comma after *elm tree*
   D. Change *in* to *at*

7. What change, if any, should be made to sentence 25?
   A. Add a comma after *work*
   B. Add a comma after *Act*
   C. Change *received* to *recieved*
   D. No change

8. What change should be made to sentence 29?
   A. Change *280* to *two-hundred-eighty*
   B. Change *tree's* to *trees*
   C. Add a comma after *branches*
   D. Change *night* to *nightly*

9. What is the most effective way to combine sentences 30 and 31?
   A. Some members of the Sons of Liberty constructed a paper obelisk, which is the same shape as the Washington Monument.
   B. Some members of the Sons of Liberty constructed a paper obelisk which is the same shape as the Washington Monument.
   C. Some members of the Sons of Liberty constructed a paper obelisk, that is the same shape as the Washington Monument.
   D. Some members of the Sons of Liberty constructed a paper obelisk; which is the same shape as the Washington Monument.

10. What change should be made to sentence 33?
    A. Delete *may*
    B. Change the comma after *obelisk* to a semicolon
    C. Delete the comma after *construction*
    D. Change *knew* to *knows*

For questions 11-15, select the best option for replacing the underlined portion of the sentence. The first option listed is always the same as the current version of the sentence.

11. Children who aren't nurtured during infancy are more likely to develop attachment disorders, <u>which can cause persisting and severely problems</u> later in life.
    A. which can cause persisting and severely problems
    B. that can cause persisting and severe problem
    C. they can cause persistent and severe problem
    D. which can cause persistent and severe problems

12. While speed is a measure of how fast an object is moving, velocity measures how fast an object is moving <u>and also indicates in what direction</u> it is traveling.
    A. and also indicates in what direction
    B. and only indicates in which direction
    C. and also indicate in which directions
    D. and only indicated in what direction

- 75 -

13. Many companies are now using social networking sites like Facebook and MySpace <u>to market there service and product.</u>
    A. to market there service and product
    B. to market their services and products
    C. and market their service and products
    D. which market their services and products

14. An autoclave is a tool used mainly in hospitals <u>to sterilizing surgical tools and hypodermic needles</u>.
    A. to sterilizing surgical tools and hypodermic needles
    B. for sterilize surgical tools and hypodermic needles
    C. to sterilize surgical tools and hypodermic needles
    D. for sterilizing the surgical tool and hypodermic needle

15. <u>The bizarre creatures known by electric eels</u> are capable of emitting an incredible 600 volts of electricity.
    A. The bizarre creatures known by electric eels
    B. A bizarre creature known as electric eels
    C. The bizarre creatures known to electric eels
    D. The bizarre creatures known as electric eels

16. Bats and dolphins use a process known as echolocation, which means they emit and receive frequencies that can help them navigate through the dark night and murky waters, and also allows them to locate food sources like insects or fish.
Rewrite, beginning with
<u>Locating food sources like insects or fish</u>
The next words will be
    A. during which they emit and receive frequencies
    B. is done through a process known as echolocation
    C. helps them navigate through the dark night
    D. is done by bats and dolphins

17. Carbon dating is an accepted method used by archaeologists to figure out the age of artifacts, even though it may not be entirely accurate if samples are contaminated or if the objects to be dated are not extremely old.
Rewrite, beginning with
<u>Even though carbon dating is not always entirely accurate,</u>
The next words will be
    A. it is an accepted method
    B. objects to be dated
    C. to figure out the age
    D. samples are contaminated

18. Chemical changes are sometimes difficult to distinguish from physical changes, but some examples of physical changes, such as melting water, chopped wood, and ripped paper, are very easy to recognize.

Rewrite, beginning with

<u>Melting water, chopped wood, and ripped paper</u>

The next words will be

    A. are sometimes difficult to distinguish

    B. are very easy to recognize

    C. are chemical changes

    D. are some examples of physical changes

19. The theory of repressed memory was developed by Sigmund Freud, and it stated that all people store memories that cannot be accessed during daily life, but can be accessed through hypnotherapy and hypnosis.

Rewrite, beginning with

<u>Developed by Sigmund Freud,</u>

The next words will be

    A. it stated that all people

    B. that cannot be accessed

    C. hypnotherapy and hypnosis

    D. the theory of repressed memory

20. Romantic poetry is an important genre, and the works are easily distinguished from other types of poetry by several characteristics, including their focus on nature and the importance that is ascribed to everyday occurrences.

Rewrite, beginning with

<u>A focus on nature and the importance that is ascribed to everyday occurrences</u>

The next words will be

    A. are easily distinguished

    B. from other types of poetry

    C. are several characteristics

    D. is an important genre

Essay

Some states have legalized the sale and use of marijuana, bringing attention to the possibility of national legalization and regulation of the drug. Please write a five-paragraph persuasive essay (approximately 350–500 words) discussing what you believe the federal government's position should be on this issue.

Answers and Explanations

Math

1. D: First, test each expression to see which satisfies the condition $x > y$. This condition is met for all the answer choices except B and C, so these need not be considered further. Next, test the remaining choices to see which satisfy the inequality $x + y > 0$. It can be seen that this inequality holds for choice A, but not for choice D, since $x + y = 3 + (-3) = 3 - 3 = 0$. In this case the sum $x + y$ is not greater than 0.

2. A: This equation represents a linear relationship that has a slope of 3.60 and passes through the origin. The table indicates that for each hour of rental, the cost increases by $3.60. This corresponds to the slope of the equation. Of course, if the bicycle is not rented at all (0 hours) there will be no charge ($0). If plotted on the Cartesian plane, the line would have a y intercept of 0. Relationship A is the only one that satisfies these criteria.

3. C: Rafael's profit on each computer is given by the difference between the price he pays and the price he charges his customer, or $800-$450. If he sells n computers in a month, his total profit will be n times this difference, or $n(800 - 450)$. However, it is necessary to subtract his fixed costs of $3000 from this to compute his final profit per month.

4. B: Subtracting 7 from both sides of the equation yields $-\frac{1}{3x} = -3$, which leads to $-9x = -1$, or $x = \frac{1}{9}$. Now we substitute this value into $\frac{1}{3x} + 3$, giving us $\frac{1}{3\left(\frac{1}{9}\right)} + 3$. This simplifies to $\frac{1}{1/3} + 3$, or $3 + 3$, which is 6.

5. B: Every possible combination of scores is a multiple of 7, since the two terms of the ratio have a sum of seven.

6. B: There are 12 inches in a foot and 3 feet in a yard. Four and a half yards is equal to 162 inches. To determine the number of 3-inche segments, divide 162 by 3.

7. A: Compute the product using the FOIL method, in which the First term, then the Outer terms, the Inner terms, and finally the Last terms are figured in sequence of multiplication. As a result, $(a+b)(a-b) = a^2 + ba - ab - b^2$. Since ab is equal to ba, the middle terms cancel each other which leaves $a^2 - b^2$.

8. A: $2^4 = 2 \times 2 \times 2 \times 2 = 16$. Therefore, $4^x = 16$; $x = 2$.

9. A: $(2x^2 + 3x + 2) - (x^2 + 2x - 3) = (2x^2 + 3x + 2) + (-1)(x^2 + 2x - 3)$. First, distribute the -1 to remove the parentheses: $2x^2 + 3x + 2 - x^2 - 2x + 3$. Next, combine like terms: $(2x^2 - x^2) + (3x - 2x) + (2 + 3) = x^2 + x + 5$.

10. C: The nth root of x is equivalent to x to the power of $\frac{1}{n}$, i.e. $\sqrt[n]{x} = x^{\frac{1}{n}}$. This means in particular that $\sqrt[3]{x} = x^{\frac{1}{3}}$, and so $\left(\sqrt[3]{(x^4)}\right)^5 = \left((x^4)^{\frac{1}{3}}\right)^5$. Raising a power to another power is equivalent to multiplying the exponents together, so this equals $x^{4 \times \frac{1}{3} \times 5} = x^{\frac{20}{3}}$.

11. C: The perimeter (P) of the quadrilateral is simply the sum of its sides, or
$$P = m + (m+2) + (m+3) + 2m$$
Combine like terms by adding the variables (m terms) together and then adding the constants resulting in:
$$P = 5m + 5$$
In this application, it appears that some of the variables do not have a number in front of them; however, the absence of a coefficient indicates multiplication by 1 hence $m = 1m$, $x = 1x$, and so on.

12. A: This is a typical plot of an inverse variation, in which the product of the dependent and independent variables, x and y, is always equal to the same value. In this case the product is always equal to 1, so the plot occupies the first and third quadrants of the coordinate plane. As x increases and approaches infinity, , y decreases and approaches zero, maintaining the constant product. In contrast, answer B is a linear plot corresponding to an equation of the form $y = x$. C is a quadratic plot corresponding to $y = x^2$. D is an exponential plot corresponding to $y = 2^x$.

13. D: The slopes of perpendicular lines are reciprocals of opposite sign. For example, in the figure below, line A has a slope of -1/2, while line B has a slope of 2.

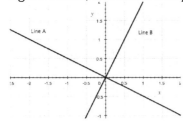

14. A: The two right triangles are similar because they share a pair of vertical angles. Vertical angles are always congruent (angle ACB and angle DCE). Obviously both right angles (angle B and angle D) are congruent. Thus, angles A and E are congruent because of the triangular sum theorem.
With similar triangles, corresponding sides will be proportional. Segment BC is ½ the length of segment CD, therefore AC will be ½ the length of CE. The length of CE can be computed from the Pythagorean theorem, since it is the hypotenuse of a right triangle for which the lengths of the other two sides are known: $CE = \sqrt{6^2 + 8^2} = \sqrt{100} = 10$.
The length of segment AC will be ½ of this value, or 5 units.

15. D: Let x stand for the length and let y stand for the width of the rectangle. Then the area is expressed as the product xy. But if the length and width are doubled to 2x and 2y respectively, the area becomes $(2x)(2y) = 4xy$, which is 4 times as large as the original rectangle. "Four times as large" is equivalent to a 300 percent increase.

16. A: Complementary angles are two angles that equal 90° when added together.

17. B: Data is said to be positively skewed when there are a higher number of lower values, indicating data that is skewed right. An approximately normal distribution shows an increase in frequency, followed by a decrease in frequency, of approximately the same rate.

18. B: Weak correlation coefficients are those with absolute values close to 0. Since −0.1 has an absolute value of 0.1 and 0.1 is closer to 0 than any of the absolute values of the other correlation coefficients, it is the weakest.

19. C: The theoretical probability of rolling a number less than 4 is the same as the theoretical probability of rolling an even number; the probability is $\frac{1}{2}$. The expected value is equal to the product of the number of rolls of 100 and the probability of $\frac{1}{2}$. Thus, it is likely that 50 of the rolls will show a number less than 4, not 75 of the rolls.

20. A: The events are dependent, since the first marble was not replaced. The sample space of the second draw will decrease by 1 because there will be one less marble to choose. The number of possible red marbles for the second draw will also decrease by 1. Thus, the probability may be written as $P(A \text{ and } B) = \frac{8}{15} \cdot \frac{7}{14}$. The probability he draws a red marble, does not replace it, and draws another red marble is $\frac{4}{15}$.

Reading

1. B: Answer choices A and C are mentioned only briefly. D is discussed, but it falls under the more general purpose of the passage, which is discussing why the Amazon Rainforest is a valuable area that should be protected.

2. C: Answer choice A is not a logical conclusion because there is no indication that Gardner ranked the intelligences in any way. Answer choice B cannot be concluded from the passage, as there is no mention of the value placed on intrapersonal intelligences in a traditional academic environment. IQ tests are not mentioned at all, so we cannot conclude anything about them based on this passage. Answer choice C is the correct choice. Those with interpersonal intelligence interact well with others, so it is reasonable to assume they would perform well in a group setting.

3. C: Answer choices A and B are touched upon only very briefly. Answer choice D is discussed, but it is encompassed by the broader purpose of the passage, which is to outline the most important considerations related to passwords.

4. B: Answer choice B is the most logical conclusion. The passage states that, "Primary sources are the more direct type of information. They are accounts of an event that are produced by individuals who were actually present." Therefore, it is reasonable to assume that an account prepared by someone who was present would be more accurate than one prepared by somebody decades later who had to rely on the accounts of others.

5. A: Answer choices B and C are mentioned only briefly, and D is not really discussed in the passage. The passage focuses mainly on discussing some of the major benefits of sleep, so that is the main purpose of the passage.

6. B: Answer choice B is the logical conclusion. The passage states that "The king controlled all of the land in his jurisdiction. He divided this among a few barons. The barons then divided up the land they were given and distributed it to knights." If the barons divided up

their lands, it would stand to reason that each baron would distribute his land to several knights. Therefore, there would have to be more knights than barons.

7. B: The author asserts both that earning money is increasingly easy and that managing money is difficult.

8. D: The author seems to believe that there are plenty of lucrative jobs for everyone.

9. A: The author insists that many people who have no trouble earning money waste it through lavish spending.

10. B: This passage is clearly intended for a non-expert adult readership.

11. C: Here, the author is speaking of money management on a personal or household level.

12. D: The author suggests that many people who believe they understand economy in fact do not.

13. A: It seems clear that the author is about to describe the correct means of personal economy.

14. D

15. C

16. B

17. B

18. A

19. D

20. A

21. B

22. C

23. D

24. D

Writing

1. C: because a comma should not be used to separate the sentence's subject (Paul Revere) and verb (ran). Choice A is incorrect because an apostrophe would make *1760s* possessive, which it is not. Choice B is incorrect because the comma is used to separate a non-essential

clause from the rest of the sentence. Choice D is incorrect because the words *busy* and *metalworking* are not a series of adjectives. Instead, *busy* is an adjective modifying the noun *metalworking shop*.

2. C: because *British* is a proper noun and should always be capitalized. Choice A is incorrect because the passage is written in past tense; therefore, *got* should remain in past tense. Choice B is incorrect because it is referring to something getting worse, rather than something that is the superlative *worst*. Choice D is incorrect because *Stamp Act* is both a proper noun and the proper name of the act.

3. C: is the correct answer because *stamp* in this sentence is not a proper noun and does not need to be capitalized. In this context, *stamp* only needs to be capitalized when it is used in the name *Stamp Act*. Choice A is incorrect because the comma sets off a non-essential phrase at the beginning of the sentence. Choice B is incorrect because the comma sets off the initial dependent clause from the independent clause in the second half of the sentence. Choice D is incorrect because *signed contract* is not a proper noun or formal name.

4. A: because *were* is referring to the plural of *colonists*. As a singular verb form, *was* is incorrect in this case. Choice B is incorrect because *parliament* is the correct spelling. Choice C is incorrect because the comma is required to set off the non-essential phrase that follows. Choice D is incorrect because *that* is used to set off a dependent phrase and should not be preceded by a comma.

5. B: because a comma and conjunction are correctly used to separate two independent clauses. Although choice A has the conjunction *and*, it is missing the required comma. Choice C is incorrect because no comma is required to separate an independent clause from a dependent clause. Choice D is incorrect because the comma creates a run-on sentence.

6. C: because a comma should not be used to separate independent clauses from essential phrases that begin with *that*. Choice A is incorrect because the Sons of Liberty staged multiple demonstrations. The reader can determine this because there is no article before the word *demonstrations*. Choice B is incorrect because a comma is not needed to separate an independent clause from a dependent clause when the clauses are connected by a conjunction. Choice D is incorrect because the tree was *in* the city of Boston, not *at* a specific location.

7. B: because a comma is needed to separate the dependent clause beginning with the word *after* from the independent clause beginning with *Paul*. Choice A is incorrect because the comma would divide a clause. Choice C is incorrect because *received* is the correct spelling. Choice D is incorrect because a comma is required after the word *Act*.

8. C: because the phrase *lighting up the sky* is non-essential and should be separated from the rest of the sentence by a comma. While the number *280* could be written out, choice A is incorrect because it should be written as *two hundred and eighty*. Choice C is incorrect because *tree's* is possessive and requires the apostrophe. Choice D is incorrect because *nightly* is an adverb, which should modify a verb. However, the word is modifying a noun and must be written as an adjective.

9. A: because a comma should be used to separate the independent clause beginning with *some members* from the non-essential phrase beginning with *which is*. Choice B is incorrect

because it is missing the comma. Choice C is incorrect because it incorrectly uses *that* instead of *which*. Choice D is incorrect because it uses a semicolon instead of a comma.

10. B: because a semicolon should be used to separate two independent clauses. Choice A is incorrect because *may* provides important meaning to the sentence. Choice C is incorrect because the comma correctly separates the two clauses. Choice D is incorrect because the passage is talking about a figure from history and should use the past tense.

11. D: Answer choice A is incorrect because *severely* is an adverb and not an adjective. B and C are incorrect because *problem* instead of the grammatically correct *problems* is used. D uses the correct, plural form *problems* and uses adjectives to describe the problems.

12. A: The sentence implies that *velocity* is used to indicate more than one value, which eliminates B and D. The phrase refers to velocity, which is singular, but the construction of choice C would correctly refer to a plural noun. Choice A agrees with the singular, noun and the *and* indicates that velocity is used to indicate more than one value.

13. B: Answer choice B uses the grammatically correct *their* instead of *there*. The *to* indicates the companies are using these sites for something, and *services* and *products* agree with each other because they are both plural.

14. C: Answer choice C states that an autoclave is a tool used *to sterilize*. A and B, which begin with *to sterilizing* and *for sterilize*, are not grammatically correct. D indicates that the machine is used to sterilize a single tool and needle, which does not make sense in the context of the sentence.

15. D: Answer choices A and C are incorrect because they imply that the bizarre creatures are something other than electric eels. The *a* in choice B does not agree with the plural *electric eels*. Choice D is best because it is grammatically correct and identifies electric eels as the bizarre creatures being discussed in the sentence.

16. B: The original sentence indicates that bats and dolphins are able to do many things, including locating food sources like insects or fish through a process known as echolocation. Answer choice B best expresses the fact that locating food is accomplished through echolocation. Answer choice C cannot logically follow the phrase. Answer choices A and D do not tell how bats and dolphins locate food.

17. A: The new sentence begins with the phrase "even though," indicating that a contrast is being constructed. "Even though carbon dating is not always entirely accurate, it is still an accepted method" provides this contrast, while the other choices do not.

18. D: Melting water, chopped wood, and ripped paper are identified in the original sentence as examples of physical changes that are easy to distinguish from chemical changes. Therefore, answer choices A and C are entirely incorrect. Answer choice B indicates that these objects are easy to recognize, but the sentence should convey that they are examples of physical changes that are easy to recognize, making this choice somewhat inaccurate. Choice D is best because it identifies the previously mentioned objects as examples of physical changes.

19. D: The only phrase that describes something developed by Sigmund Freud is D. Answer choice A does not identify what the *it* is referring to, and B cannot logically follow the given phrase. Answer choice C describes ways to access repressed memories, but these were not developed by Freud.

20. C: A focus on nature and ascribing importance to everyday occurrences are identified in the original sentence as important characteristics of Romantic poetry. Answer choice C clearly identifies them as characteristics, and is the only choice that can logically follow the given phrase.

Practice Test #2

Practice Questions

Math

1. A combination lock uses a 3-digit code. Each digit can be any one of the ten available integers 0-9. How many different combinations are possible?
   A. 1000
   B. 30
   C. 81
   D. 100

2. The cost, in dollars, of shipping x computers to California for sale is 3000 + 100x. The amount received when selling these computers is 400x dollars. What is the least number of computers that must be shipped and sold so that the amount received is at least equal to the shipping cost?
   A. 10
   B. 15
   C. 20
   D. 25

3. If $(3/s) = 7$ and $(4/t) = 12$, then $s - t =$
   A. -1/7
   B. 2/12
   C. 2/7
   D. 2/21

4. If the average of 7 and x is equal to the average of 9, 4, and x, what is the value of x?
   A. 4
   B. 5
   C. 6
   D. 7

5. How many integers are solutions of the inequality $|x| < 4$?
   A. An infinite number
   B. 0
   C. 3
   D. 7

6. For what real number x is it true that $3(2x - 10) = x$?
   A. -6
   B. -5
   C. 5
   D. 6

7. Solve the following equation: $(y + 1)(y + 2)(y + 3)$
   A. $y^2 + 3y + 2$
   B. $3y^2 + 6y + 3$
   C. $y^3 + 6y^2 + 11y + 6$
   D. $8y^3 + 6y + 8$

8. Which of the following is *not* a factor of $x^3 - 3x^2 - 4x + 12$?
   A. $x - 2$
   B. $x + 2$
   C. $x - 3$
   D. $x + 3$

9. Simplify $\frac{x^6}{y^4} \times x^2 y^3$.
   A. $x^4 y$
   B. $\frac{x^4}{y}$
   C. $x^8 y$
   D. $\frac{x^8}{y}$

10. $(x + 2)(x - 3) = ?$
    A. $x^2 - 1$
    B. $x^2 - 6$
    C. $x^2 - x - 6$
    D. $x^2 - 5x - 1$

11. In the following figure, angle b = 120°. What is the measurement of angle a?

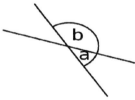

   A. 40°
   B. 60°
   C. 90°
   D. 100°

12. Which of the following figures has rotational symmetry?

A.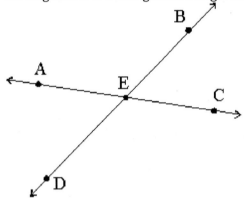

B.

C.

D.

13. Angle AEC is a straight line. Angle BEC is 45°. What is the measure for angle AEB?

A. Angle AEB is 90°
B. Angle AEB is 115°
C. Angle AEB is 135°
D. Angle AEB is 180°

14. If the measures of the three angles in a triangle are 2 : 6 : 10, what is the measure of the smallest angle?

A. 20 degrees
B. 40 degrees
C. 60 degrees
D. 80 degrees

15.

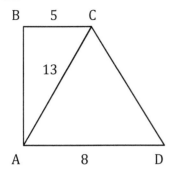

In the figure above, what is the area of triangular region ACD?
   A. 13
   B. 30
   C. 48
   D. 60

16. If the area of a rectangular game board is 336 square inches and its perimeter is 76 inches, what is the length of each of the shorter sides?
   A. 10 inches
   B. 14 inches
   C. 19 inches
   D. 24 inches

17. Given the histograms shown below, which of the following statements is true?

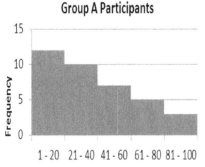
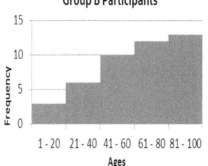

   A. Group A is negatively skewed and has a mean that is less than the mean of Group B.
   B. Group A is positively skewed and has a mean that is more than the mean of Group B.
   C. Group B is negatively skewed and has a mean that is more than the mean of Group A.
   D. Group B is positively skewed and has a mean that is less than the mean of Group A.

18. Which of the following best represents the line of best fit for the data shown in the scatter plot below?

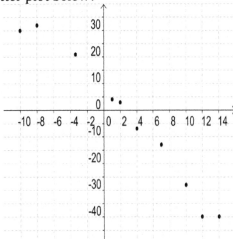

A. $y = -3.2x + 5.1$
B. $y = -2.4x + 10.3$
C. $y = -4.7x - 5.3$
D. $y = -8.2x + 3.4$

19. What is the probability that Ana draws a jack, replaces the card, and then draws an ace card?

A. $\frac{1}{52}$

B. $\frac{3}{208}$

C. $\frac{1}{169}$

D. $\frac{17}{52}$

20. What is the expected value of drawing a card from a deck when the cards are labeled 1 – 5?

A. 1.5
B. 2
C. 2.5
D. 3

Reading

Directions for questions 1 – 6
Read the statement or passage and then choose the best answer to the question. Answer the question based on what is stated or implied in the statement or passage.

1. A bird's feathers are extremely important, and when they clean and smooth them, it is known as preening. Birds in the wild preen their feathers on a regular basis. This is true of most captive birds as well, but not all. For example, some birds do not preen their feathers at all. This problem is most common in birds that are taken from their mothers at a very young age. Presumably, the absence of preening is due to the fact that they were never shown how to do it properly. A more common problem among captive birds is excessive preening. Some birds may pull out large numbers of their feathers or bite them down to the skin. It should be noted that wild birds never exhibit this kind of behavior. There are several suggestions about how the problem of excessive preening can be solved. Giving birds baths or placing them in an area that has more activity to prevent boredom are suggestions. However, these measures are often not sufficient to solve the problem.

The purpose of the passage is
A. to give an overview of abnormal preening in birds.
B. to compare captive birds to wild birds.
C. to discuss why preening is important.
D. to explain how excessive preening problems can be solved.

2. Hibernation in animals is an extremely fascinating phenomenon, one that biologists are not yet close to understanding fully. However, it is quite easy to understand why animals hibernate during the cold winter months. Usually, it is because their food is quite scarce during this time. Animals that are herbivores will find the winters extremely tough, because all of the vegetation will have died off by the time winter arrives. Hibernation is essentially a way of dealing with this food shortage. Animals like birds rely on seeds and small insects for sustenance. Obviously, these will also be quite scarce in the winter when the ground becomes covered and frozen. Many birds address their upcoming food shortage in quite a different way: they migrate to warmer areas where their sources of food will be plentiful.

The main reason animals hibernate is
A. to travel to a warmer area where food will be more plentiful.
B. to cut down on their food consumption during the winter months.
C. to avoid the harsh weather that occurs during the winter months.
D. to avoid food shortages that occur during the winter months.

3. At one time, the use of leeches to treat medical problems was quite common. If a person suffered from a snake bite or a bee sting, leeches were believed to be capable of removing the poison from the body if they were placed on top of the wound. They have also been used for blood letting and to stop hemorrhages, although neither of these leech treatments would be considered acceptable by present-day physicians. Today, leeches are still used on a limited basis. Most often, leeches are used to drain blood from clogged veins. This results in little pain for the patient and also ensures the patient's blood will not clot while it is being drained.

The main purpose of the passage is

    A. to discuss the benefits of using leeches to treat blocked veins.

    B. to give an overview of how leeches have been used throughout history.

    C. to compare which uses of leeches are effective and which are not.

    D. to explain how leeches can be used to remove poison from the body.

4. When online file-sharing programs emerged, the music industry changed forever. Perhaps the first widely-used music file sharing program was Napster. It allowed users to sign up to use the service at no charge. Then, they could download music files from other users all over the world by simply typing in what song or album they wanted. Obviously, this was bad news for music artists and record labels because they weren't making any profits from downloaded music. Eventually, Napster was shut down. While it later reinvented itself as a paying service, other free music-sharing sites cropped up almost immediately. Even though several sites and individual users have been charged, there are still countless individuals who log onto these sites to obtain free music.

The main problem associated with peer file-sharing sites is

    A. it is hard to locate users to criminally charge them.

    B. there are too many of them currently in existence.

    C. they prevent artists and labels from earning money.

    D. they allow users to sign up for the service free of charge.

5. The so-called anti-aging industry is worth a staggering amount of money in North America. Women are sold all sorts of creams and ointments, and are promised that these will make them look younger over time. Unfortunately, these claims are entirely false. Lotions cannot penetrate to the inner layers of the skin where wrinkles typically form. Therefore, no over-the-counter creams are effective at erasing lines and wrinkles.

According to the author, the anti-aging industry

    A. targets its products at men and women equally.

    B. sells products that are highly effective.

    C. is still a relatively small industry.

    D. sells goods that do not do what they promise.

6. There is a clear formula that many students are taught when it comes to writing essays. The first is to develop an introduction, which outlines what will be discussed in the work. It also includes the thesis statement. Next comes the supporting paragraphs. Each paragraph contains a topic sentence, supporting evidence, and finally a type of mini-conclusion that restates the point of the paragraph. Finally, the conclusion sums up the purpose of the paper and emphasizes that the thesis statement was proven.

After the topic sentence,

    A. a thesis statement is included.
    B. supporting evidence is presented.
    C. the conclusion is stated.
    D. the author outlines what will be discussed.

Questions 7 - 13 are based on the following passage:

For those of you not in the know in the world of invented languages, Esperanto was created in the late 1800s by a Mr. Ludwik Zamenhof of Poland. Zamenhof bemoaned the tension created by the literal inability of we humans to understand each other. In Esperanto he sought to provide a sort of neutral universal second language that privileged no one linguistically, confining us all only by our ability to be articulate, rather than by our familiarity with whatever language happens to be spoken at a given time.

While not the world-wide form of communication Zamenhof and other Esperantists have hoped for, Esperanto has grown impressively since its inception. Estimates of numbers of speakers range from 100,000 to 2 million, in 115 different countries; native speakers are estimated to number more than 1000. Many books have been translated and written in Esperanto, and two movies have been made in Esperanto – including Incubus starring William Shatner.

Reasons to Learn Esperanto:
It's Easy. A common argument for learning Esperanto is the ease of learning it: it's phonetic, grammatically regular, and a relatively small amount of words can be combined to create additional words -- so you need to know less vocabulary to sound smart than you would in other languages. In addition to being able to be learned many times more quickly than anything else, studies show that learning Esperanto increases people's ability to learn a next language.

You Can Stay in People's Houses for Free. Some of these Esperanto-speakers really put their money where their mouths are when it comes to supporting international understanding. There's a list Esperantists can put themselves on called the *Pasporta Serva*; speak Esperanto and, bang, you can stay with any of those fellow speakers for free. The list currently has around 1350 hosts in more than 85 countries. Does any other language come with that kind of perk?

I am Esperanto. A final reason to pin a green 5-pointed star (symbol of Esperanto) to your shirt and try and learn this crazy human-made language is to support the ideals that motivated Zamenhof to create the thing in the first place. He wanted to help usher in peace among cultures by giving people a place to be on equal footing, at least linguistically. In this time of tensions and divisions between pretty much every group you can find, that seems like a goal worth sharing. So, go ahead and call yourself Esperanto – it means, in Esperanto, "one who hopes."

7. According to the author, estimates of Esperanto speakers range from:
   A. 115 to 1000
   B. 100,000 to 2 million
   C. around 1350
   D. 85 to 1350

8. Which of the following is <u>not</u> a reason given by the author for learning Esperanto?
   A. Esperanto speakers can stay in some other speakers' homes for free
   B. It is phonetic
   C. It increases speakers' ability to learn a next language.
   D. It is spoken by most Europeans

9. According to the author, why did Zamenhof create Esperanto?
   A. To give people a place to be on equal footing and thereby help create peace   among cultures
   B. To assist people in staying with other speakers around the world
   C. To combine what he thought were the best elements of Spanish and English in   one language
   D. To eliminate political differences

10. According to the author, in how many countries is Esperanto spoken, and how many countries are represented on the *Pasporta Serva*?
    A. 115/ more than 1000
    B. 1350/more than 85
    C. 115/ more than 85
    D. 1350/ more than 1000

11. The author writes that "he sought to provide a sort of neutral universal second language that privileged no one linguistically…" Which of the following words is most synonymous with the word "privileged" as used in that sentence?
    A. benefited
    B. hindered
    C. advantage
    D. fortunate

12. What are Esperanto speakers called?
    A. Esperantos
    B. Esperantis
    C. Esperantists
    D. Esperantons

13. According to the author, what have studies shown about Esperanto?
    A. That it is spoken in 115 countries
    B. That learning it increases people's ability to learn a next language
    C. That it has grown impressively since its inception
    D. That it increases global understanding and communication

Questions 14 - 18 are based on the following passage:

It could be argued that all American war movies take as their governing paradigm that of the Western, and that we, as viewers, don't think critically enough about this fact. The virtuous hero in the white hat, the evil villain in the black hat, the community threatened by violence; these are the obvious elements of the paradigm. In addition, the hero is highly skilled at warfare, though reluctant to use it, the community is made up of morally upstanding citizens, and there is no place for violence in the community: the hero himself must leave the community he has saved once the battle is complete. This way of seeing the world has soaked into our storytelling of battle and conflict. It's hard to find a U.S.-made war movie that, for example, presents the enemy as complex and potentially fighting a legitimate cause, or that presents the hero (usually the U.S.) as anything other than supremely morally worthy. It is important to step back and think about the assumptions and frameworks that shape the stories we're exposed to; if we're careless and unquestioning, we absorb biases and world views with which we may not agree.

14. The primary purpose of this passage is to:
    A. analyze an interesting feature of American cinema.
    B. refute the Western paradigm.
    C. suggest a way that war movies could be made better.
    D. suggest that viewers think critically about underlying assumptions in the movies we watch.

15. The author claims that it is hard to find a U.S. made movie that "presents the hero (usually the U.S.) as anything other than supremely morally worthy." Does the author imply that she:
    A. believes the hero should always appear to be morally worthy.
    B. believes the hero should never appear to be morally worthy.
    C. believes the hero should be more nuanced and less unconditionally good.
    D. believes the hero is an uninteresting character.

16. Which of the following is not an example given by the author of an element of the Western paradigm:
    A. Hero highly skilled at warfare
    B. Evil villain in black hat
    C. Everyone riding horses
    D. Community made up of upstanding citizens

17. Which of the following is part of the world view, with which we may not agree, that the author implies we might absorb from these movies if we're careless and unquestioning:
    A. Enemies of the U.S. do not ever fight for legitimate causes.
    B. The community is morally bankrupt.
    C. The U.S. is complex.
    D. The U.S. is not skilled at warfare.

18. The author writes that "the virtuous hero in the white hat, the evil villain in the black hat, the community threatened by violence; these are the obvious elements of the paradigm." Which of the following words is most synonymous with the word "paradigm" as used in that sentence?
    A. story
    B. moral
    C. pattern
    D. example

Questions 19 – 21 are based on the following passage:
        Black History Month is unnecessary. In a place and time in which we
        overwhelmingly elected an African American president, we can and should
        move to a post-racial approach to education. As *Detroit Free Press* columnist
        Rochelle Riley wrote in a February 1 column calling for an end to Black
        History Month, "I propose that, for the first time in American history, this
        country has reached a point where we can stop celebrating separately, stop
        learning separately, stop being American separately."
        In addition to being unnecessary, the idea that African American history
        should be focused on in a given month suggests that it belongs in that month
        alone. It is important to instead incorporate African American history into
        what is taught every day as American history. It needs to be recreated as
        part of mainstream thought and not as an optional, often irrelevant, side
        note. We should focus efforts on pushing schools to diversify and broaden
        their curricula.
        There are a number of other reasons to abolish it: first, it has become a
        shallow commercial ritual that does not even succeed in its (limited and
        misguided) goal of focusing for one month on a sophisticated, intelligent
        appraisal of the contributions and experiences of African Americans
        throughout history. Second, there is a paternalistic flavor to the mandated
        bestowing of a month in which to study African American history that is
        overcome if we instead assert the need for a comprehensive curriculum.
        Third, the idea of Black History Month suggests that the knowledge
        imparted in that month is for African Americans only, rather than for all
        people.

19. The author's primary purpose is to:
    A. argue that Black History Month should not be so commercial.
    B. argue that Black History Month should be abolished.
    C. argue that Black History Month should be maintained.
    D. suggest that African American history should be taught in two months rather than just one.

20. It can be inferred that the term "post-racial" in the second sentence is an approach that:
    A. is not based on or organized around concepts of race.
    B. treats race as one factor, but not the most important, in determining an individual's experience.
    C. considers race after considering all other elements of a person's identity.
    D. prohibits discussion of race.

21. Which of the following does the author not give as a reason for abolishing Black History Month?
    A. It has become a shallow ritual.
    B. There is a paternalistic feel to being granted one month of focus.
    C. It suggests that the month's education is only for African Americans.
    D. No one learns anything during the month.

Questions 22 - 24 are based on the following passage:

On April 30, 1803, the United States bought the Louisiana Territory from the French. Astounded and excited by the offer of a sale and all that it would mean, it took less than a month to hear the offer and determine to buy it for $15 million. Right away the United States had more than twice the amount of land as before, giving the country more of a chance to become powerful. They had to move in military and governmental power in this region, but even as this was happening they had very little knowledge about the area. They did not even really know where the land boundaries were, nor did they have any how many people lived there. They needed to explore.

22. Based on the facts in the passage, what prediction could you make about the time immediately following the Louisiana Purchase?
    A. Explorers were already on the way to the region.
    B. The government wanted to become powerful.
    C. People in government would make sure explorers went to the region.
    D. Explorers would want to be paid for their work.

23. Why did the United States decide to buy the Louisiana Territory?
    A. They wanted to be more powerful.
    B. They wanted to find out the land boundaries.
    C. They wanted to know how many people lived there.
    D. They were astounded.

24. The author writes that "astounded and excited by the offer of a sale and all that it would mean ..." Which of the following words is most synonymous with the word "astounded" as used in that sentence?
    A. eager
    B. confused
    C. greedy
    D. shocked

Writing

Landon's German teacher has assigned a research project on the culture and history of Germany. Landon has made a poster and written detailed captions for each set of pictures on the poster. He would like your help revising and improving the captions. After you read Landon's essay, answer questions 1 - 10.

<u>Berlin</u>

(1) For almost 30 years, the Berlin Wall divided Berlin in two. (2) On November 9, 1989, citizens from both sides of the city joined together to break down the wall and reunite the city. (3) Today, most of the wall has fallen, but a line of bricks snake across the city, marking its old path.

(4) Although bombing during World War II destroyed most of Berlins buildings, the city has been rebuilt as a cultural center. (5) It has art, history, and science museums, as well as famous historical monuments.

(6) The majestic Brandenburg Gate was built in 1791 as a symbols of peace. (7) For many years, it was part of the Berlin Wall and reminded people of the divisions between east and west. (8) Today, the Brandenburg Gate symbolizes reunification and freedom. (9) Near the Brandenburg Gate is the German parliament building, called the Reichstag. (10) It was built in 1894 and was at the center of many important events in German politics. (11) Today, visitors can take an elevator up to the sparkling glass dome at the top of the Reichstag for a view of the city.

Ich bin ein Berliner

(12) On June 26, 1963, President John F. Kennedy visited West Berlin. (13) His visit took place a few years after the Berlin Wall was built and tensions between the United States and Communist East Germany were running high. (14) He gave an inspiring speech about freedom and democracy to the people of democratic West Berlin that ended with words of unity: "Ich bin ein Berliner." (15) He meant to say, "I am a citizen of Berlin," but his words really meant, "I am a doughnut." (16) A Berliner is a jelly doughnut popular in Germany. (17) The Germans in the audience appreciated President Kennedy's support, and cheered his message of freedom enthusiastically.

Cuisine

(18) German cuisine is known for its hearty, meat and potato dishes. (19) Families often enjoy a rich Sunday dinner of roast meat, potatoes, and cabbage. (20) A typical Sunday dinner might feature juicy Rinderrouladen, creamy Kartoffelpuree, and sweet Apfelkuchen. (21) In English, that would be stuffed beef rolls, mashed potatoes, and apple cake.

(22) Germans eat their heaviest meal of the day at lunchtime. (23) School cafeterias usually serve hearty stews and side dishes. (24) For dinner, families often eat thin slices of whole wheat bread with sausage, sliced meat, and cheese.

(25) Many Germans enjoy late afternoon Kaffee. (26) They visit a neighborhood café and relax with a cup of coffee and slice of creamy, rich cake. (27) Bakeries dot the streets of German towns and cities, selling from small sandwiches to rich pastries. (28) The Amerikaner cookie, a bakery favorite, is a cakey sugar cookie topped with a vanilla and chocolate glaze. (29) The Americaner got its name because it looks like New York City's famous black and white cookies.

1. What could be deleted from sentence 2 without changing the meaning?
   A. 1989
   B. from both sides of the city
   C. together
   D. break down

2. What change should be made to sentence 4?
   A. Change *Although* to *However*
   B. Add a comma after *World War II*
   C. Change *Berlins* to *Berlin's*
   D. Change *has* to *had*

3. What change should be made to sentence 6?
   A. Change *Gate* to *gate*
   B Change *was* to *were*
   C. Insert a comma after *1791*
   D. Change *symbols* to *symbol*

4. What change should be made to sentence 13?
   A. Change *years* to *year's*
   B. Add a comma after *built*
   C. Add a comma after *States*
   D. Change *were* to *was*

5. What change should be made to sentence 17?
   A. Insert commas after *Germans* and *audience*
   B. Change *appreciated* to *apreciated*
   C. Delete the comma after *support*
   D. Change *enthusiastically* to *enthusiaticaly*

6. What change should be made to sentence 18?
   A. Change *German* to *Germany*
   B. Change *is known* to *knew*
   C. Change *its* to *it's*
   D. Delete the comma after *hearty*

7. What is the most effective way to combine sentences 18 and 19?
   A. German cuisine is known for its hearty, meat and potato dishes but families often enjoy a rich Sunday dinner of roast meat, potatoes, and cabbage.
   B. German cuisine is known for its hearty, meat and potato dishes, but families often enjoy a rich Sunday dinner of roast meat, potatoes, and cabbage.
   C. German cuisine is known for its hearty, meat and potato dishes, and families often enjoy a rich Sunday dinner of roast meat, potatoes and cabbage.
   D. German cuisine is known for its hearty, meat and potato dishes, and families often enjoy a rich Sunday dinner of roast meat, potatoes, and cabbage.

8. What is the most concise way to combine sentences 20 and 21 without confusing the reader?

    A. A typical Sunday dinner might feature juicy Rinderrouladen, which are stuffed beef rolls, creamy Kartoffelpuree, which are mashed potatoes, and sweet Apfelkuchen, which is apple cake.

    B. A typical Sunday dinner might feature juicy Rinderrouladen (stuffed beef rolls), creamy Kartoffelpuree (mashed potatoes), and sweet Apfelkuchen (apple cake).

    C. A typical Sunday dinner might feature juicy Rinderrouladen, creamy Kartoffelpuree, and sweet Apfelkuchen, and these are stuffed beef rolls, mashed potatoes, and apple cake.

    D. A typical Sunday dinner might feature juicy Rinderrouladen, creamy Kartoffelpuree, and sweet Apfelkuchen.

9. What change should be made to sentence 27?

    A. Insert *that* after *Bakeries*

    B. Insert *big* after *of*

    C. Insert *everything* after *selling*

    D. Insert *and* after *to*

10. What change, if any, should be made to sentence 29?

    A. Change *Americaner* to *Amerikaner*

    B. Change *name* to *names*

    C. Change *City's* to *Cities*

    D. No change

For questions 11-15, select the best option for replacing the underlined portion of the sentence. The first option listed is always the same as the current version of the sentence.

11. <u>A key factor taken into account during city planning is</u> where major services and amenities will be located.

    A. A key factor taken into account during city planning is

    B. Key factors taken into account during city planning is

    C. A key factor taking into account during city planning is

    D. Key factors, taken into accounting during city planning are

12. <u>Jupiter with its numerous moons, and Great Red Spot,</u> has been studied extensively by astronomers.

    A. Jupiter with its numerous moons, and Great Red Spot,

    B. Jupiter with, its numerous moons and Great Red Spot,

    C. Jupiter, with its numerous moons and Great Red Spot,

    D. Jupiter with, its numerous moons, and Great Red Spot,

13. Many gardeners are now making their own backyard compost, <u>which is not only cheap, but also helps to cut down on landfill waste.</u>

    A. which is not only cheap, but also helps to cut down on landfill waste

    B. which is not only cheaper, but also cuts down on landfill's waste

    C. which is, not only cheap, but also, helps to cut down on landfill waste

    D. which is not only done cheaply, but is also cutting down on landfills wastes

14. <u>The growth of the security industry can be large attributable</u> to the fact that people are less trusting of others than they once were.

    A. The growth of the security industry can be large attributable

    B. The growing of the securities industry can be largely attributable

    C. The growth on the security industry can be large attributed

    D. The growth of the security industry can be largely attributed

15. Claude Monet was a famous painter <u>who's well-known painting includes</u> Starry Night and Water Lilly Pond.

    A. who's well-known painting includes

    B. whose well-known painting including

    C. whose well-known paintings include

    D. who well-known paintings include

16. The Sugar Act was implemented in 1764 by England, and it required individuals residing in the colonies of the United States to pay a tax on sugar, as well as on dyes and other goods.

Rewrite, beginning with

<u>Implemented in 1764 by England</u>

The next words will be

    A. the Sugar Act

    B. it required individuals

    C. in the colonies

    D. on sugar

17. Oil spill, as the phrase suggests, refers to the accidental introduction of oil into environments, and even though it can refer to land spills, the phrase is usually understood to refer to spills in water.

Rewrite, beginning with

<u>Even though the phrase "oil spill" is usually understood to refer to spills in water</u>

The next words will be

    A. as the name suggests

    B. it can refer to land spills

    C. and the introduction of oil

    D. known as oil spills

18. Radar was first used in 1904, and at that time all it was capable of was determining whether objects were present, but now it can determine the size and shape of an object, among other things, as well.

Rewrite, beginning with

<u>Although once only capable of determining the presence of objects,</u>

The next words will be

    A. radar was first used

    B. among other things

    C. radar can now determine

    D. the size and shape of an object

19. Placebos are often used in drug studies, and the effectiveness of a drug can be determined by measuring whether people with illnesses or diseases show significantly more improvement when they are given a real drug rather than a placebo.

Rewrite, beginning with

<u>By measuring whether people with illnesses show significantly more improvement when given a real drug,</u>

The next words will be

    A. the effectiveness of a drug

    B. placebos can be used in drug studies

    C. it is rather than a placebo

    D. is often used in drug studies

20. Employees value salary and good benefits in a job, but many also consider having an enjoyable job important, so it's difficult to say what the majority of people value most in a career.

Rewrite, beginning with

<u>While many people consider having an enjoyable job important,</u>

The next words will be

    A. it's what the majority of people

    B. it's difficult to say

    C. salary and good benefits

    D. other employees value

Essay

Preemptive war has long been discussed as an option to prevent certain countries that are viewed as dangerous or unstable from acquiring nuclear weapons. Please write a five-paragraph persuasive essay (approximately 350–500 words) discussing whether you support or oppose the idea of a preemptive war for this purpose.

Answers and Explanations

Math

1. A: In this probability problem, there are three independent events (the codes for each digit), each with ten possible outcomes (the numerals 0-9). Since the events are independent, the total possible outcomes equals the product of the possible outcomes for each of the three events, that is $P = P_1 \times P_2 \times P_3 = 10 \times 10 \times 10 = 1000$
This makes sense when you also relate the problem to a sequence, beginning with the combinations 0-0-0, 0-0-1, 0-0-2......In ascending order, the last 3 digit combination would be 9-9-9. Although it may seem that there would be 999 possible combinations, you must include the initial combination, 0-0-0.

2. A: Setting the cost of shipping equal to the amount received gives us the equation $3,000 + 100x = 400x$. Subtract 100x from both sides to get $3,000 = 300x$, then divide both sides by 300 to see that $x = 10$.

3. D: Multiply both sides of the first equation by s to get 3 = 7s, then divide both sides by 7 to find that $s = \frac{3}{7}$. Multiply both sides of the second equation by t to get 4 = 12t, then divide both sides by 12 to find that $t = \frac{1}{3}$. To find the difference, we must convert to a common denominator. In this case, the common denominator is 21. Multiplying by appropriate fractional equivalents of 1, we find that $\frac{3}{7}\left(\frac{3}{3}\right) = \frac{9}{21}$ and $\frac{1}{3}\left(\frac{7}{7}\right) = \frac{7}{21}$. Therefore $-t = \frac{9}{21} - \frac{7}{21} = \frac{2}{21}$.

4. B: The average of 7 and x is 7 + x divided by 2. The average of 9, 4, and x is 9 + 4 + x divided by 3. (7+x)/2 = (9+4+x)/3. Simplify the problem and eliminate the denominators by multiplying the first side by 3 and the second side by 2. For the first equation, (21 + 3x)/6. For the second equation, (18 + 8 + 2x)/6. Since the denominators are the same, they can be eliminated, leaving 21 + 3x = 26 + 2x. Solving for x gets x = 26-21. x = 5.

5. D: There are 7 integers whose absolute value is less than 4: -3, -2, -1, 0, 1, 2, 3.
6. D: To solve 3(2x – 10) = x, first multiply the left side out. 6x – 30 = x. Therefore, 5x = 30, and x = 6.

7. C: This equation is asking you to multiply three algebraic expressions. When multiplying more than two expressions, multiply any two expressions (using the foil method), then multiply the result by the third expression. Start by multiplying:
$(y + 1)(y + 2) = (y \times y) + (y \times 2) + (1 \times y) + (1 \times 2)$
$= y^2 + 2y + y + 2$
$= y^2 + 3y + 2$
Then multiply the result by the third expression:
$(y^2 + 3y + 2)(y + 3) = (y^2 + 3y + 2)(y) + (y^2 + 3y + 2)(3)$
$= (y^3 + 3y^2 + 2y) + (3y^2 + 9y + 6)$
$= y^3 + 3y^2 + 2y + 3y^2 + 9y + 6$
$= y^3 + 3y^2 + 3y^2 + 9y + 2y + 6$
$= y^3 + 6y^2 + 11y + 6$

8. D: Note that the first two terms and the last two terms of $x^3 - 3x^2 - 4x + 12$ are each divisible by $x - 3$. Thus $x^3 - 3x^2 - 4x + 12 = x^2(x - 3) - 4(x - 3) = (x^2 - 4)(x - 3)$. $x^2 - 4$ is a difference of squares, and since in general $x^2 - a^2 = (x + a)(x - a)$, we know $x^2 - 4 = (x + 2)(x - 2)$. The full factorization of $x^3 - 3x^2 - 4x + 12$ is therefore $(x + 2)(x - 2)(x - 3)$.

Alternatively, instead of factoring the polynomial, we could have divided the polynomial $x^3 - 3x^2 - 4x + 12$ by the expression contained in each answer choice. Of those listed, only the expression x+3 yields a nonzero remainder when divided into $x^3 - 3x^2 - 4x + 12$, so it is not a factor.

9. D: $\frac{x^6}{y^4} \times x^2y^3 = x^6y^{-4} \times x^2y^3 = (x^6x^2)(y^{-4}y^3) = x^{6+2}y^{-4+3} = x^8y^{-1} = \frac{x^8}{y}$.

10. C: A method commonly taught to multiply binomials is the "FOIL" method, an acronym for First, Outer, Inner, Last: multiply the first terms of each factor, then the outer terms, and so forth. Applied to $(x + 2)(x - 3)$, this yields $(x)(x) + (x)(-3) + (2)(x) + (2)(-3) = x^2 - 3x + 2x - 6 = x^2 - x - 6$.

11. B: These are supplementary angles. That means that the two angles will add up to a total of 180°, which is the angle of a straight line. To solve, subtract as follows:
b = 180° - 120°
b = 60

12. C: Rotational symmetry is defined as a figure that looks exactly the same after being rotated any amount. Answer choice D is the only example given that would stay the same if rotated.

13. C: A straight line is 180°. Subtract to solve: 180° - 45° = 135°

14. A: The sum of the measures of the three angles of any triangle is 180. The equation of the angles of this triangle can be written as 2x + 6x + 10x = 180, or 18x = 180. Therefore, x = 10. Therefore, the measure of the smallest angle is 20.

15. C: Using the Pythagorean Theorem, we first find AB.
AB² + BC² = AC²
AB² + 5² = 13²
AB² + 25 = 169
AB² = 144
AB = 12
Next, we draw a perpendicular bisector from C to AD, forming segment CE, which is the height of triangle ACD and is equal to segment AB. Thus, the height of the triangle is 12.

16. B: Using the formula for the perimeter of a rectangle, we know that P = 2*l* + 2*w*. Substituting the value given, we get 76 = 2*l* + 2*w* or 38 = *l* + *w*. We can now solve for *l*: 38 – *w* = *l*.
Using the formula for the area of a rectangle, we know that A = *lw*. Substituting the value given, we get 336 = *lw*.
If we substitute the 38 – *w* we found in the first step for *l*, we get (38–*w*)*w* = 336. Thus:
38*w* – *w*² = 336

$0 = w^2 - 38w + 336$
$0 = (w - 14)(w - 24)$
$w = 14$ or 24

The shorter of these two possibilities is 14.

      A. Incorrect: $24 - 14$
      B. Correct
      C. Incorrect: $76/4$
      D. Incorrect: length of the longer sides

17. C: Group B is negatively skewed since there are more high scores. With more high scores, the mean for Group B will be higher.

18. A: The correlation is negative with a slope of approximately −3 and a y-intercept of approximately 5. Choices B and C can be eliminated, since a y-intercept of 10.3 is too high and a y-intercept of −5.3 is too low. Choice D may also be eliminated since the slope of −8.2 is too steep for the slope shown on the graph.

19. C: The probability of independent events, A and B, may be found using the formula, $P(A \text{ and } B) = P(A) \cdot P(B)$. Thus, the probability she draws a jack, replaces it, and then draws an ace card may be represented as $P(A \text{ and } B) = \frac{4}{52} \cdot \frac{4}{52}$, which simplifies to $P(A \text{ and } B) = \frac{1}{169}$.

20. D: The expected value is equal to the sum of the products of each card value and its probability. Thus, the expected value is $\left(1 \cdot \frac{1}{5}\right) + \left(2 \cdot \frac{1}{5}\right) + \left(3 \cdot \frac{1}{5}\right) + \left(4 \cdot \frac{1}{5}\right) + \left(5 \cdot \frac{1}{5}\right)$, which equals 3.

Reading

1. A: Answer choice B is not correct, because wild birds are not discussed at length. Answer choice C is not really discussed, and D is touched upon only briefly. The passage focuses on lack of preening and excessive preening, which are both examples of abnormal preening behavior. The main purpose of the passage is to discuss abnormal preening in birds.

2. D: The passage states that "Animals that are herbivores will find the winters extremely tough, because all of the vegetation will have died off by the time winter arrives. Hibernation is essentially a way of dealing with this food shortage." Therefore, D is the correct answer. Answer choice A is the purpose of migration, and answer choices B and C are not mentioned.

3. B: Answer choices A, C, and D are all mentioned in the passage, but they are part of the overall purpose, which is to give an overview of how leeches have been used throughout history.

4. C: The passage states that "Obviously, this was bad news for music artists and record labels because they weren't making any profits from downloaded music." Therefore, answer

- 106 -

Copyright © Mometrix Media. You have been licensed one copy of this document for personal use only. Any other reproduction or redistribution is strictly prohibited. All rights reserved.

choice C is the correct choice. None of the other choices are identified as problems associated with file-sharing sites.

5. D: The passage states "Women are sold all sorts of creams and ointments, and are promised that these will make them look younger over time. Unfortunately, these claims are entirely false. Lotions can not penetrate to the inner layers of the skin, which is where wrinkles form." Therefore, these goods do not deliver what they promise.

6. B: The topic sentence is placed at the beginning of each supporting paragraph. Supporting evidence is presented after the topic sentence in each supporting paragraph. The passage states "Next come the supporting paragraphs. Each paragraph contains a topic sentence, supporting evidence, and finally a type of mini-conclusion that restates the point of the paragraph."

7. B

8. D

9. A: Answer (B) incorrect because, although it is a benefit the author claims come from learning Esperanto, the author does not state that it is the reason the language was initially developed. Answers (C) and (D) are incorrect as they were never brought up in the text at all.

10. C

11. A: In the sentence quoted, the author uses "privileged" to mean benefited or favored. Answers (B) and (C) are not meanings of the word privileged in any situation. Answers (D) and (E) are both meanings of the word privileged but are not appropriate in this context.

12. C

13. B: The only answer option about which the author claimed a study had shown something is that Esperanto increased one's ability to learn a next language.

14. D: The point of the passage is to suggest that viewers should think more critically about assumptions and frameworks (such as the Western paradigm) that underlie the stories in movies they watch.

15. C: The author recommends that viewers think more critically about frameworks that underlie stories in movies; she argues that, if not, viewers may absorb biases with which they do not agree. An example the author gives of that bias is that it is hard to find a movie in which the hero is not supremely morally worthy. The author's identification of this as a bias implies that she thinks it is not the right choice. Her comment about the difficulty of finding a portrayal of an enemy that allows the enemy to be complex suggests that the author believes that more nuance and less absolutes would be an improvement in the U.S. storytelling of war.

16. C: The author said nothing about horseback riding.

17. A: The author suggests that these movies rarely show enemies of the U.S. to be complex or fighting for a legitimate cause.

18. C

19. B: The entire passage makes the argument that Black History Month should be abolished, offering various reasons why this is the best course of action.

20. A: The context of the sentence suggests that post-racial refers to an approach in which race is not a useful or positive organizing principle.

21. D: The author of Passage 1 never suggests that people do not learn about African American history during Black History Month.

22. C: People in government knew that the purchase would make the country more powerful, but the last sentence specifically states that they needed to explore. Answer choice C is the best prediction of what would occur next. Answer choices A, D and E infer too much, since you cannot assume any of these based on this passage given. Answer choice B is simply a statement that does not predict anything for the future.

23. A: While all of the answer choices are in the passage, only answer choice A answers the question as it is written. The desire to become more powerful is listed in the passage as one of the reasons that the United States decided to buy the land.

24. D

Writing

1. C: because the word *together* reinforces the word *join* but is not required; *joined together* is slightly redundant. Choice A is incorrect because the year is required to help the reader know when these events are taking place. Choice B is incorrect because the phrase *from both sides of the city* tells the reader that citizens from both East Berlin and West Berlin participated. Choice D is incorrect because *break down* makes it clear that the wall was torn down.

2. C: because *Berlin* is a possessive that modifies *buildings* (the buildings are in Berlin). Choice A is incorrect because the word *however* is a conjunctive that should stand on its own and be followed by a comma. The word *although* correctly sets up the dependent clause that begins the sentence. Choice B is incorrect because *during World War II* is part of the subject and should not be separated by a comma from the verb *destroyed*. Choice D is incorrect because the verb should be the present tense *has*. Present tense is required because the city is still rebuilt.

3. D: because the article *a* indicates that *symbol* should be singular rather than plural. Choice A is incorrect because *gate* is part of the proper noun *Brandenburg Gate*. Choice B is incorrect because the subject of the sentence is singular, which means the verb must be singular. Choice C is incorrect because a comma is not required after the year because it is essential to the sentence.

4. B: because the conjunction *and* is separating two independent clauses. When this happens, a comma is required before the conjunction. Choice A is incorrect because the sentence is talking about *years*, which is plural, rather than possessive. Choice C is incorrect because a comma is not needed between the *and* in a two-item series. Choice D is incorrect because the subject *tensions* is plural, which means the verb *were* needs to remain in the plural form.

5. C: because the conjunction *and* connects an independent clause and a dependent clause. When these two types of clauses are connected, a comma should not be used. Choice A is not correct because the prepositional phrase *in the audience* is essential and should not be separated by commas. Choices B and D are incorrect because both words are spelled correctly in the original passage.

6. D: because a comma should not separate an adjective from the noun it modifies. Choice A is incorrect because the word *German* is an adjective that is correctly modifying *cuisine*, while *Germany* is a noun. Choice B is incorrect because the sentence is constructed as a passive sentence and needs the passive verb form *is known*. Choice C is incorrect because *it's* means *it is* and is not a possessive.

7. D: because a comma and the conjunction *and* are required to combine the sentences. *And* is a better choice than *but* because the second sentence is a continuation of the first rather than a contradiction. Choices A and B are incorrect because the conjunction *but* doesn't fit the meaning of the sentences. Choice A is also missing the required comma. Choice C uses the correct conjunction, *and*, but is missing the comma.

8. B: is correct because it uses parentheses to define the German words. This version is both the least wordy choice and also one that defines the unknown words. Choices A and C also define the unknown words, but they are longer and wordier than choice B. Choice C is the most concise, but it does not define the German words, which might confuse a reader who does not understand German.

9. C: because the word *everything* is the object of the clause and the sentence would be incomplete without it. Choice A is incorrect because the word *that* would turn the first part of the sentence into a complex subject rather than a subject and verb. Choice B is incorrect because *big* changes the meaning of the sentence. While the towns may be big, it is not required to fix the sentence. Choice D is incorrect because *rich* is an adjective that modifies the noun *pastries*; these words should not be separated by *and*.

10. A: is the correct answer because *Amerikaner* should be spelled with a 'k.' The reader can determine this spelling by looking at the previous sentence. Choice B is incorrect because *name* is referring to a singular subject. Choice C is incorrect because the word *City's* should be singular possessive, not plural. Choice D is incorrect because it misspells *Amerikaner* as *Americaner*.

11. A: Answer choice B is incorrect because the plural *key factors* and the singular *is* do not agree. The *taking* in choice C makes it incorrect. Choice D has a misplaced comma. Choice A makes sense and the singular *a key factor* and *is* agree with each other.

12. C: Choice C is the only choice that has correctly placed commas. The *numerous moons* and the *Great Red Spot* both refer to the planet Jupiter, which is maintained in answer choice C.

13. A: Answer choice B is incorrect because of the misplaced apostrophe. C has two unnecessary commas. Answer choice D is too wordy, and *landfills wastes* sounds quite awkward. Answer choice A is succinct, the comma is in the correct place, and it expresses the information is a clear way that is not awkward.

14. D: Answer choices A and C are incorrect because *large* is used in front of *attributable* and *attributed.* Both of these phrases are grammatically incorrect. B describes *the growing of the securities industry*, which is quite awkward. D is the best choice because it refers to *the growth of the security industry* and uses the phrase *largely attributed*, which is grammatically correct.

15. C: The correct way to refer to a person, in this case Monet, is through the use of the pronoun *whose*, which eliminates A and D. Two paintings are identified, so the plural form must be used, eliminating choice B. Choice C uses *whose* and *paintings*, indicating there is more than one, making it the correct choice.

16. A: The Sugar Act is identified in the first sentence as something that was implemented in 1764 by England. Therefore, answer choice A is the best choice. Answer choice B does not indicate what was implemented. Answer choice C indicates where but not what was implemented, and D does not tell the reader what was implemented.

17. B: The phrase "even though" indicates a contrast. Answer choice A is more of an agreement than a contrast. Answer choice C is somewhat redundant, and D cannot logically follow the given phrase. Answer choice B provides a contrast because the given phrase talks about spills in water, while choice B talks about spills on land. It is also a logical choice because "it" in choice B refers to "the phrase" that is mentioned in the given phrase.

18. C: C is the only choice that provides a distinction between then and now. The given phrase says that radar was *once* used to determine the presence of objects, and C indicates that radar can *now* determine other things as well.

19. A: The word "by" indicates a cause/effect relationship. By measuring whether people respond significantly more favorably when given a real drug, something is being accomplished. Answer choices C and D do not imply this relationship. Answer choice B does not make logical sense in the context of the sentence. Answer choice A states "the effectiveness of a drug," which is a good choice because it could logically be followed with a phrase like "can be determined."

20. D: The word "while" is used to establish a contrast, making D the obvious choice. The given phrase speaks about *some people*, while D identifies *other employees*, which creates an effective contrast.

Practice Test #3

Practice Questions

Math

1. If 2x + 3y = 13 and 4x − y = 5, then 3x + 2y =
   - A. 3
   - B. 6
   - C. 12
   - D. 24

2. If a movie reached the 90-minute mark 12 minutes ago, what minute mark had it reached *m* minutes ago?
   - A. *m* − 102
   - B. *m* − 78
   - C. 102 − *m*
   - D. 78 − *m*

3. If x > 2500, then the value of $\frac{x}{1-2x}$ is closest to
   - A. $-\frac{50}{99}$
   - B. $-\frac{1}{2}0$
   - C. $\frac{50}{99}$
   - D. $\frac{1}{2}$

4. If 520 ÷ x = 40n, then which of the following is equal to *nx*?
   - A. 13
   - B. 26
   - C. 40
   - D. 13x

5. If *a* − 16 = 8b + 6, what does *a* + 3 equal?
   - A. b + 3
   - B. 8b + 9
   - C. 8b + 22
   - D. 8b + 25

6. Janice weighs *x* pounds. Elaina weighs 23 pounds more than Janice. June weighs 14 pounds more than Janice. In terms of *x*, what is the sum of their weights minus 25 pounds?
   - A. 3x + 37
   - B. 3x + 12
   - C. x + 12
   - D. 3x - 25

7. If $x > 2$, then $\left(\frac{x^2-5x+6}{x+1}\right) \times \left(\frac{x+1}{x-2}\right) =$

   A. . $x + 1$

   B. $x - 3$

   C. $\frac{x^2+2x+1}{x-2}$

   D. $\frac{x^2-2x-3}{x+1}$

8. What is $\frac{x^3+2x}{x+3}$ when $= -1$?

   A. $-\frac{3}{2}$

   B. $-\frac{2}{3}$

   C. $\frac{1}{2}$

   D. $\frac{3}{4}$

9. $(x + 6)(x - 6) =$

   A. $x^2 - 12x - 36$

   B. $x^2 + 12x - 36$

   C. $x^2 + 12x + 36$

   D. $x^2 - 36$

10. If $x + 2y = 3$ and $-x - 3y = 4$, then $x =$

   A. 1

   B. 5

   C. 7

   D. 17

Use the figure below to answer questions 11, 12, and 13.

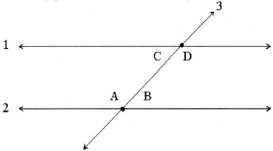

11. Which of the following statements is true about the figure above?

   A. Lines 1 and 2 are parallel.

   B. Lines 1 and 3 are parallel.

   C. Lines 1 and 2 intersect.

   D. Line 1 bisects line 3.

12. In the figure above, which of the following is a pair of alternate interior angles?

   A. angle A and angle B

   B. angle A and angle C

   C. angle B and angle D

   D. angle A and angle D

13. In the figure above, which of the following is an obtuse angle?
    A. line 1
    B. line 3
    C. angle A
    D. angle B

14. Which of the following letters has a vertical line of symmetry?
    A. V
    B. K
    C B
    D. L

15.

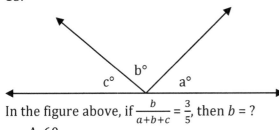

In the figure above, if $\frac{b}{a+b+c} = \frac{3}{5}$, then $b = ?$
    A. 60
    B. 72
    C. 108
    D. 120

16. If the radius of circle O is one-quarter the diameter of circle P, what is the ratio of the circumference of circle O to the circumference of circle P?
    A. $\frac{1}{4}$
    B. $\frac{1}{2}$
    C. 2
    D. 4

17. Suppose two variables show a correlation of 0.9. Which of the following statements *best* describes the relationship?
    A. The variables show a strong correlation.
    B. The variables show some correlation, which is neither weak nor strong.
    C. The variables show a weak correlation.
    D. The variables show a perfect correlation.

18. Edward draws a card from a deck of cards, does not replace it, and then draws another card. What is the probability that he draws a heart and then a spade?
    A. $\frac{1}{16}$
    B. $\frac{1}{2}$
    C. $\frac{1}{17}$
    D. $\frac{13}{204}$

19. Suppose Ashley will receive a $6,000 scholarship if she chooses University A, a $4,500 scholarship if she chooses University B, and a $5,500 scholarship if she chooses University C. The probabilities that she will attend each university are equal. Which of the following best represents the expected value for the scholarship amount she will receive?

    A. $4,833
    B. $5,155
    C. $5,333
    D. $5,525

20. Nia spends $5 on a raffle ticket. If she wins, she will win $500. A total of 250 raffle tickets were sold. What is the expected value?

    A. −$2
    B. −$3
    C. −$5
    D. −$7

Reading

Directions for questions 1 – 6

Read the statement or passage and then choose the best answer to the question. Answer the question based on what is stated or implied in the statement or passage.

1. The importance of a comfortable work space cannot be overstated. Developing a comfortable work environment is relatively simple for employers. Ergonomic chairs, large computer screens, personal desk space, and some level of privacy are all essential. This involves some expense, but not a great deal. Not surprisingly, employees are happier in this type of environment, but it is the employers who really benefit. Reduced sick time, higher levels of employee satisfaction, higher productivity, and more creativity have all been observed.

The main idea expressed in this passage is

    A. a comfortable work space is not as important as people say.
    B. developing a comfortable work space is easy.
    C. establishing a comfortable work space is not expensive.
    D. employers benefit greatly when they provide comfortable work spaces.

2. Planning weddings is tough. One important part of the planning process is choosing bridesmaid dresses. Although there used to be a lot of rules when it came to picking out a color, many of them are not observed any more. However, one that is still observed is that the bridesmaids should not wear the same color as the bride. The most popular colors for bridesmaid dresses in recent years have been white and black.

It can be concluded that

    A. picking dresses is the hardest part of planning a wedding.
    B. many brides are choosing to wear colors other than white.
    C. most bridesmaids are allowed to choose their own dress.
    D. bridesmaids were not traditionally allowed to wear black.

3. Those so-called green fuels may not be as environmentally friendly as once thought. For example, producing natural gas is a much more labor intensive process than producing an equal amount of conventional gasoline. Also, producing natural gas involves burning fossil fuels. Transporting natural gas also involves burning fossil fuels.

The weakness of green fuels is that
    A. they are not as abundant as conventional fuel.
    B. they require a lot more work to produce.
    C. burning them releases fossil fuels.
    D. they must be transported greater distances.

4. The media has done a lot to promote racism in North America. For example, it was found that the majority of crimes discussed on the nightly news featured African American suspects. However, when the total number of crimes committed in North American was examined, it was found that white people were also suspects 50% of the time.

If the above information were true, it could be concluded that
    A. there are more white criminals than African American criminals.
    B. most people believe that African Americans commit more crimes.
    C. many crimes committed by white people are not discussed on the news.
    D. the total number of crimes committed has decreased in the last several years.

5. Many people feel that the use of stem cells in research is unethical. However, they fail to realize that such research could lead to cures for some of the world's most troubling diseases. Diseases like Parkinson's and MS could possibly be cured through the use of stem cells, and those with spinal cord injuries could possibly walk again. Therefore, it is entirely ethical to engage in stem cell research aimed at easing the suffering of those who have life-altering conditions.

The main purpose of the passage is
    A. to discuss why people believe stem cell research is unethical.
    B. to discuss the possible benefits of stem cell research.
    C. to identify diseases that have been cured through stem cell research.
    D. to argue that not conducting stem cell research is unethical.

6. Many people do not know the difference between precision and accuracy. While accuracy means that something is correct, precision simply means that you are able to duplicate results and that they are consistent. For example, if there was a glass of liquid that was 100 degrees, an accurate measurement would be one that was close to this temperature. However, if you measured the temperature five times, and came up with a measurement of exactly 50 degrees each time, your measurement would be extremely precise, but not accurate.

The term accurate results refers to
    A. results that are correct.
    B. results that are consistent.
    C. results that can be duplicated.
    D. results that are measurable.

Questions 7 - 11 are based on the following passage:

Who Was This Man?

"You have a visitor, you see," said Monsieur Defarge.

"What did you say?"

"Here is a visitor."

The shoemaker looked up as before, but without removing a hand from his work.

"Come!" said Defarge. "Here is monsieur, who knows a well-made shoe when he sees one. Show him that shoe you are working at. Take it, monsieur."

Mr. Lorry took it in his hand.

"Tell monsieur what kind of shoe it is, and the maker's name."

There was a longer pause than usual, before the shoemaker replied: "I forget what it was you asked me. What did you say?"

"I said, couldn't you describe the kind of shoe, for monsieur's information?"

"It is a lady's shoe. It is a young lady's walking-shoe. It is in the present mode. I never saw the mode. I have had a pattern in my hand."

He glanced at the shoe with some little passing touch of pride.

"And the maker's name?" said Defarge.

Now that he had no work to hold, he laid the knuckles of the right hand in the hollow of the left, and then the knuckles of the left hand in the hollow of the right, and then passed a hand across his bearded chin, and so on in regular changes, without a moment's intermission. The task of recalling him from the vagrancy into which he always sank when he had spoken, was like recalling some very weak person from a swoon, or endeavouring, in the hope of some disclosure, to stay the spirit of a fast-dying man.

"Did you ask me for my name?"

"Assuredly I did."

"One Hundred and Five, North Tower."

"Is that all?"

"One Hundred and Five, North Tower."

With a weary sound that was not a sigh, nor a groan, he bent to work again, until the silence was again broken.

"You are not a shoemaker by trade?" said Mr. Lorry, looking steadfastly at him.

His haggard eyes turned to Defarge as if he would have transferred the question to him: but as no help came from that quarter, they turned back on the questioner when they had sought the ground.

"I am not a shoemaker by trade? No, I was not a shoemaker by trade. I-I learnt it here. I taught myself. I asked leave to ... "

He lapsed away, even for minutes, ringing those measured changes on his hands the whole time. His eyes came slowly back, at last, to the face from which they had wandered; when they rested on it, he started, and resumed, in the manner of a sleeper that moment awake, reverting to a subject of last night.

"I asked leave to teach myself, and I got it with much difficulty after a long while, and I have made shoes ever since."

—Excerpted from *A Tale of Two Cities* by Charles Dickens

7. Monsieur Defarge and Mr. Lorry are visiting
    A. an art gallery in Paris.
    B. a man who has been ill.
    C. a member of the British government.
    D. a doctor making hospital calls.

8. Based on the name he gives, the reader can infer that the man
    A. has spent time in a prison tower.
    B. has been traveling throughout Europe.
    C. has been homeless a long time.
    D. first left home as a young man.

9. Which of the following is NOT a sign of the man's mental condition?
    A. his inability to complete a thought
    B. his identifying himself by a location instead of a name
    C. the repetitive motion of his hands
    D. his cheerful laughter

10. The man has asked to learn the trade of
    A. woodcarving.
    B. glassblowing.
    C. shoemaking.
    D. dressmaking.

11. What can the reader infer about the identity of Monsieur Defarge?
    A. He is the unkind jailer at the prison.
    B. He is a friend keeping the man safe.
    C. He is the man's loving son or grandson.
    D. He is a cruel doctor in a hospital.

Questions 12 - 15 are based on the following passages:

Passage 1:
Fairy tales, fictional stories that involve magical occurrences and imaginary creatures like trolls, elves, giants, and talking animals, are found in similar forms throughout the world. This occurs when a story with an origin in a particular location spreads geographically to, over time, far-flung lands. All variations of the same story must logically come from a single source. As language, ideas, and goods travel from place to place through the movement of peoples, stories that catch human imagination travel as well through human retelling.

Passage 2:
Fairy tales capture basic, fundamental human desires and fears. They represent the most essential form of fictionalized human experience: the bad characters are pure evil, the good characters are pure good, the romance of royalty (and of commoners becoming royalty) is celebrated, etc. Given the nature of the fairy tale genre, it is not surprising that many different cultures come up with similar versions of the same essential story.

12. On what point would the authors of both passages agree?
   A. Fairy tales share a common origin.
   B. The same fairy tale may develop independently in a number of different cultures.
   C. There are often common elements in fairy tales from different cultures.
   D. Fairy tales capture basic human fears.

13. What does the "nature of the fairy tale genre" refer to in Passage 2?
   A. The representation of basic human experience
   B. Good characters being pure good and bad characters being pure evil
   C. Different cultures coming up with similar versions of the same story
   D. Commoners becoming royalty

14. Which of the following is not an example of something the author of Passage 1 claims travels from place to place through human movement?
   A. Fairy tales
   B. Language
   C. Ideas
   D. Foods

15. Which of the following is not an example of something that the author of Passage 1 states might be found in a fairy tale?
   A. Trolls
   B. Witches
   C. Talking animals
   D. Giants

Questions 16 - 21 are based on the following passage:

Peanut allergy is the most prevalent food allergy in the United States, affecting around one and a half million people, and it is potentially on the rise in children in the United States. While thought to be the most common cause of food-related death, deaths from food allergies are very rare. The allergy typically begins at a very young age and remains present for life for most people. Approximately one-fifth to one-quarter of children with a peanut allergy, however, outgrow it. Treatment involves careful avoidance of peanuts or any food that may contain peanut pieces or oils. For some sufferers, exposure to even the smallest amount of peanut product can trigger a serious reaction.

Symptoms of peanut allergy can include skin reactions, itching around the mouth, digestive problems, shortness of breath, and runny or stuffy nose. The most severe peanut allergies can result in anaphylaxis, which requires immediate treatment with epinephrine. Up to one-third of people with peanut allergies have severe reactions. Without treatment, anaphylactic shock can result in death due to obstruction of the airway, or heart failure. Signs of anaphylaxis include constriction of airways and difficulty breathing, shock, a rapid pulse, and dizziness or lightheadedness.
As of yet, there is no treatment to prevent or cure allergic reactions to peanuts. In May of 2008, however, Duke University Medical Center food

Copyright © Mometrix Media. You have been licensed one copy of this document for personal use only. Any other reproduction or redistribution is strictly prohibited. All rights reserved.

allergy experts announced that they expect to offer a treatment for peanut allergies within five years.

Scientists do not know for sure why peanut proteins induce allergic reactions, nor do they know why some people develop peanut allergies while others do not. There is a strong genetic component to allergies: if one of a child's parents has an allergy, the child has an almost 50% chance of developing an allergy. If both parents have an allergy, the odds increase to about 70%.

Someone suffering from a peanut allergy needs to be cautious about the foods he or she eats and the products he or she puts on his or her skin. Common foods that should be checked for peanut content are ground nuts, cereals, granola, grain breads, energy bars, and salad dressings. Store prepared cookies, pastries, and frozen desserts like ice cream can also contain peanuts. Additionally, many cuisines use peanuts in cooking – watch for peanut content in African, Chinese, Indonesian, Mexican, Thai, and Vietnamese dishes.

Parents of children with peanut allergies should notify key people (child care providers, school personnel, etc.) that their child has a peanut allergy, explain peanut allergy symptoms to them, make sure that the child's epinephrine auto injector is always available, write an action plan of care for their child when he or she has an allergic reaction to peanuts, have their child wear a medical alert bracelet or necklace, and discourage their child from sharing foods.

16. According to the passage, approximately what percentage of people with peanut allergies have severe reactions?
    A. Up to 11%
    B. Up to 22%
    C. Up to 33%
    D. Up to 44%

17. By what date do Duke University allergy experts expect to offer a treatment for peanut allergies?
    A. 2008
    B. 2009
    C. 2010
    D. 2013

18. Which of the following is not a type of cuisine the passage suggests often contains peanuts?
    A. African
    B. Italian
    C. Vietnamese
    D. Mexican

19. Which allergy does the article state is thought to be the most common cause of food-related death?
    A. Peanut
    B. Tree nut
    C. Bee sting
    D. Poison oak

20. It can be inferred from the passage that children with peanut allergies should be discouraged from sharing food because:
    A. Peanut allergies can be contagious.
    B. People suffering from peanut allergies are more susceptible to bad hygiene.
    C. Many foods contain peanut content and it is important to be very careful when you don't know what you're eating.
    D. Scientists don't know why some people develop peanut allergies.

21. Which of the following does the passage not state is a sign of anaphylaxis?
    A. running or stuffy nose
    B. shock
    C. a rapid pulse
    D. constriction of airways

Questions 22 - 24 refer to the following passage:

> "His pride," said Miss Lucas, "does not offend me so much as pride often does, because there is an excuse for it. One cannot wonder that so very fine a young man, with family, fortune, everything in his favour, should think highly of himself. If I may so express it, he has a right to be proud."
>
> "That is very true," replied Elizabeth, "and I could easily forgive his pride, if he had not mortified mine."
>
> "Pride," observed Mary, who piqued herself upon the solidity of her reflections, "is a very common failing I believe. By all that I have ever read, I am convinced that it is very common indeed, that human nature is particularly prone to it, and that there are very few of us who do not cherish a feeling of self-complacency on the score of some quality or other, real or imaginary. Vanity and pride are different things, though the words are often used synonymously. A person may be proud without being vain. Pride relates more to our opinion of ourselves, vanity to what we would have others think of us."

22. Why doesn't the gentleman's pride offend Miss Lucas?
    A. She admires his vanity.
    B. He is handsome and rich.
    C. It is human nature to be proud.
    D. He is poor and homeless.

- 120 -

23. Which sentence best states the theme of this passage?
    A. Pride and vanity are offensive.
    B. Fame and fortune can make a person proud.
    C. Every person is proud in one way or another.
    D. Pride can bring you fortune.

24. According to the passage, what is the difference between pride and vanity?
    A. Pride relates to a person's abilities; vanity relates to a person's looks.
    B. Men are proud; women are vain.
    C. Pride and vanity are synonymous.
    D. Pride is what you think of yourself; vanity is what you want others to think of you.

Writing

Margot's high school may be adopting a dress code. Margot is against this idea and has written an article for her school newspaper arguing against the dress code. Margot wrote the article and would like your help revising and improving the essay. After you read the article, answer questions 1 - 10.

(1) Mrs. Conwer, the Jackson High principal, announced last week that Jackson High is considering a student dress code. (2) She is saying that some of the students are wearing to school is being distracting and inappropriate. (3) For example, she says that some of the boys like to wear their pants too low and that some of the girls like to wear very short skirts. (4) I don't agree that there is a problem. (5) Furthermore, I think there are several reasons why it is important that Jackson High does not have a dress code.

(6) When people are in high school, they are teenagers. (7) Being a teenager means that your at a time in life when you are exploring new things and learning about yourself. (8) Many teens also like to express themselves. (9) For example, some people I know keep a blog where they write about things that are important to them. (10) Other people play in a band and can express themselves through music. (11) A lot of teens express themselves through fashion. (12) Since many teens start earning their own money, they can buy their own clothes and choose the fashions that they want. (13) If Jackson High adopts a dress code the students won't be able to express themselves. (14) Self expression is important and are often taught at Jackson High. (15) Ms. Riley, my dance teacher, tells me to express myself through dance. (16) Mr. Hunter, my English teacher, tells me to express myself through writing. (17) Taking away expression through fashion is hypocritical because it goes against what is taught in many classes.

(18) A dress code at Jackson High will never please everyone. (19) Who gets to decide what is appropriate and what is not? (20) What happens if the students disagree with the code? (21) In school, we learn about respecting different opinions and making compromises. (22) However, if Mrs. Conwer or just a couple of teacher's choose the dress code, they will be ignoring the students. (23) Jackson High should stop ignoring the lessons that we learn in our classes every day.

(24) How can Jackson High make sure that students dress appropriately if it doesn't have a dress code? (25) That's what some teachers have said to me. (26) I think the answer is obvious. (27) Teach us, the students, how people are supposed to dress in the real world when they have jobs. (28) Explain why certain choices might be inappropriate. (29) Than let us make our own decisions. (30) That's what we learn in all our classes, and that's how it should be for the dress code.

1. What is the most effective way to rewrite sentence 2?
   A. Some of the outfits students wear to school, she is saying, are distracting and not appropriate.
   B. The outfits are distracting and inappropriate, she says, that students wear to school.
   C. She says that some of the outfits that students wear to school are distracting and inappropriate.
   D. She says that it is distracting and inappropriate that students wear outfits to school.

2. What change, if any, should be made to sentence 7?
   A. Change *your* to *you're*
   B. Insert a comma before *and*
   C. Change *about* to *on*
   D. No change

3. What is the most effective way to combine sentences 11 and 12?
   A. A lot of teens express themselves through fashion, and since many teens start earning their own money, they can buy their own clothes and choose the fashions that they want.
   B. A lot of teens express themselves through fashion and since many teens start earning their own money, they can buy their own clothes and choose the fashions that they want.
   C. A lot of teens express themselves through fashion, but since many teens start earning their own money, they can buy their own clothes and choose the fashions that they want.
   D. A lot of teens express themselves through fashion but since many teens start earning their own money, they can buy their own clothes and choose the fashions that they want.

4. What change should be made to sentence 13?
   A. Change *if* to *because*
   B. Add a comma after *code*
   C. Change *students* to *students'*
   D. Change *themselves* to *theirselves*

5. What change should be made in sentence 14?
   A. Change *expression* to *expresion*
   B. Insert a comma before *and*
   C. Delete *are*
   D. Insert *the* after *at*

6. What transition should be added to the beginning of sentence 18?
   A. However
   B. Furthermore
   C First of all
   D. Therefore

7. What change should be made to sentence 22?
   A. Change *however* to *nevertheless*
   B. Change ***a couple*** to *several*
   C. Change *teacher's* to *teachers*
   D. Delete the comma after ***code***

8. What change should be made in sentence 27?
   A. Delete the comma after *us*
   B. Change *suppossed* to *supposed*
   C. Change *real world* to *real-world*
   D. Change *jobs* to *job's*

9. What change, if any, should be made to sentence 28?
   A. Change *explain* to *explaining*
   B. Insert *not* after *might*
   C. Change *inappropriate* to *inapropriate*
   D. No change

10. What change should be made in sentence 29?
    A. Change *than* to *then*
    B. Insert *you* before *let*
    C. Insert *to* after *us*
    D. Change *decisions* to *descisions*

For questions 11-15, select the best option for replacing the underlined portion of the sentence.
The first option listed is always the same as the current version of the sentence.

11. If he stops to consider the ramifications of this decision, <u>it is probable that he will rethink his original decision a while longer</u>.
    A. it is probable that he will rethink his original decision.
    B. he will rethink his original decision over again.
    C. he probably will rethink his original decision.
    D. he will most likely rethink his original decision for a bit.

12. When you get <u>older," she said "you will no doubt</u> understand what I mean."
    A. older," she said "you will no doubt
    B. older" she said "you will no doubt
    C. older," she said, "you will no doubt
    D. older," she said "you will not

13. <u>Dr. Anderson strolled past the nurses, examining a bottle of pills.</u>
   A. Dr. Anderson strolled past the nurses, examining a bottle of pills.
   B. Dr. Anderson strolled past the nurses examining a bottle of pills.
   C. Examining a bottle of pills Dr. Anderson strolled past the nurses.
   D. Examining a bottle of pills, Dr. Anderson strolled past the nurses.

14. Karl and Henry <u>raced to the reservoir, climbed the ladder, and then they dove into</u> the cool water.
   A. raced to the reservoir, climbed the ladder, and then they dove into
   B. first raced to the reservoir, climbed the ladder, and then they dove into
   C. raced to the reservoir, they climbed the ladder, and then they dove into
   D. raced to the reservoir, climbed the ladder, and dove into

15. Did either <u>Tracy or Vanessa realize that her decision would be</u> so momentous?
   A. Tracy or Vanessa realize that her decision would be
   B. Tracy or Vanessa realize that each of their decision was
   C. Tracy or Vanessa realize that her or her decision would be
   D. Tracy or Vanessa realize that their decision would be

16. The Burmese python is a large species of snake that is native to parts of southern Asia, althoughthe snake has recently begun infesting the Florida Everglades and causing environmental concerns by devouring endangered species.
Rewrite the sentence, beginning with the phrase, *The Burmese python has recently caused environmental concerns in the Florida Everglades*. The words that follow will be:
   A. because it is devouring endangered species in Florida
   B. where it has made a home for itself away from its origins in southern Asia
   C. by leaving its native home of southern Asia with an infestation of its natural prey
   D. and is altering the delicate balance of species in that area

17. In the wild, the Burmese python typically grows to around twelve feet in length, but in captivity the snakes can often grow much longer than that, to upwards of fifteen or twenty feet in length.
Rewrite the sentence, beginning with the phrase, *Burmese pythons in captivity can grow to be as long as fifteen or twenty feet*. The words that follow will be:
   A. as a result of the controlled environment that allows them to eat more
   B. while it is typically shorter in the wild
   C. but in the wild are shorter and may only be twelve feet long
   D. which is much longer than a python in the wild grows to be

18. Florida biologists and environmentalists blame the exotic animals industry for the snake's introduction into the Everglades, because many snake owners are unable or unwilling to continue taking care of the creature once it grows too large and becomes too expensive.
Rewrite the sentence, beginning with the phrase, *The Burmese python can grow large and become too expensive for snake owners to maintain*. The words that follow will be:
   A. and Florida biologists and environmentalists blame the exotic animals industry
   B. so the python has been introduced into the Everglades
   C. leaving the exotic animals industry at risk in the United States
   D. resulting in abandoned snakes that have infested the Everglades

- 124 -

19. Lawmakers called for action against owning Burmese pythons after a pet python got out of its cage in a Florida home and killed a young child while she was sleeping, a situation that left responsible snake owners objecting and claiming that this was an isolated event.

Rewrite the sentence, beginning with the phrase, *Responsible Burmese python owners have claimed that the death of a young child in Florida after a python attack was an isolated event.* The words that follow will be:

    A. but lawmakers have called for action against owning the pythons

    B. because the python accidentally got out of its cage and attacked the child

    C. that does not reflect accurately on conscientious snake owners

    D. resulting in angry lawmakers who called for a prohibition of Burmese pythons

20. Biologists were initially concerned that the Burmese python could spread throughout much of the United States, due to its ability to adapt to its environment, but recent evidence suggests that the snake is content to remain within the Everglades.

Rewrite the sentence, beginning with the phrase, *Recent evidence suggests that the Burmese python is content to remain within the Everglades.* The words that follow will be:

    A. due to its ability to adapt to its environment

    B. and comes as a surprise to biologists who believed the snake would spread outside Florida

    C. despite concerns that the snake could spread throughout much of the United States

    D. because it is unable to adapt to cooler environments outside of south Florida

Essay

NSA wiretapping and spying policies have been a topic of interest lately with much discussion taking place over the need for security as it relates to the right to individual privacy. Please write a five-paragraph persuasive essay (approximately 350–500 words) discussing whether you support or oppose government collection of private data for the purpose of national security.

Answers and Explanations

Math

1. C: Solving for y in the second equation gives y = 4x-5. If we plug this into the first equation we get 2x + 3(4x-5) = 13. Solving for this equation gives us 14x = 28, or x = 2. Then, plug the value of x into either equation to solve for y. y = 3. Therefore, 3x + 2y = 12.

2. C: The movie is now at the 90 + 12 = 102-minute mark. Therefore, m minutes ago, it had reached the 102 – m mark.
     A. Incorrect: Reverses constant and variable.
     B. Incorrect: Subtracts 12 from 90 instead of adding and reverses constant and variable.
     C. Correct
     D. Incorrect: Subtracts 12 from 90 instead of adding.

3. B: For all large values of x, the value of $\frac{x}{1-2x}$ will be very close to the value of $\frac{x}{-2x} = -\frac{1}{2}$.
     A. Incorrect: Less than –1/2, so not closest
     B. Correct
     C. Incorrect: Wrong sign; greater than 1/2, so not closest
     D. Incorrect: Wrong sign

4. A: If $520 \div x = 40n$, then
    $(40n)(x) = 520$ or
    $40nx = 520$
    $nx = 13$.

5. D: Isolate a: $a = 8b + 6 + 16$. Thus, $a = 8b + 22$. Next add 3 to both side of the equation: $a + 3 = 8b + 22 + 3 = 8b + 25$.

6. B: Translate this word problem into a mathematical equation. Let Janice's weight = x. Let Elaina's weight = $x + 23$. Let June's weight = $x + 14$. Add their weights together and subtract 25 pounds:
    $= x + x + 23 + x + 14 - 25$
    $= 3x + 37 - 25$
    $= 3x + 12$

7. B: $\left(\frac{x^2-5x+6}{x+1}\right) \times \left(\frac{x+1}{x-2}\right) = \frac{(x^2-5x+6)\times(x+1)}{(x+1)\times(x-2)}$. Before carrying out the multiplication of the polynomials, notice that there is a factor of $x + 1$ in both the numerator and denominator, so the expression reduces to $\frac{x^2-5x+6}{x-2}$. We can simplify further by factoring the numerator. One way to factor a quadratic expression with a leading coefficient of 1 is to look for two numbers that add to the coefficient of x (in this case -5) and multiply to the constant term (in this case 6). Two such numbers are -2 and -3: $(-2) + (-3) = -5$ and $(-2) \times (-3) = 6$. So $x^2 - 5x + 6 = (x - 2)(x - 3)$. That means $\frac{x^2-5x+6}{x-2} = \frac{(x-2)(x-3)}{x-2}$. The $x - 2$ in the numerator and denominator can cancel, so we are left with just $x - 3$. (Note that if $x = -1$ or $x = 2$, the obtained simplified expression would not be true: either value of x would

- 127 -

result in a denominator of zero in the original expression, so the whole expression would be undefined. Therefore, it is necessary to state that these values of x are excluded from the domain. For a domain of $x > 2$, both -1 and 2 are excluded as possible values of x.)

8. A: To evaluate $\frac{x^3+2x}{x+3}$ at $= -1$, substitute in -1 for x in the expression: $\frac{(-1)^3+2(-1)}{(-1)+3} = \frac{(-1)+(-2)}{2} = \frac{-3}{2} = -\frac{3}{2}$.

9. D: Use the rule that $(a+b)(a-b) = a^2 - b^2$ or multiply the bionomials using the FOIL method: multiply together the First term of each factor, then the Outer, then the Inner, then the Last, and add the products together.
$(x+6)(x-6) = x \times x + x \times (-6) + 6 \times x + 6 \times (-6) = x^2 - 6x + 6x - 36 = x^2 - 36$.

10. D: There are several ways to solve a system of equations like this. One is by substitution. If $x + 2y = 3$, then $x = -2y + 3$. Substituting that into the other equation, $-x - 3y = 4$, we get $-(-2y + 3) - 3y = 4 \Rightarrow 2y - 3 - 3y = 4 \Rightarrow -y - 3 = 4 \Rightarrow -y = 7 \Rightarrow y = -7$. Now, putting that value for y back into one of the original equations, we get $x + 2(-7) = 3 \Rightarrow x - 14 = 3 \Rightarrow x = 17$.

11. A: Lines 1 and 2 are parallel. If the parallel lines continued on into infinity, they would never cross. To *intersect* means that the lines cross. *Bisect* means that a line cuts another line or figure in two equal halves. To *correspond* means to match.

12. D: The degree measurement for alternate interior angles is exactly the same. In the figure, there are two pairs of alternate interior angles: B and C; A and D.

13. C: An obtuse angle is one that is more than 90° (a right angle) and less than 180°. Answer choices A, B and C are not angles. Answer choice E, angle B, is an acute angle since it is small than a 90° angle.

14. A: If you draw a vertical line down the center of the letter V, the two sides will be symmetrical.

15. C: The angles a, b, and c form a straight line, so $a + b + c$ = 180. Substituting 180 for $a + b + c$ in the proportion, we have:
$$\frac{b}{180} = \frac{3}{5}$$

By cross-multiplying, we can solve for b: $5b = 3(180)$ or $b = 108$.
  A. Incorrect: 180/3
  B. Incorrect: $180 - b$
  C. Correct
  D. Incorrect: $180 - (180/3)$

16. B: The radius of circle O is one-fourth the diameter of circle P. The diameter is twice the radius, or d = 2r. So $r_o = \frac{1}{4}(2r_p) = \frac{1}{2}r_p$.
The circumference of circle P = $2\pi\, r_p$.
The circumference of circle O = $2\pi\, r_o = 2\pi\left(\frac{1}{2}r_p\right) = \pi\, r_p$.

The ratio of circle O's circumference to circle P's is $(\pi r_p)/(2\pi r_p) = \frac{1}{2}$.

    A. Incorrect: Doesn't convert diameter to radius.

    B. Correct

    C. Incorrect: Finds ratio of circle P's circumference to circle O's.

    D. Incorrect: Doesn't convert diameter to radius; Finds ratio of circle P's circumference to circle O's.

17. A: A correlation of 0.9 is a strong correlation. Recall the closer a correlation coefficient is to −1 or 1, the stronger the correlation. A correlation of −1 or 1 is perfect.

18. D: Since he does not replace the first card, the events are dependent. The sample space will decrease by 1 for the second draw because there will be one less card to choose. Thus, the probability may be written as $P(A \text{ and } B) = \frac{13}{52} \cdot \frac{13}{51}$, or $P(A \text{ and } B) = \frac{169}{2652}$ or $\frac{13}{204}$.

19. C: The expected value is equal to the sum of the products of the scholarship amounts and probability she will attend each college, or $\frac{1}{3}$. Thus, the expected value is $\left(6000 \cdot \frac{1}{3}\right) + \left(4500 \cdot \frac{1}{3}\right) + \left(5500 \cdot \frac{1}{3}\right)$, which equals 5,333. So, she can expect to receive $5,333.

20. B: The expected value is equal to the sum of the product of the amount of the net profit, or $495, and the probability of winning and the product of the amount of the loss, or −$5, and the probability of losing. The expected value is $\left(495 \cdot \frac{1}{250}\right) + \left((-5) \cdot \frac{249}{250}\right)$, which equals −3. Thus, the expected value is −$3.

Reading

1. D: The main idea discussed in the passage is that employers benefit the most from establishing a comfortable work space. The author points out that it is not extremely expensive, then identifies all of the benefits for employers: better productivity, less absenteeism, etc.

2. B: It can be concluded that many brides are choosing to wear colors other than white based on two statements in the passage. First, we know that bridesmaids do not wear the same color as the bride. Secondly, it is stated that white is a popular color for bridesmaid dresses. Therefore, since the color of the bridesmaid dress is not the same as the bride's dress, it can be concluded that the bride's dress is not white.

3. B: Many green fuels require more work to produce than conventional fuels. The passage states "producing natural gas is a much more labor-intensive process than producing an equal amount of conventional gasoline. Producing natural gas also involves burning fossil fuels."

4. C: This conclusion can be made based on two statements. First, the passage states that "the majority of crimes discussed on the nightly news featured African American suspects." Second, "it was found that white people were also suspects 50% of the time." Therefore, if half of all suspects are white, but the majority of suspects on the news are African American,

it is reasonable to conclude that the news chooses not to report crimes that involve white suspects.

5. B: The main purpose of the passage is to discuss the possible benefits of stem cell research. The author states that many people feel it is unethical, but most of the passage is devoted to discussing the possible benefits of stem cell research. Cures for diseases and being able to repair spinal cord injuries are the possible benefits identified.

6. A: Accuracy is the same as correctness. The passage states "accuracy means that something is correct" and "if there was a glass of liquid that was 100 degrees, an accurate measurement would be one that was close to this temperature."

7. B: The passage refers to the nameless shoemaker's haggard eyes, his inability to focus on a question, his repetitive motions, and his inability to give his name. There is no indication of any art or gallery. The setting is Paris; the passage does not indicate that. Thus choice A is incorrect. The man being described is not identified as British or as a member of government, so choice C is incorrect. The man is making shoes, not hospital calls; therefore, choice D is incorrect. Although the man is making shoes by hand, there is no sign that he is a fashion designer.

8. A: The man gives his name as One Hundred and Five, North Tower, an address, not a personal name. The reference to a tower suggests a prison. Option B is an incorrect choice; the man has not apparently been out of the North Tower in many years. Nor is option C correct because the man is not precisely homeless. Nothing in the passage tells the reader when the man left home, so option D can be eliminated.

9. D: The man does not laugh in this passage. Choice A is clearly stated in the passage. He has lapses in conversation with Mr. Lorry. It is also clear in the passage that the man has no remembrance of a given personal name, so choice B can be eliminated. The repeated motion of his hands when they do not hold the shoe is a telling sign of derangement, so choice C is incorrect.

10. C: The man is working on a lady's walking-shoe when his visitors arrive and states that he had learned the trade, which was not his original manner of work, at his own request since arriving at the prison. He even expresses some pride in the quality of his work, which is based on a pattern because he has never seen the current mode of shoe. There is no indication that he is engaged in carving wood, blowing glass, or dressmaking. All of the other choices are clearly false.

11. B: Defarge is somehow the man's keeper and is concerned with his well-being. The first choice suggests unkindness, which is clearly not the case—Defarge is neutral at best. That option can be eliminated. He does not appear to be a family member, so choice C can be eliminated as well. These is also no suggestion of cruelty nor of a profession nor of a definite setting, leaving choice D untenable. A man in this setting is unlikely to have any money.

12. C: Since both authors are explaining in the passages how the same story may come to be in different cultures, it is clear they both accept that there are often common elements in fairy tales from different cultures.

13. A: The author of Passage 2 claims that the essence and nature of fairy tales is their representation of basic human experience. It is this assertion that leads the author to believe that the same story could develop independently in different places.

14. D: The author does not mention the movement of food in the passage.

15. B: The author never mentions witches in the passage.

16. C: The second paragraph of the passage notes that "up to one-third of people with peanut allergies have severe reactions." Since one-third is approximately 33%, (C) is the correct choice.

17. D: The second paragraph of the passage notes that in 2008, Duke experts stated that they expect to offer treatment in five years. Five years from 2008 is 2013.

18. B: The last sentence in paragraph five lists the cuisines in which one should watch for peanuts. Italian is not listed.

19. A: The second sentence of the first paragraph states that peanut allergy is the most common cause of food-related death.

20. C: The passage implies that it is not always easy to know which foods have traces of peanuts in them and that it's important to make sure you know what you're eating. This is hard or impossible if you share someone else's food.

21. A: Paragraph two gives examples of symptoms of peanut allergies and, more specifically, examples of symptoms of anaphylaxis. A running or stuffy nose is given as a symptom of the former, but not of the latter.

22. B: In the first paragraph, Miss Lucas states that "so very fine a young man, with family, fortune, every thing in his favour, should think highly of himself. If I may so express it, he has a *right* to be proud." Basically, she feels he deserves to be proud because he is physically attractive, comes from a good family, has money, and is successful. The best choice is (B).

23. C: A theme is a message or lesson conveyed by a written text. The message is usually about life, society or human nature. This particular excerpt is exploring pride as it relates to human nature. Mary's observations on pride are the best summary of the theme of this passage. "By all that I have ever read, I am convinced that it is very common indeed, that human nature is particularly prone to it." The best answer choice is (C).

24. D: Paragraph 3 gives the answer to this question. According to Mary, pride is an opinion of yourself, and vanity is what we want others to think of us.

Writing

1. C: because this version begins with a subject and verb and is followed by a clause. Choice A is incorrect because the words are out of order and don't logically follow the previous sentence. Sentence 2 should begin with 'She says' because it is the school principal's opinion being expressed. This choice is also incorrect because it uses the words *not appropriate*

instead of *inappropriate*. Choice B is incorrect because the clause "that students wear to schools" should come after the word *outfits*. Choice D is incorrect because the word order changes the meaning of the sentence by stating that any outfits are distracting and inappropriate.

2. A: is correct because *your* is the possessive of *you* while *you're* is a conjunction that stands for *you are*. Because it makes sense to substitute *you are* for *you're*, choice A is correct. Choice B is incorrect because a comma is only required before *and* if it is concluding a series of three or more items. Choice C is incorrect because it is correct to write *learn about* but incorrect to write *learn on*. Choice D is incorrect because *your* should be written as the conjunction *you're*.

3. A: because it uses correct punctuation and a logical conjunction. Because the conjunction *and* connects two independent clauses (meaning that they can stand on their own as sentences), there must be a comma before the conjunction. Therefore, choices B and D are incorrect because they are missing this comma. While choice C does have a comma before the conjunction, it uses the conjunction *but* rather than *and*. *But* implies that the two clauses contradict each other. *And* is a better choice because the two clauses are connected and support each other.

4. B: is correct because the phrase *If Jackson high adopts a dress code* is a dependent clause that is followed by an independent clause. Because there is no conjunction, these two clauses must be separated by a comma. Choice A is incorrect because the word *because* would only be used if the dress code had already been adopted. Choice C is incorrect because *students'* would require the word to be a possessive, even though the sentence does not show the students possessing anything. Choice D is incorrect because *theirselves* is not a real word.

5. C: because the verb *are* does not match the subject, *self expression*, which is singular. Choice A is incorrect because *expression* is already written with the correct spelling. Choice B is incorrect because the conjunction *and* is connecting an independent clause with a dependent clause. When *and* is used in this way, there should not be a comma before the conjunction. Choice D is incorrect because an article is not needed before the name of the school, which is a proper noun.

6. B: is correct because the word *furthermore* shows that the sentence will present additional support for the writer's argument. Choice A is incorrect because *however* indicates that the following sentence will contradict what came before. Choice C is incorrect because the sentence is not presenting the first point in the writer's argument. Choice D is incorrect because the sentence is not presenting a conclusion, but an additional point.

7. C: because *teacher's* is not being used as a possessive. Instead, it's being used as a plural noun and therefore should not have an apostrophe. Choice A is incorrect because *however* is a better transition to sentence 22 due to the sentence showing a contrast with a previous point. Choice B is incorrect because the word *of* should not follow *several*. Choice D is incorrect because the comma correctly separates a dependent clause from an independent clause.

8. B: is correct because the correct spelling of the word only has a single *s*. Choice A is incorrect because the comma is required to set off the non-essential clause *the students*.

Choice C is incorrect because *real* is an adjective modifying *world*, and it is incorrect to put a hyphen in between an adjective and a noun. Choice D is incorrect because *jobs* is a plural noun, not a possessive.

9. **D:** is correct because the sentence does not have any errors. Choice A is incorrect because sentences should not begin with a declarative verb. Choice B is incorrect because *not* changes the meaning of the sentence to the opposite of the writer's point. Choice C is incorrect because *inappropriate* is spelled correctly.

10. **A:** because *than* is a comparison word while *then* indicates a conclusion. Choice B is incorrect because *you* indicates that the writer is addressing a specific person, which is not the case. Choice D is incorrect because *decisions* is already written with the correct spelling.

11. **C:** The original sentence is redundant and wordy.

12. **C:** The syntax of the original sentence is fine, but a comma after *said* but before the open-quotation mark is required.

13. **D:** In the original sentence, the modifier is placed too far away from the word it modifies.

14. **D:** The verb structure should be consistent in a sentence with parallel structures.

15. **A:** The singular pronoun *her* is appropriate since the antecedents are joined by *or*. Also, the subjunctive verb form is required to indicate something indefinite.

16. **A:** Answer choice A best completes statement in the rewritten sentence by making the immediate connection between the environmental concerns and the reason for them. Answer choice B could work within the context of the sentence, but it does not create a sufficient link between the environmental concerns and their causes. Answer choice C provides information that is not contained within the original sentence, and answer choice D also adds information by noting that the "delicate balance" is altered. While this might be inferred from the original sentence, it cannot be added to the rewritten sentence.

17. **C:** Answer choice C accurately adds the statement of contrast about the python being shorter in the wild. Answer choice A adds information to the original sentence. Answer choice B is technically correct but does not contain as much information as answer choice C and is thus not the best choice. Answer choice D is also technically correct but does not provide the substance of the information that answer choice C contains.

18. **D:** Answer choice D creates the necessary link between the snake owners and the infestation of pythons in the Everglades. Answer choice A contains accurate information, but the sentence does not flow smoothly from one idea to the next. Answer choice B is true but is vague and fails to create a sufficient link between ideas. Answer choice C contains details that make no sense within the context of the sentence.

19. **A:** Answer choice A provides the sense of contrast that is contained within the original sentence by showing the differences between the responsible snake owners and the lawmakers. Answer choice B offers information that is contained within the original sentence but fails to provide a clear link between ideas. Answer choice C essentially repeats the information that is in the rewritten statement and is thus repetitive. Answer choice D,

though correct, does not make a great deal of sense following up the information in the rewritten statement.

20. C: Answer choice C effectively restates the sentence by capturing the entire mood of the original. Answer choice A adds correct information, but it is incomplete with respect to the original idea. Answer choice B may be inferred to a degree, but there is not enough information in the original sentence to claim that the biologists were "surprised" about the results – only that they were "concerned" about the potential. Answer choice D adds information that is not within the original sentence.

Practice Test #4

Practice Questions

Math

1. A regular toilet uses 3.2 gallons of water per flush. A low flow toilet uses 1.6 gallons of water per flush. What is the difference between the number of gallons used by the regular toilet and the low flow toilet after 375 flushes?
   A. 100 gallons
   B. 525 gallons
   C. 600 gallons
   D. 1,200 gallons

2. Solve for n in the following equation: $4n - p = 3r$
   A. 3r/4 - p
   B. p + 3r
   C. 3r/4 + p
   D. 3r/4 + p/4

3. What is $|x| + |x - 2|$ when $x = 1$?
   A. 0
   B. 1
   C. 2
   D. 3

4. Which of the following inequalities is correct?
   A. $\frac{1}{3} < \frac{2}{7} < \frac{5}{12}$
   B. $\frac{2}{7} < \frac{1}{3} < \frac{5}{12}$
   C. $\frac{5}{12} < \frac{2}{7} < \frac{1}{3}$
   D. $\frac{5}{12} < \frac{1}{3} < \frac{2}{7}$

5. If $6q + 3 = 8q - 7$, what is q?
   A. $-\frac{5}{7}$
   B. $\frac{5}{7}$
   C. 5
   D. -7

6. A communications company charges $5.00 for the first ten minutes of a call and $1.20 for each minute thereafter. Which of the following equations correctly relates the price in dollars, d, to the number of minutes, m (when $m \geq 10$)?

A. $d = 5 + 1.2m$
B. $d = 5 + 1.2(m - 10)$
C. $d = 5m + 1.2(m + 10)$
D. $d = (m + 10)(5 + 1.2)$

7. $\dfrac{x^2}{y^2} + \dfrac{x}{y^3} =$

A. $\dfrac{x^3 + x}{y^3}$

B. $\dfrac{x^2 + xy}{y^3}$

C. $\dfrac{x^2 y + xy}{y^3}$

D. $\dfrac{x^2 y + x}{y^3}$

8. How many solutions are there to the equation $|x^2 - 2| = x$?

A. 0
B. 1
C. 2
D. 4

9. Which of the following represents the factors of the expression, $x^2 - 3x - 40$?

A. $(x - 8)(x + 5)$
B. $(x - 7)(x + 4)$
C. $(x + 10)(x - 4)$
D. $(x + 6)(x - 9)$

10. Given the equation, $2^x = 64$, what is the value of x?

A. 4
B. 5
C. 6
D. 7

11. In the figure below, angles b and d are equal. What is the degree measure of angle d?

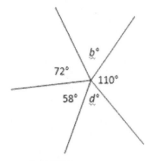

A. 120°
B. 80°
C 60°
D. 30°

12. What is the area of the parallelogram in the figure pictured below?

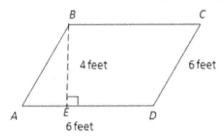

A. 10 square feet
B. 16 square feet
C. 24 square feet
D. 36 square feet

13. Find the value of x in the figure pictured below:

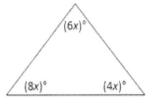

A. 10
B. 16
C. 18
D. 60

14. A rectangle is twice as long as it is wide. If its area is 200 cm², what is its width?
A. 10 cm
B. 20 cm
C. $10\sqrt{2}$ cm
D. $20\sqrt{2}$ cm

15. A building has a number of floors of equal height, as well as a thirty-foot spire above them all. If the height of each floor in feet is h, and there are n floors in the building, which of the following represents the building's total height in feet?
A. $n + h + 30$
B. $nh + 30$
C. $30n + h$
D. $30h + n$

16. Which of the following figures show parallelogram $WXYZ$ being carried onto its image $W'X'Y'Z'$ by a reflection across the x-axis?

A.

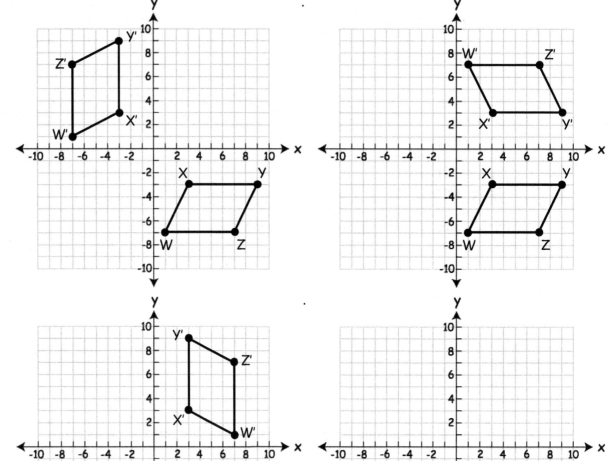

B.

17. Which of the following measures is unaffected by a skewed distribution?
    A. mean
    B. median
    C. standard deviation
    D. range

18. Which of the following correlation coefficients represents a weak correlation?
    A. −0.9
    B. 0.2
    C. −0.7
    D. 0.8

19. Elisha spins a spinner with 8 equally-spaced sections labeled 1 – 8. What is the probability that the spinner lands on either a number greater than 5 or on 2?

    A. $\frac{3}{64}$

    B. $\frac{1}{2}$

    C. $\frac{1}{8}$

    D. $\frac{3}{8}$

20. A bag contains 2 red marbles, 3 blue marbles, and 5 green marbles. What is the probability Gitta draws a red marble, does not replace it, and then draws another red marble?

    A. $\frac{1}{25}$

    B. $\frac{1}{45}$

    C. $\frac{2}{45}$

    D. $\frac{14}{45}$

Reading

Directions for questions 1 – 6
Read the statement or passage and then choose the best answer to the question. Answer the question based on what is stated or implied in the statement or passage.

1. Literacy rates are lower today than they were fifteen years ago. Then, most people learned to read through the use of phonics. Today, whole language programs are favored by many educators.
If these statements are true, it can be concluded that
    A. whole language is more effective at teaching people to read than phonics.
    B. phonics is more effective at teaching people to read than whole language.
    C. literacy rates will probably continue to decline over the next 15 years.
    D. the definition of what it means to be literate is much stricter now.

2. George Washington was a remarkable man. He was born in 1732. Shortly before becoming the President of the United States in 1789, Washington was an important leader in the American Revolutionary War from 1775 to 1783. After retiring, he returned to Mount Vernon in 1797. A short time later, John Adams made him commander in chief of the United States Army again. This was done in anticipation that the country might go to war with France.
Almost immediately after serving as a leader in the American Revolutionary War
    A. Washington returned to Mount Vernon.
    B. Washington was made commander in chief of the U.S. Army.
    C. Washington became the President of the United States.
    D. Washington decided to go into retirement.

3. During the 1970s, a new type of pet became popular in North America. Although they were actually just brine shrimp, they were marketed as "Sea Monkeys." They don't actually look like monkeys at all, but were branded as such due to their long tails. When sea monkeys first began to be sold in the United States, they were sold under the brand name "Instant Life." Later, when they became known as sea monkeys, the cartoon drawings that were featured in comic books showed creatures that resembled humans more than shrimp. The creative marketing of these creatures can only be described as genius, and at the height of their popularity in the 1970s, they could be found in as many as one in five homes.
Based on the information in the passage, it can be inferred that
    A. Sea monkeys were more popular when they were marketed as "instant life."
    B. Sea monkeys wouldn't have been as popular if they had been marketed as "brine shrimp."
    C. Most people thought they were actually purchasing monkeys that lived in the sea.
    D. There are more homes today that have sea monkeys than there were in the 1970s.

4. Before the battle between CDs and MP3s, there was a rivalry during the 1960s between the four-track and the eight-track tape. Four-track tapes were invented in the early 1960s by Earl Muntz, an entrepreneur from California. Later, Bill Lear designed the eight-track tape. This latter invention was similar in size to the four-track tape, but it could store and play twice as many songs. Lear had close ties with the motor company Ford, and he convinced them to include eight-track players in their vehicles, which definitely helped the eight-track tape to achieve a high level of popularity. Soon after, they began being used in homes, and the four-track tape all but disappeared.

The main difference between the four-track and eight-track tape was
    A. The four-track tape was much larger than the eight-track tape.
    B. The eight-track tape cost a lot more to produce than the four-track tape.
    C. The eight-track tape could hold more songs than the four-track tape.
    D. The four-track tape was usually included in Ford vehicles.

5. It is natural for humans to have fears, but when those fears are completely irrational and begin to interfere with everyday activities they are known as phobias. Agoraphobia is a serious phobia, and it can be devastating for those who suffer from it. Contrary to popular belief, agoraphobia is not simply a fear of open spaces. Rather, the agoraphobic fears being in a place that he feels is unsafe. Depending on the severity of the problem, the agoraphobic might fear going to the mall, walking down the street, or even walking to the mailbox. Often, the agoraphobic will view his home as the safest possible place to be, and he may even be reluctant to leave his house. Treatments for this condition include medication and behavioral therapy.

An agoraphobic would feel safest
    A. In their yard.
    B. In their house.
    C. In a mall.
    D. On the sidewalk.

6. The butterfly effect is a somewhat poorly understood mathematical concept, primarily because it is interpreted and presented incorrectly by the popular media. It refers to systems, and how initial conditions can influence the ultimate outcome of an event. The best way to understand the concept is through an example. You have two rubber balls. There are two inches between them, and you release them. Where will they end up? Well, that depends. If they're in a sloped, sealed container, they will end up two inches away from each other at the end of the slope. If it's the top of a mountain, however, they may end up miles away from each other. They could bounce off rocks; one could get stuck in a snow bank while the other continues down the slope; one could enter a river and get swept away. The fact that even a tiny initial difference can have a significant overall impact is known as the butterfly effect.

The purpose of this passage is
    A. To discuss what could happen to two rubber balls released on top of a mountain.
    B. To show why you can predict what will happen to two objects in a sloped, sealed container.
    C. To discuss the primary reason why the butterfly effect is a poorly understood concept.
    D. To give an example of how small changes at the beginning of an event can have large effects.

Questions 7 - 15 are based on the following passage:

Daylight Saving Time (DST) is the practice of changing clocks so that afternoons have more daylight and mornings have less. Clocks are adjusted forward one hour in the spring and one hour backward in the fall. The main purpose of the change is to make better use of daylight.

DST began with the goal of conservation. Benjamin Franklin suggested it as a method of saving on candles. It was used during both World Wars to save energy for military needs. Although DST's potential to save energy was a primary reason behind its implementation, research into its effects on energy conservation are contradictory and unclear.

Beneficiaries of DST include all activities that can benefit from more sunlight after working hours, such as shopping and sports. A 1984 issue of *Fortune* magazine estimated that a seven-week extension of DST would yield an additional $30 million for 7-Eleven stores. Public safety may be increased by the use of DST: some research suggests that traffic fatalities may be reduced when there is additional afternoon sunlight.
On the other hand, DST complicates timekeeping and some computer systems. Tools with built-in time-keeping functions such as medical devices can be affected negatively. Agricultural and evening entertainment interests have historically opposed DST.

DST can affect health, both positively and negatively. It provides more afternoon sunlight in which to get exercise. It also impacts sunlight exposure; this is good for getting vitamin D, but bad in that it can increase skin cancer risk. DST may also disrupt sleep.

Today, daylight saving time has been adopted by more than one billion people in about 70 countries. DST is generally not observed in countries near the equator because sunrise times do not vary much there. Asia and Africa do not generally observe it. Some countries, such as Brazil, observe it only in some regions.

DST can lead to peculiar situations. One of these occurred in November, 2007 when a woman in North Carolina gave birth to one twin at 1:32 a.m. and, 34 minutes later, to the second twin. Because of DST and the time change at 2:00 a.m., the second twin was officially born at 1:06, 26 minutes earlier than her brother.

7. According to the passage, what is the main purpose of DST?
   A. To increase public safety
   B. To benefit retail businesses
   C. To make better use of daylight
   D. To promote good health

8. Which of the following is not mentioned in the passage as a negative effect of DST?
    A. Energy conservation
    B. Complications with time keeping
    C. Complications with computer systems
    D. Increased skin cancer risk

9. The article states that DST involves:
    A. Adjusting clocks forward one hour in the spring and the fall.
    B. Adjusting clocks backward one hour in the spring and the fall.
    C. Adjusting clocks forward in the fall and backward in the spring.
    D. Adjusting clocks forward in the spring and backward in the fall.

10. Which interests have historically opposed DST, according to the passage?
    A. retail businesses and sports
    B. evening entertainment and agriculture
    C. 7-Eleven and health
    D. medical devices and computing

11. According to the article, increased sunlight exposure:
    A. is only good for health.
    B. is only bad for health.
    C. has no effect on health.
    D. can be both good and bad for health.

12. In what region does the article state DST is observed only in some regions?
    A. The equator
    B. Asia
    C. Africa
    D. Brazil

13. What is an example given in the passage of a peculiar situation that DST has caused?
    A. sleep disruption
    B. driving confusion
    C. twin birth order complications
    D. countries with DST only in certain regions

14. According to the passage, a 1984 magazine article estimated that a seven-week extension of DST would provide 7-Eleven stores with an extra $30 million. Approximately how much extra money is that per week of the extension?
    A. 42,000
    B. 420,000
    C. 4,200,000
    D. 42,000,000

15. For what purpose did Benjamin Franklin first suggest DST?
    A. to save money for military needs
    B. to save candles
    C. to reduce traffic fatalities
    D. to promote reading

Questions 16 - 21 refer to the following passage:

Tips for Eating Calcium Rich Foods

- Include milk as a beverage at meals. Choose fat-free or low-fat milk.
- If you usually drink whole milk, switch gradually to fat-free milk to lower saturated fat and calories. Try reduced fat (2%), then low-fat (1%), and finally fat-free (skim).
- If you drink cappuccinos or lattes—ask for them with fat-free (skim) milk.
- Add fat-free or low-fat milk instead of water to oatmeal and hot cereals
- Use fat-free or low-fat milk when making condensed cream soups (such as cream of tomato).
- Have fat-free or low-fat yogurt as a snack.
- Make a dip for fruits or vegetables from yogurt.
- Make fruit-yogurt smoothies in the blender.
- For dessert, make chocolate or butterscotch pudding with fat-free or low-fat milk.
- Top cut-up fruit with flavored yogurt for a quick dessert.
- Top casseroles, soups, stews, or vegetables with shredded low-fat cheese.
- Top a baked potato with fat-free or low-fat yogurt.

  For those who choose not to consume milk products
- If you avoid milk because of lactose intolerance, the most reliable way to get the health benefits of milk is to choose lactose-free alternatives within the milk group, such as cheese, yogurt, or lactose-free milk, or to consume the enzyme lactase before consuming milk products.
- Calcium choices for those who do not consume milk products include:
  o Calcium fortified juices, cereals, breads, soy beverages, or rice beverages
  o Canned fish (sardines, salmon with bones) soybeans and other soy products, some other dried beans, and some leafy greens.

16. According to the passage, how can you lower saturated fat and calories in your diet?
    A. Add fat-free milk to oatmeal instead of water.
    B. Switch to fat-free milk.
    C. Drink calcium-fortified juice.
    D. Make yogurt dip.

17. What device does the author use to organize the passage?
    A. headings
    B. captions
    C diagrams
    D. labels

18. How much fat does reduced fat milk contain?
    A. 0 percent
    B. 1 percent
    C 2 percent
    D. 3 percent

19. Which of the following is true about calcium rich foods?
    I. Canned salmon with bones contains calcium.
    II. Cheese is a lactose-free food.
    III. Condensed soup made with water is a calcium rich food.
    A. I only
    B. I and II only
    C. II and III only
    D. III only

20. What information should the author include to help clarify information in the passage?
    A. The fat content of yogurt.
    B. How much calcium is in fortified juice.
    C. Which leafy greens contain calcium.
    D. The definition of lactose intolerance.

21. The style of this passage is most like that found in a(n)
    A. tourist guidebook.
    B. health textbook.
    C. encyclopedia.
    D. friendly letter.

Questions 22 - 24 pertain to the following passage:

Leaving

Even though Martin and Beth's steps were muffled by the falling snow, Beth could still hear the faint crunch of leaves underneath. The hushed woods had often made Beth feel safe and at peace, but these days they just made her feel lonely.

"I'm glad we decided to hike the trail, Martin. It's so quiet and pretty."

"Sure."

Beth couldn't understand how it happened, but over the past few months this silence had grown between them, weighing down their relationship. Of course, there was that thing with Mary, but Beth had forgiven Martin. They moved on. It was in the past.

"Do you want to see a movie tonight?" asked Beth. "There's a new one showing at the downtown theater."

"Whatever you want."

She wanted her husband back. She wanted the laughter and games. She wanted the late-night talks over coffee. She wanted to forget Mary and Martin together. She wanted to feel some sort of <u>rapport</u> again.

"Is everything alright, Martin?"

"I'm fine. Just tired."

"We didn't have to come; we could have stayed at home."

"It's fine."

Beth closed her eyes, tilted her head back, and breathed in the crisp air. "Fine" once meant "very good," or "precious." Now, it is a meaningless word, an excuse not to tell other people what's on your mind. "Fine" had hung in the air between them for months now, a softly falling word that hid them from each other. Beth wasn't even sure she knew Martin anymore, but

- 145 -

she was confident that it was only a matter of time before everything was not "fine," only a matter of time before he told her...

"I have to leave."

"Huh? What?"

"I got a page. My patient is going into cardiac arrest."

"I wish you didn't have to leave."

"I'm sorry, but I have to go."

"I know."

22. It is reasonable to infer that Martin and Beth's relationship is strained because:
    A. Martin recently lost his job.
    B. Martin was unfaithful to Beth.
    C. Martin works too much.
    D. Martin does not want to go to the movies.

23. Based on the passage, it is reasonable to infer that Martin is a:
    A. mechanic.
    B. medical doctor.
    C. dentist.
    D. film director.

24. The best definition of the underlined word *rapport* is:
    A. a close relationship.
    B. a sense of well-being.
    C. a common goal.
    D. loneliness.

Writing

Jordan's English class is reading a book set in the 1920s. In order to better understand that decade, his English teacher has assigned a research essay on one aspect of that time period. Jordan has written an essay on early pilots but needs help revising and improving the essay. After you read the essay, answer questions 1 - 10.

(1) After Orville and Wilbur Wright have flown their first airplane in 1903, the age of flying slowly began. (2) Many new pilots learned how to fly in World War I, which the United States joined in 1917. (3) During the war, the American public loved hearing stories about the daring pilots and their air fights. (4) But after the war ended, many Americans thought that men and women belonged on the ground and not in the air.

(5) In the years after the war and through the Roaring Twenties, Americas pilots found themselves without jobs. (6) Some of them gave up flying altogether. (7) Pilot Eddie Rickenbacker, who used to be called America's Ace of Aces, became a car salesman. (8) But other pilots found new and creative things to do with their airplanes.

(9) Pilot Casey Jones used his airplane to help get news across the country. (10) When a big news story broke, Jones flew news photos to newspapers in different cities. (11) Another pilot, Roscoe Turner traveled around the country with a lion cub in his plane. (12) The cub was the mascot of an oil company, and Turner convinced the company that flying the cub around would be a good advertisement. (13) The Humane Society wasn't very happy about this idea, and they convinced Turner to make sure the lion cub always wore a parachute.

(14) Other pilots took people for short airplane rides, often charging five dollars for a five-minute ride (by comparison, you could buy a loaf of bread for about ten cents in 1920). (15) These pilots, called barnstormers, often used dangerous tricks to get customers: two barnstormers once stood on a plane's wings and played tennis while the plane flew at 70 miles per hour! (16) Many barnstormers advertised their shows as a 'flying circus.'

(17) During the 1920s, the U.S. Post Office developed airmail. (18) Before airmail, the post traveled on trains and can take weeks to reach a destination. (19) Flying for the post office was dangerous work. (20) Early pilots didn't have sophistocated instruments and safety equipment on their planes. (21) Many of them had to bail out and use their parachutes when their planes iced up in the cold air or had other trouble.

(22) The most famous pilot of the 1920s, Charles A. Lindbergh, began as a postal pilot. (23) In May 1927, he participated in an air race to fly across the Atlantic Ocean. (24) The prize was $25,000, but the dangers were extensive. (25) Named Nungesser and Coli, two French pilots had recently tried to fly across the Atlantic.

(26) They disappeared.

(27) The newspapers called Charles Lindbergh "the dark horse" to win the race. (28) He had already set a record by making the fastest solo flight between St. Louis, Missouri, and, San Diego, California. (29) Lindbergh's record-setting flight took 23 hours and 15 minutes; today, a flight between St. Louis and San Diego takes about four hours.

(30) After several weather delays, Lindbergh took off in his small plane, The Spirit of St. Louis, on May 20, 1927. (31) He made it across the Atlantic Ocean and arrived in France after 33 hours and 30 minutes of non-stop flight; today, a flight from New York to Paris would take about seven hours.

(32) The flight was taxing. (33) Because Lindbergh flew alone, he had to stay awake for the entire trip. (34) He knew that he couldn't have made it across without a great plane. (35) He said, "I feel that the monoplane was as much a part of the trip as myself."

(36) Lindbergh's trip set off a golden age for aviation. (37) The same people who were nervous about airplanes at the beginning of the 1920s came out by the thousands to cheer Lindbergh. (38) The age of pilots doing odd jobs and dangerous stunt work had ended.

1. What change should be made to sentence 1?
    A. Add a comma after *Wright*
    B. Change *have flown* to *flew*
    C. Change *first* to *1ˢᵗ*
    D. Delete the comma after *1903*

2. What change should be made to sentence 5?
    A. Change *years* to *year's*
    B. Delete the comma after *Twenties*
    C. Change *Americas* to *America's*
    D. Change *themselves* to *theirselves*

3. What change should be made in sentence 11?
    A. Delete the comma before *Roscoe*
    B. Add a comma after *Turner*
    C. Change *with* to *as*
    D. Change *plane* to *airplane*

4. What change should be made to sentence 15?
    A. Change *barnstormers* to *barnstormer*
    B. Change the colon after *customers* to a semicolon
    C. Change *plane's* to *planes*
    D. Change *while* to *when*

5. What change should be made to sentence 18?
    A. Delete the comma after *airmail*
    B. Change *traveled* to *travelled*
    C. Change *can* to *could*
    D. Change *a* to *it's*

6. What change should be made to sentence 20?
    A. Change *pilots* to *pilot's*
    B. Change sophistocated to sophisticated
    C. Add a comma after *instruments*
    D. Change *their* to *they're*

7. What's the most effective way to rewrite sentence 25?

    A. Two French pilots, named Nungesser and Coli, had recently tried to fly across the Atlantic.
    B. Two French pilots Nungesser and Coli had recently tried to fly across the Atlantic.
    C. Recently having tried to fly across the Atlantic, two French pilots were named Nungesser and Coli.
    D. No change

8. What change should be made to sentence 28?
    A. Delete the comma after *St. Louis*
    B. Delete the comma after *Missouri*
    C. Delete the comma after *and*
    D. Delete the comma after *San Diego*

9. How could sentences 34 and 35 best be combined?
    A. He knew that he couldn't have made it across without a great plane and he said, "I feel that the monoplane was as much a part of the trip as myself."
    B. He knew that he couldn't have made it across without a great plane, he said, "I feel that the monoplane was as much a part of the trip as myself."
    C. He knew that he couldn't have made it across without a great plane and says, "I feel that the monoplane was as much a part of the trip as myself."
    D. He knew that he couldn't have made it across without a great plane and said, "I feel that the monoplane was as much a part of the trip as myself."

10. What transition could be added at the beginning of sentence 36?
    A. In conclusion
    B. Furthermore
    C. Therefore
    D. Additionally

For questions 11-15, select the best option for replacing the underlined portion of the sentence. The first option listed is always the same as the current version of the sentence.

11. Despite their lucky escape, <u>Jason and his brother could not hardly enjoy themselves</u>.
    A. Jason and his brother could not hardly enjoy themselves.
    B. Jason and his brother could not enjoy themselves.
    C. Jason and Jason's brother could not hardly enjoy themselves.
    D. Jason and his brother could not enjoy them.

12. Stew recipes call <u>for rosemary, parsley, thyme, and these sort of herbs.</u>
    A. for rosemary, parsley, thyme, and these sort of herbs.
    B. for: rosemary; parsley; thyme; and these sort of herbs.
    C. for rosemary, parsley, thyme, and these sorts of herbs.
    D. for rosemary, parsley, thyme, and this sorts of herbs.

13. Mr. King, <u>an individual of considerable influence, created a personal fortune and gave back</u> to the community.
    A. an individual of considerable influence, created a personal fortune and gave back
    B. an individual of considerable influence, he created a personal fortune and gave back
    C. an individual of considerable influence created a personal fortune and gave back
    D. an individual of considerable influence, created a personal fortune and gave it back

14. <u>She is the person whose opinion matters the most.</u>
    A. She is the person whose opinion matters the most.
    B. She is the person to whom opinion matters the most.
    C. She is the person who matters the most, in my opinion.
    D. She is the person for whom opinion matters the most.

15. Minerals are nutritionally significant elements <u>that assist to make your body</u> work properly.
    A. that assist to make your body
    B. that help your body
    C. that making your body
    D. that work to make your body

16. The most prolific predator in the Florida Everglades has always been the alligator, which preys on local birds and wildlife, while the introduction of the Burmese python adds another, and often insatiable, predator to compete with the alligator.
Rewrite the sentence, beginning with the phrase, *The introduction of the Burmese python to the Everglades adds another predator to compete with the alligator.* The words that follow will be:
    A. which has always been the most prolific predator in the Everglades
    B. thus leaving the local birds and wildlife in serious danger of becoming endangered
    C. and the alligator was never as serious a predator as the python has become
    D. which does not have the python's reputation for being insatiable

17. Not only does the Burmese python compete with the alligator for prey, but it also competes with the alligator as prey, because pythons have been known to engorge full-grown alligators, thus placing the python at the top of the food chain and leaving them with no native predators in the Everglades.
Rewrite the sentence, beginning with the phrase, *The Burmese python is now at the top of the food chain in the Everglades and has no native predator.* The words that follow will be:
    A. so it competes with the alligator as prey
    B. as evidence shows that pythons are capable of engorging full-grown alligators
    C. although the python still competes with alligators for prey
    D. leaving the Everglades with a serious imbalance of predators

18. Biologists and environmentalists recognize the considerable dangers of the python's expansion in the Everglades as it consumes endangered creatures native to that area, and in one instance researchers were shocked to discover that the tracking device for a tagged rodent led them to the python who had already consumed the unlucky creature.
Rewrite the sentence, beginning with the phrase, *Researchers in the Everglades were shocked to discover that the tracking device for a tagged rodent led them to the python who had already consumed the unlucky creature.* The words that follow will be:
    A. thus showing how the python is destroying endangered species within the Everglades
    B. causing concerns that the python expansion might be more dangerous than biologists and environmentalists originally believed
    C. which was one of the few of its species that had managed to survive the python expansion in the Everglades
    D. leaving biologists and environmentalists to recognize the considerable dangers of the python's expansion in the Everglades

19. In an attempt at controlling the python, Florida dispatched hunters to destroy as many pythons as possible, but after several months of searching the hunters were only able to make a dent in the python population of thousands by killing several dozen.
Rewrite the sentence, beginning with the phrase, *The python population of thousands was reduced only be several dozen.* The words that follow will be:
    A. even after many months of searching for and destroying the creatures
    B. because the hunters were only given a few months for the task and needed more time to destroy as many pythons as possible
    C. after the hunters sent to destroy as many pythons as possible failed to make a dent in the number
    D. resulting in concerns that more hunters were needed to locate and destroy as many pythons as possible

20. Although eradication is preferred when non-native species are introduced into the United States, researchers have found that is it virtually impossible, and controlling the species becomes the only real option in avoiding the destruction of native habitats and endangered species.

Rewrite the sentence, beginning with the phrase, *Controlling an invasive species is the only real option in avoiding the destruction of native habitats and endangered species*. The words that follow will be:

    A. because the total eradication of non-native species that are introduced into the United States is virtually impossible

    B. because the total eradication of non-native species that are introduced into the United States is generally frowned upon

    C. although researchers prefer the total eradication of non-native species and continue to make efforts to destroy the python in the Everglades

    D. in spite of the many attempts at totally eradicating the non-native species that are introduced into the United States

Essay

There is an ongoing struggle between those who would like to develop the oil reserves in Alaska and the Gulf of Mexico to help the US gain energy independence and those who oppose doing so because of possible environmental consequences. Please write a five-paragraph persuasive essay (approximately 350–500 words) discussing whether you support or oppose developing the oil reserves.

Answers and Explanations

Math

1. C: To solve this problem, first calculate how many gallons each toilet uses in 375 flushes:
3.2 X 375 = 1,200 gallons
1.6 X 375 = 600 gallons
The problem is asking for the difference, so find the difference between the regular toilet and the low-flow toilet:
1,200 – 600 = 600 gallons. Note that you could also find the difference in water use for one flush, and then multiply that amount by 375:
3.2 – 1.6 = 1.6
1.6 X 375 = 600.

2. D: To solve for n, you have to isolate that variable by putting all of the other terms of the equation, including coefficients, integers, and variables on the other side of the equal sign. Add p to each side of the equation:

$$4n - p = 3r$$
$$4n - p + p = 3r + p$$
$$4n = 3r + p$$

Divide each term by 4:

$$\frac{4n}{4} = \frac{3r}{4} + \frac{p}{4}$$
$$n = \frac{3r}{4} + \frac{p}{4}$$

3. C: $|x| + |x - 2| = |1| + |1 - 2| = |1| + |-1| = 1 + 1 = 2$.

4. B: One way to compare fractions is to convert them to equivalent fractions which have common denominators. In this case the lowest common denominator of the three fractions is $7 \times 12 = 84$. Converting each of the fractions to this denominator, $\frac{1}{3} = \frac{1 \times 28}{3 \times 28} = \frac{28}{84}$, $\frac{2}{7} = \frac{2 \times 12}{7 \times 12} = \frac{24}{84}$, and $\frac{5}{12} = \frac{5 \times 7}{12 \times 7} = \frac{35}{84}$. Since $24 < 28 < 35$, it must be the case that $\frac{2}{7} < \frac{1}{3} < \frac{5}{12}$.

5. C: $6q + 3 = 8q - 7 \Rightarrow 6q + 3 + 7 = 8q \Rightarrow 6q + 10 = 8q \Rightarrow 10 = 8q - 6q \Rightarrow 10 = 2q \Rightarrow q = 5$.

6. B: The charge is $1.20 for each minute *past* the first ten minutes. The number of minutes after the first ten minutes is $m - 10$, so this amount charged for the part of the phone call exceeding 10 minutes is $1.2(m - 10)$. Adding this to the $5.00 charge for the first ten minutes gives $d = 5 + 1.2(m - 10)$.

7. D: To add the two fractions, first rewrite them with the least common denominator, which is in this case y^3. $\frac{x}{y^3}$ already has this denominator, and we can rewrite $\frac{x^2}{y^2}$ as $\frac{x^2 \times y}{y^2 \times y} = \frac{x^2 y}{y^3}$. Thus, $\frac{x^2}{y^2} + \frac{x}{y^3} = \frac{x^2 y}{y^3} + \frac{x}{y^3} = \frac{x^2 y + x}{y^3}$.

8. C: To solve an equation with an absolute value like $|x^2 - 2| = x$, we can treat it as two separate cases. If $x^2 - 2$ is positive, $|x^2 - 2| = x^2 - 2$, and the equation becomes simply $x^2 - 2 = x$, which can be rewritten as the quadratic equation $x^2 - x - 2 = 0$. Since the leading coefficient is 1, we can factor this quadratic equation by finding two numbers that add to the coefficient of x (-1) and multiply to the constant term (-2); the two qualifying numbers are 1 and -2, and the equation factors to $(x + 1)(x - 2) = 0$, yielding the solutions $x = -1$ and $x = 2$. If $x^2 - 2$ is negative, then $|x^2 - 2| = -(x^2 - 2)$, and the equation becomes $-(x^2 - 2) = x$, which we can rewrite as $x^2 + x + 2 = 0$. Again, this can be factored, as $(x - 1)(x + 2) = 0$, yielding the two additional solutions $x = 1$ and $x = -2$. However, this method of solving equations with an absolute value may result in spurious solutions, so we should check all these solutions in the original equation to make sure that they are genuine. $|1^2 - 2| = |-1| = 1$ and $|2^2 - 2| = |2| = 2$, so $x = 1$ and $x = 2$ are valid solutions to the equation. However, $|(-1)^2 - 2| = |-1| = 1 \neq -1$ and $|(-2)^2 - 2| = |-2| = 2 \neq -2$, so $x = -1$ and $x = -2$ are not solutions. The equation has two valid solutions.

9. A: The expression may be factored as $(x - 8)(x + 5)$. The factorization may be checked by distributing each term in the first factor over each term in the second factor. Doing so gives $x^2 + 5x - 8x - 40$, which can be rewritten as $x^2 - 3x - 40$.

10. C: The power to which 2 is raised to give 64 is 6; $2^6 = 64$. Thus, $x = 6$.

11. C: Angles around a point add up to 360 degrees. Add the degrees of the given angles: 72° + 110° + 58° = 240°. Then subtract from 360° - 240° = 120°. Remember to divide 120° in half, since the question is asking for the degree measure of one angle, angle d.

12. C: The area of a parallelogram is base X height or $A = bh$, where b is the length of a side and h is the length of an altitude to that side. In this problem,
$A = 6$ x 4; $A = 24$. Remember, use the length of BE, not the length of CD for the height.

13. A: The sum of the measures of the angels in a triangle equals 180°. Use the numbers given in the figure to make the following equation:
$6x + 8x + 4x = 180$
$18x = 180$
$x = 10$

14. A: The area A of a rectangle is equal to its length l times its width w: $A = l \times w$. The rectangle is twice as long as it is wide, so $l = 2w$. By replacing l with its equivalent $2w$, the area of this rectangle can be written as $A = 2w \times w = 2w^2$. So $2w^2 = 200$ cm^2; $w^2 = 100$ cm^2; $w = \sqrt{100 \text{ cm}^2} = 10$ cm.

15. B: If there are n floors, and each floor has a height of h feet, then to find the total height of the floors, we just multiply the number of floors by the height of each floor: nh. To find the total height of the building, we must also add the height of the spire, 30 feet. So, the building's total height in feet is $nh + 30$.

16. C: A reflection is a transformation producing a mirror image. A figure reflected over the x-axis will have its vertices in the form (x, y) transformed to $(x, -y)$. The point W at (1,-7) reflects to W' at (1,7). Only Answer C shows $WXYZ$ being carried onto its image $W'X'Y'Z'$ by

a reflection across the *x*-axis. Answer A shows a reflection across the line *y* = *x*. Answer B shows a 90° counterclockwise rotation about the origin. Answer D shows a reflection across the *y*-axis.

17. B: The median is unaffected by a skewed distribution, or data with extreme outliers. The median represents the value, at which 50% of the scores fall above and 50% of the scores fall below. The mean, standard deviation, and range are all impacted by non-normal data.

18. B: Correlation coefficients range from −1 to 1, with values close to −1 or 1, representing strong relationships. Thus, a correlation coefficient of 0.2 represents a weak correlation.

19. B: The probability of mutually exclusive events, A or B, occurring may be written as $P(A \text{ or } B) = P(A) + P(B)$. Thus, $P(A \text{ or } B) = \frac{3}{8} + \frac{1}{8}$ or $\frac{1}{2}$.

20. B: The events are dependent since the first marble was not replaced. The sample space of the second draw will decrease by 1 because there will be one less marble to choose. The number of possible red marbles for the second draw will also decrease by 1. Thus, the probability may be written as $P(A \text{ and } B) = \frac{2}{10} \cdot \frac{1}{9}$. Thus, the probability she draws a red marble, does not replace it, and draws another red marble is $\frac{1}{45}$.

Reading

1. B: It can be concluded that phonics is a more effective way to learn to read for two reasons. First, the passage states that literacy rates are lower now than they were 15 years ago, meaning that more people knew how to read 15 years ago. Then, the passage states that phonics was the main way people learned how to read then. Therefore, based on these two facts, it can be concluded that phonics is more effective.

2. C: The passage states that "Shortly before becoming the President of the United States in 1789, Washington was an important leader in the American Revolutionary War from 1775 to 1783."

3. B: In describing the marketing of "sea monkeys," the author describes it as creative genius, and attributes their popularity to the drawings and advertisements that appeared in comic books. It is reasonable to conclude that without the branding and (somewhat misleading) ads, they wouldn't have been as popular. Marketing them under the less exciting brand name "brine shrimp" likely wouldn't have resulted in as many sales.

4. C: A is incorrect because the passage states they were similar in size. The cost of production is not mentioned, eliminating B as a possibility. D is incorrect because it was the eight-track tape that was included in these vehicles. C is correct because the passage states the eight-track tape could store and play twice as many songs.

5. B: The passage states that, "Often, the agoraphobic will view his home as the safest possible place to be, and he may even be reluctant to leave his house," making B the correct choice.

6. D: B and C are only briefly mentioned, allowing them to be eliminated as possibilities. Although the passage does discuss what could happen to two balls released at the top of a mountain, that is not the purpose of the passage, so A can be eliminated. The purpose is to show how small differences (in this case two inches between two rubber balls) can have large effects. This is essentially what the butterfly effect is, and the purpose of the passage is to give an example to demonstrate this principle.

7. C: The first paragraph states that the main purpose of DST it to make better use of daylight.

8. A: Energy conservation is discussed as a possible benefit of DST, not a negative effect of it.

9. D: The first paragraph states that DST involves setting clocks forward one hour in the spring and one hour backward in the fall.

10. B: The last sentence in paragraph four notes that agricultural and evening entertainment interests have historically been opposed to DST.

11. D: The passage gives examples of both good and bad effects extra daylight can have on health.

12. D: The sixth paragraph notes that DST is observed in only some regions of Brazil.

13. C: The last paragraph of the passage notes that DST can lead to peculiar situations, and relays an anecdote about the effect of DST on the birth order of twins.

14. C: If $30,000,000 is gained over 7 weeks, each week has a gain of 1/7 of that, or $4,200,000.

15. B: In the second paragraph, the author asserts that Benjamin Franklin suggested DST as a way to save candles.

16. B: Tip number 2 best answers this detail question. The tip recommends that those who drink whole milk gradually switch to fat-free milk. Since the question asks about ways to reduce saturated fat and calories, using skim milk in the place of water does not address the issue being raised.

17. A: The author uses headings to organize the passage. While the headings are bold print, such font is not used to organize the passage (i.e. notify the reader of what information is forthcoming), but rather to draw the reader's eyes to the headings.

18. C: Tip number 2 bests answers this detail question. Reduced fat milk contains 2% fat.

19. B: Statement I and Statement II are both true statements about calcium rich foods. Canned fish, including salmon with bones, is recommended as a calcium rich food. Cheese is mentioned as a lactose-free alternative within the milk group. Statement III is false. According to the passage, condensed cream soups should be made with milk, not water.

20. D: The best choice for this question is choice (D). The other options would clarify information for minor details within the passage and would provide little new information

for the reader. However, food recommendations for those who do not consume milk products are listed under a separate heading, and lactose intolerance is the only reason listed. The reader can deduce that this is a main idea in the passage and the definition of "lactose intolerance" would help explain this main idea to the reader.

21. B: The author's style is to give facts and details in a bulleted list. Of the options given, you are most likely to find this style in a health textbook. A tourist guidebook would most likely make recommendations about where to eat, not what to eat. An encyclopedia would list and define individual foods. A friendly letter would have a date, salutation, and a closing.

22. B: This question is concerned with the main idea of the passage. Although the passage is not explicit about why Martin and Beth's relationship is strained, by eliminating a number of answer choices, the right answer can easily be found. Choice A can be eliminated because Martin has not lost his job—he receives a page at the end of the passage concerning one of his patients. Choice B is not contradicted by the passage, but all that the reader is told is that Martin and Mary were once together. Choice C can be eliminated because the passage does not indicate how much Martin works. Choice D can be eliminated because Martin tells Beth that if she wants to go to the movies, they can go. Choice E can be eliminated because the passage does not tell the reader how much Beth talks. The best choice, then, is B.

23. B: This question asks the reader to make a conclusion based on details from the passage. The reader knows that (1) Martin wears a pager for his job, (2) he has patients, and (3) one of his patients is going into cardiac arrest. Choices A, D, and E can be eliminated because mechanics, film directors, and television producers do not see patients. Choice C seems like a possibility. After all, dentists see patients. Choice B is the best choice because if a person goes into cardiac arrest it is more likely a medical doctor rather than a dentist would be paged.

24. A: This question asks for the best definition of "rapport." A "rapport" is a relationship based on mutual understanding. With this in mind, Choice A might be a good answer, even though it is not an exact match. Choice B can be eliminated because it does not describe a relationship. Choice C can be eliminated because individuals can have a relationship based on mutual understanding without sharing a common goal. Choices D and E can be eliminated because loneliness or boredom have nothing to do with the definition of "rapport."

Writing

1. B: is the correct answer because the verb should be in past tense rather than present tense. Choice A is incorrect because a comma should not separate the subject and verb of a sentence. Choice C is incorrect because it is better to write out *first* than it is to use numerical digits. Choice D is incorrect because a comma is required to separate the dependent clause at the beginning of the sentence from the independent clause at the end of the sentence.

2. C: because *America's* is possessive. The sentence is referring to the pilots who lived in America. Choice A is incorrect because *years* is plural and not possessive. Choice B is incorrect because the comma correctly separates the dependent clause at the beginning of

the sentence from the independent clause at the end of the sentence. Choice D is incorrect because *theirselves* is not a real word.

3. B: is correct because a comma is needed to offset the non-essential clause *Roscoe Turner*. Choice A is incorrect because *Roscoe Turner* is a non-essential clause; it is not required to understand the meaning of the sentence. The clause should be offset by commas on both sides. Choice C is incorrect because *as* would change the meaning of the sentence to imply that Roscoe Turner dressed as a lion cub. Choice D is incorrect because the words *plane* and *airplane* can be used interchangeably.

4. B: because a semicolon is used to separate two related independent clauses. In contrast, a colon is used to set off lists. Choice A is incorrect because *barnstormers* is referring to multiple pilots and should remain in the plural. Choice C is incorrect because *plane's* is correctly written as a possessive. Choice D is incorrect because *while* implies that the barnstormers played tennis at the same time as the plane flew.

5. C: is correct because the passage is discussing the past. Therefore, the past tense *could* is preferable over the present tense *can*. Choice A is incorrect because the comma is needed to set off the phrase at the beginning of the sentence. Choice B is incorrect because *traveled* only has a single *l*. Although both *a* and *its* could be used in this sentence, choice D is incorrect because *it's* is a conjunction for *it is* and would be incorrect if used in this part of the sentence.

6. B: because *sophisticated* is the correct spelling. Choice A is incorrect because *pilots* is not a possessive in this context. Choice C is incorrect because a comma is not needed to separate a list that only has two items. Choice D is incorrect because *their* is a possessive, which fits the sentence. *They're* refers to *they are*, which does not work in this sentence.

7. A: is correct because this word order best conveys the meaning of the sentence in a concise manner. Choice B is incorrect because *Nungesser and Coli* is a non-essential phrase and needs to be separated from the rest of the sentence with commas. Choice C inverts the order to the sentence and makes it more awkward; it is better to have a simple subject and verb at the beginning of a sentence. Choice D is incorrect because the word order confuses the sentence's meaning.

8. B: because a comma is rarely needed after the word *and*. A comma would only be required if a non-essential phrase followed *and*. However, the word *and* in this sentence simply separates a two-item series. The other commas are correct because commas should be used both before and after a state's name.

9. D: is correct because it uses the correct punctuation and verb tense. Choice A is incorrect because the conjunction *and* separates two independent clauses; when the conjunction is used in this way, a comma must come before it. Choice B is incorrect because there is no conjunction between the two independent clauses, making the answer choice a run-on sentence. Choice C is incorrect because the passage is written in the past tense but *says* is incorrectly written in the present tense.

10. A: is the best answer choice because *in conclusion* sums up the essay and leads into the final paragraph. Choices B and D are incorrect because the words *furthermore* and *additionally* indicate that an additional argument will be made. However, sentence 35

begins a concluding paragraph. Choice C is incorrect because the word *therefore* should be used as a conclusion to a specific point rather than the conclusion of an entire essay.

11. B: The combination of *hardly* and *not* constitutes a double negative.

12. C: The plural demonstrative adjective *these* should be used with the plural noun *sorts*.

13. A: This sentence contains a number of parallel structures that must be treated consistently.

14. A: In this sentence, *whose* is the appropriate possessive pronoun to modify *opinion*.

15. B: Answer choice B is precise and clear. Answer choice A keeps the meaning, but is awkward and wordy. Answer choice C uses the wrong verb tense. Answer choice D would put the word *work* into the sentence twice. It is not completely incorrect, but it is not the best choice.

16. A: Answer choice A correctly adds the necessary information about the alligator's traditional role within the Everglades. Answer choice B reassembles the information from the original sentence but does not provide the key detail about the alligator's place in the Everglades. Answer choices C and D add information that cannot be inferred from the original sentence.

17. B: Answer choice B provides the full information that is needed to complete the original idea. Answer choice A provides only partial information and is thus insufficient. Answer choice C is repetitive and does not offer any new information to complete the original idea. Answer choice D offers inferred information, but as this is not contained within the original sentence, it cannot be added.

18. D: Answer choice D adds the correct information about the concern that follows the python's expansion within the Everglades, without adding inferred information. Answer choice A is correct but is not necessarily effective in explaining the substance of the reason for concern. Answer choice B adds information that cannot be clearly inferred (i.e., what biologists and environmentalists originally believed about the python in the Everglades). Answer choice C adds information that has no place in the original sentence.

19. C: Answer choice C effectively links the ideas contained in the original sentence. Answer choice A is accurate but ineffective and incomplete, because it fails to explain *who* was doing the searching and destroying. Answer choices B and D add judgment statements that are not in the original sentence.

20. A: Answer choice A sufficiently links the ideas in the original sentence, connecting the reality of control with the hope for eradication. Answer choice B contradicts information that is not in the original sentence; that is to say, the original sentence states clearly that "eradication is preferred," not frowned upon. Answer choice C is partially correct but becomes incorrect with the added information about researchers continuing to search for means of eradication. Answer choice D contains correct information but does not encompass the full meaning of the original sentence and leaves out valuable information (i.e., the virtual impossibility of eradication).

Practice Test #5

Practice Questions

Math

1. Which of the following graphs represents the inequality $-2 < x \le 4$?

A.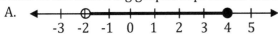
     -3 -2 -1 0 1 2 3 4 5

B.
     -3 -2 -1 0 1 2 3 4 5

C.
     -3 -2 -1 0 1 2 3 4 5

D.
     -3 -2 -1 0 1 2 3 4 5

2. Which of the following is equivalent to $3 - 2x < 5$?

A. $x < 1$
B. $x > 1$
C. $x < -1$
D. $x > -1$

3. A certain exam has 30 questions. A student gets 1 point for each question he gets right and loses half a point for a question he answers incorrectly; he neither gains nor loses any points for a question left blank. If C is the number of questions a student gets right and B is the number of questions he leaves blank, which of the following represents his score on the exam?

A. $C - \frac{1}{2}B$

B. $C - \frac{1}{2}(30 - B)$

C. $C - \frac{1}{2}(30 - B - C)$

D. $(30 - C) - \frac{1}{2}(30 - B)$

4. Every person attending a certain meeting hands out a business card to every other person at the meeting. If there are a total of 30 cards handed out, how many people are at the meeting?

A. 5
B. 6
C. 10
D. 15

5. $x(y - 2) + y(3 - x) =$
    A. $xy + y$
    B. $-2x + 3y$
    C. $2xy - 2x + 3y$
    D. $xy + 3y - x - 2$

6. At a school carnival, three students spend an average of $10. Six other students spend an average of $4. What is the average amount of money spent by all nine students?
    A. $5
    B. $6
    C. $7
    D. $8

7. The formula for finding the volume of a cone is $V = \frac{1}{3}\pi r^2 h$. Which of the following equations is correctly solved for r?
    A. $r = \frac{1}{3}\pi h$

    B. $r = \sqrt{\frac{3V}{\pi h}}$

    C. $r = \frac{V}{\frac{1}{3}\pi h}$

    D. $r = V - \frac{1}{3}\pi h$

8. Given the equation, $\frac{2}{x+4} = \frac{3}{x}$, what is the value of x?
    A. 10
    B. 12
    C. −12
    D. −14

9. What is the solution to the equation, $4\sqrt{x} + 8 = 24$?
    A. $x = 2$
    B. $x = 4$
    C. $x = 12$
    D. $x = 16$

10. Which of the following represents the solution of the following system of linear equations: $\begin{matrix} 5x + 9y = -7 \\ 2x - 4y = 20 \end{matrix}$?
    A. $x = 3, y = 2$
    B. $x = 4, y = 3$
    C. $x = 4, y = -3$
    D. $x = 3, y = -2$

11. In the figure pictured below, $AD = 5$ and $AB = 12$, what is the length of AC (not shown)?

    A. 10
    B. 13
    C. 17
    D. 60

12. In the figure pictured below, find the value of x:

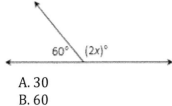

    A. 30
    B. 60
    C. 100
    D. 120

13. What is a good estimate of the circumference of the circle in the figure pictured below?

    A. 12
    B. 24
    C. 36
    D. 48

14. Based on the figure below, describe how rectangle $ABCD$ can be carried onto its image $A'B'C'D'$.

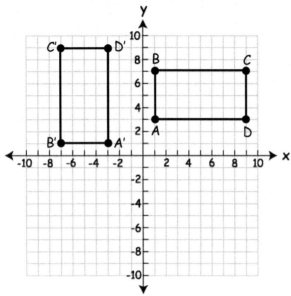

    A. Reflection across the x-axis
    B. Reflection across the y-axis
    C. Rotation 90° clockwise about the origin
    D. Rotation 90° counterclockwise about the origin

15. Examine the triangles below:

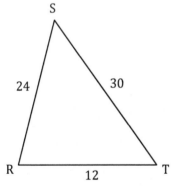
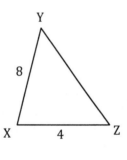

In order for ΔRST to be similar to ΔXYZ, what must be the length of $\overline{YZ}$?
    A. 10
    B. 14
    C. 15
    D. 22

16. Two hikers start at a ranger station and leave at the same time. One hiker heads due west at 3 miles/hour. The other hiker heads due north at 4 miles/hour. How far apart are the hikers after 2 hours of hiking?
    A. 5 miles
    B.. 7 miles
    C. 10 miles
    D. 14 miles

17. Which frequency table is represented by the histogram shown below?

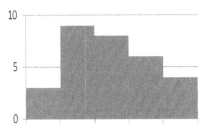

A.

Interval	Frequency
1 – 10	3
11 – 20	9
21 – 30	8
31 – 40	6
41 – 50	4

C.

Interval	Frequency
1 – 10	3
11 – 20	9
21 – 30	8
31 – 40	5
41 – 50	4

B.

Interval	Frequency
1 – 10	3
11 – 20	8
21 – 30	8
31 – 40	6
41 – 50	3

D.

Interval	Frequency
1 – 10	2
11 – 20	9
21 – 30	8
31 – 40	6
41 – 50	4

18. Abram rolls a die. What is the probability he rolls an even number or a number greater than 4?
    A. $\frac{2}{3}$
    B. $\frac{1}{6}$
    C. $\frac{3}{4}$
    D. $\frac{5}{6}$

19. What is the expected value of spinning a spinner with 10 equally-spaced sections labeled 1 – 10?
    A. 4.5
    B. 5
    C. 5.5
    D. 6

20. Amanda rolls a die. She will lose $6 if the die lands on a 3 or 5. She will win $3 if the die lands on a 1 or 2. She will lose $9 if the die lands on a 4 or 6. What is the expected value?
    A. −$2
    B. −$4
    C. −$5
    D. −$6

Reading

Directions for questions 1 – 6
Read the statement or passage and then choose the best answer to the question. Answer the question based on what is stated or implied in the statement or passage.

1. Wells provide water for drinking, bathing, and cleaning to many people across the world. When wells are being dug, there are several issues that must be taken into account to minimize the chance of potential problems down the road. First, it's important to be aware that groundwater levels differ, depending on the season. In general, groundwater levels will be higher during the winter. So if a well is being dug during the winter, it should be deep enough to remain functional during the summer, when water levels are lower. Well water that is used is replaced by melting snow and rain. If the well owners are using the water faster than it can be replaced, however, the water levels will be lowered. The only way to remedy this, aside from waiting for the groundwater to be replenished naturally, is to deepen the well.

From this passage, it can be concluded that
    A. It is better to have a well that is too deep than one that is too shallow.
    B. Most well owners will face significant water shortages every year.
    C. Most people who dig wells during the winter do not make them deep enough.
    D. Well water is safe to use for bathing and cleaning, but is not suitable for drinking.

2. Today's low-fat craze has led many people to assume that all fats are unhealthy, but this is simply not the case. Fat is an essential component of any healthy diet because it provides energy and helps the body process nutrients. While all fats should be consumed in moderation, there are good and bad fats. Good fats are what are known as unsaturated fats. They are found in olive oil, fatty fish like salmon, and nuts. Bad fats are saturated and trans fats. They are found in foods like butter, bacon, and ice cream. Consumption of foods that contain trans or saturated fats should be restricted or avoided altogether.

The main purpose of this passage is to
    A. Explain why fat is important for the body.
    B. Discuss some of the main sources of good fats.
    C. Talk about the different types of fats.
    D. Discuss examples of foods that should be avoided.

3. Satire is a genre that originated in the ancient world and is still popular today. Although satire is often humorous, its purposes and intentions go well beyond simply making people laugh. Satire is a way for the playwright, author, or television producer to criticize society, human nature, and individuals that he holds in contempt. Satire as we know it today developed in Ancient Greece and Rome. There were three main types. The first, Menippean satire, focused on criticizing aspects of human nature. This was done by introducing stereotypical, one-dimensional characters. Horatian satire can be viewed as gentle satire. It made fun of people and their habits, but in a way that was not offensive. Juvenalian satire was written is such a way that the audience would experience feelings of disgust and aversion when they saw the characters and their actions. Some of the most popular satires today are fake news shows, like the *Daily Show* and the *Colbert Report*, and satirical comic strips like *Doonesbury*.

The main purpose of the passage is

    A. To discuss the history of satire.

    B. To present the major types of satire.

    C. To discuss modern examples of satire.

    D. To present the purposes of satire.

4. Many people believe that how we express our feelings is mainly determined by our upbringing and culture. Undoubtedly, this is true in some cases. In North America, for example, it is customary to shake hands when we meet somebody to express acceptance, whereas in other countries they may simply bow slightly to indicate this. Many feelings, however, are expressed in similar ways by people all over the world. These emotions include, fear, anger, happiness, disgust, and sorrow. For example, if a person is experiencing fear, their eyes will widen and their pupils will dilate. This reaction is largely involuntary. The finding that people express many feelings in a similar manner, regardless of where they are from, indicates that facial expressions are influenced more by evolution than culture.

Based on the passage, it can be concluded that

    A. People often can't hide what they are feeling.

    B. People from other parts of the world express happiness differently.

    C. Fear is the only emotion that is felt by everybody in the worlD.

    D. Acceptance is a feeling invented by man.

5. Cities are typically warmer than the surrounding countryside, a phenomenon known as the heat island effect. There are numerous causes of this phenomenon, including emissions from cars and buildings. This creates a mini greenhouse effect. In rural areas, the standing water in marshes and ponds evaporates, which cools the air slightly. This does not occur to the same extent in the city. The tall buildings in the center of most cities block winds that would provide some relief from the excessive heat. Finally, the color and material of most roads and buildings absorbs rather than reflects heat. Although planting trees and using building materials that reflect heat may alleviate the problem somewhat, it will by no means eliminate it.

The main purpose of the passage is to

    A. Talk about how the problem of heat island can be solved.

    B. Argue that cities should make an effort to plant more trees.

    C. Present the major causes of the problem of heat island.

    D. Contrast the city environment to that of the countryside.

6. Marsupials resemble mammals in a number of ways. For one thing, they are warm-blooded creatures. They have hair, and the mothers feed their young by producing milk. However, one thing that separates marsupials from mammals is that their young are born when they are not yet fully-developed. Most are born after only about four or five weeks. They finish their development in the pouch of their mother. Some of the more commonly known marsupials are koalas, kangaroos, and opossums. They are a diverse group, with many members having little in common besides their reproductive traits.

A major difference between marsupials and mammals is
    A. Marsupials have hair, while mammals do not.
    B. Mammals are a much more diverse group than marsupials.
    C. Marsupials are born at an earlier stage of development.
    D. Mammals feed their young by producing milk.

Questions 7 - 11 are based on the following passage:

Harriet Tubman was a runaway slave from Maryland who became known as the "Moses of her people." Over the course of 10 years, and at great personal risk, she led hundreds of slaves to freedom along the Underground Railroad, a secret network of safe houses where runaway slaves could stay on their journey north to freedom. She later became a leader in the abolitionist movement, and during the Civil War she was a spy for the federal forces in South Carolina as well as a nurse.

Harriet Tubman's name at birth was Araminta Ross. She was one of 11 children of Harriet and Benjamin Ross born into slavery in Dorchester County, Maryland. As a child, Ross was "hired out" by her master as a nursemaid for a small baby. Ross had to stay awake all night so that the baby wouldn't cry and wake the mother. If Ross fell asleep, the baby's mother whipped her. From a very young age, Ross was determined to gain her freedom.

As a slave, Araminta Ross was scarred for life when she refused to help in the punishment of another young slave. A young man had gone to the store without permission, and when he returned, the overseer wanted to whip him. He asked Ross to help but she refused. When the young man started to run away, the overseer picked up a heavy iron weight and threw it at him. He missed the young man and hit Ross instead. The weight nearly crushed her skull and left a deep scar. She was unconscious for days, and suffered from seizures for the rest of her life.

In 1844, Ross married a free black named John Tubman and took his last name. She also changed her first name, taking her mother's name, Harriet. In 1849, worried that she and the other slaves on the plantation were going to be sold, Tubman decided to run away. Her husband refused to go with her, so she set out with her two brothers, and followed the North Star in the sky to guide her north to freedom. Her brothers became frightened and turned back, but she continued on and reached Philadelphia. There she found work as a household servant and saved her money so she could return to help others escape.

- 168 -

7. This passage is mainly about
   A. slaves in the Civil War.
   B. how slaves escaped along the Underground Railroad.
   C. Harriet Tubman's role as an abolitionist leader.
   D. Harriet Tubman's life as a slave.

8. The author of the passage describes Harriet Tubman's life as a slave to show
   A. why she wanted to escape slavery.
   B. why she was a spy during the Civil War.
   C. why she suffered from seizures.
   D. how she loved babies.

9. Harriet Tubman's seizures were caused by
   A. a whipping.
   B. a severe head injury.
   C. loss of sleep.
   D. a birth defect.

10. How is this passage structured?
   A. cause and effect
   B. problem and solution
   C. chronological order
   D. compare and contrast

11. How did Araminta Ross come to be known as Harriet Tubman?
   A. She took her husband's last name and changed her first name to her mother's name.
   B. She was named after the plantation owner's wife.
   C. She changed her name because she was wanted as an Underground Railroad runner.
   D. She changed her name to remain anonymous as a Civil War spy.

Questions 12 - 16 are based on the following passage:

> There will come soft rains and the smell of the ground,
> And swallows circling with their shimmering sound;
> And frogs in the pools singing at night,
> And wild plum trees in tremulous white;
> Robins will wear their feathery fire
> Whistling their whims on a low fence-wire;
> And not one will know of the war, not one
> Will care at last when it is done.
> Not one would mind, neither bird nor tree
> If mankind perished utterly;
> And Spring herself, when she woke at dawn,
> Would scarcely know that we were gone.

12. How many stanzas does this poem have?
   A. 2
   B. 4
   C. 6
   D. 10

13. Which line uses personification?
   A. Line 2
   B. Line 4
   C. Line 7
   D. Line 11

14. The "we" used in line 12 refers to
   A. all of mankind.
   B. the victors of the war.
   C. Americans.
   D. the poet and the reader.

15. This poem is an example of a(n)
   A. sonnet.
   B. rhymed verse.
   C. free verse.
   D. lyric.

16. Which of these statements offers the best summary of the poem?
   A. Nature does not care about the affairs of mankind.
   B. It is the government's responsibility to fight a war.
   C. War has a devastating impact on nature.
   D. Wars should not be fought in the spring.

Questions 17 - 20 refer to the following passage:

Grapes are one of the oldest cultivated fruits. Hieroglyphics show that Egyptians were involved in grape and wine production. Also, the early Romans were known to have developed many grape varieties.

Grapes have been grown in California for more than 200 years. The tradition of viticulture (growing grapes) began in 1769 when Spanish friars established missions throughout California.

In California, the boom in grapes planted for eating arose in the early 1800s. William Wolfskill, founder of California's citrus industry, planted the first table grape vineyard in 1839 near Los Angeles.

By the 1850s, the United States had officially acquired California from Mexico and 80,000 gold prospectors had moved to the region, a few of them realizing that there was money in grapes as well as in gold.

Today, California wine, table grapes and raisins are all important agricultural commodities, with approximately 700,000 acres planted in vineyards.

About 85% of California's table grape production is in the southern San Joaquin Valley region with the Coachella Valley region accounting for most of the remaining production.

17. This passage is mainly about
    A. how Egyptians grew wine grapes.
    B. how to make raisins from grapes.
    C. William Wolfskill's life as a farmer.
    D. the history of growing grapes in California.

18. The best title for this passage is
    A. Early Wine Production.
    B. California Table Grapes.
    C. Viticulture in California.
    D. The California Missions.

19. Most of California's table grapes are grown in
    A. the San Joaquin Valley region.
    B. the Coachella Valley region.
    C. Los Angeles.
    D. the California missions.

20. William Wolfskill is credited with
    A. deciphering hieroglyphics about grape and wine production.
    B. helping the United States acquire California.
    C. planting the first table grape vineyard in California.
    D. farming 700,000 acres of vineyards.

Questions 21 - 24 pertain to the following passage:

How are Hypotheses Confirmed?

Most scientists agree that while the scientific method is an invaluable methodological tool, it is not a failsafe method for arriving at objective truth. It is debatable, for example, whether a hypothesis can actually be confirmed by evidence.

When a hypothesis is of the form "All x are y," it is commonly believed that a piece of evidence that is both x and y confirms the hypothesis. For example, for the hypothesis "All monkeys are hairy," a particular monkey that is hairy is thought to be a confirming piece of evidence for the hypothesis. A problem arises when one encounters evidence that disproves a hypothesis: while no scientist would argue that one piece of evidence proves a hypothesis, it is possible for one piece of evidence to disprove a hypothesis. To return to the monkey example, one hairless monkey out of one billion hairy monkeys disproves the hypothesis "All monkeys are hairy." Single pieces of evidence, then, seem to affect a given hypothesis in radically different ways. For this reason, the confirmation of hypotheses is better described as probabilistic.

Hypotheses that can only be proven or disproven based on evidence need to be based on probability because sample sets for such hypotheses are too large. In the monkey example, every single

- 171 -

monkey in the history of monkeys would need to be examined before the hypothesis could be proven or disproven. By making confirmation a function of probability, one may make provisional or working conclusions that allow for the possibility of a given hypothesis being <u>disconfirmed</u> in the future. In the monkey case, then, encountering a hairy monkey would slightly raise the probability that "all monkeys are hairy," while encountering a hairless monkey would slightly decrease the probability that "all monkeys are hairy." This method of confirming hypotheses is both counterintuitive and controversial, but it allows for evidence to equitably affect hypotheses and it does not require infinite sample sets for confirmation or disconfirmation.

21. What is the main idea of the second paragraph?
    A. One hairy monkey proves the hypothesis "All monkeys are hairy."
    B. The same piece of evidence can both confirm and disconfirm a hypothesis.
    C. Confirming and disconfirming evidence affect hypotheses differently.
    D. The scientific method is not a failsafe method for arriving at objective truth.

22. A synonym for the underlined word, <u>disconfirmed</u>, would be:
    A. proven
    B. dissipated
    C. distilled
    D. disproven

23. Which of the following is true of hypotheses of the form "All x are y"?
    A. Something that is neither x nor y disproves the hypothesis.
    B. Something that is both x and y disproves the hypothesis.
    C. Something that is x but not y disproves the hypothesis.
    D. Something that is y but not x disproves the hypothesis.

24. Using the same reasoning as that in the passage, an automobile with eighteen wheels does what to the following hypothesis: "All automobiles have only four wheels"?
    A. It proves the hypothesis.
    B. It raises the hypothesis's probability.
    C. It disproves the hypothesis.
    D. It decreases the hypothesis's probability.

Writing

Alberto wrote this essay about a memorable teacher. He would like you to read his paper and look for corrections and improvements he should make. When you finish reading, answer questions 1 - 10.

(1) I had the same teacher for both third and 4th grades, which were difficult years for me. (2) My teacher and I did not get along, and I don't think she liked me. (3) Every day, I thought she was treating me unfairly and being mean. (4) Because I felt that way, I think I acted out and stopped doing my work. (5) In the middle of fourth grade, my family moved to a new town, and I had Mr. Shanbourne as my new teacher.

(6) From the very first day in Mr. Shanbourne's class, I was on guard. (7) I was expecting to hate my teacher and for him to hate me back when I started his class. (8) Mr. Shanbourne took me by surprise right away when he asked me if I wanted to stand up and introduce myself. (9) I said no, probably in a surly voice, and he just nodded and began teaching the first lesson of the day.

(10) I wasn't sure how to take this. (11) My old teacher forced me to do things and gave me detention if I didn't. (12) She loved detention and gave it to me for anything I did--talking back, working too loudly, forgetting an assignment. (13) Mr. Shanbourne obviously didn't believe in detention, and I tried him! (14) During my first two weeks at my new school I did my best to get in trouble. (15) I zoned out in class, turned work in late, talked out in class, and handed in assignments after the due date. (16) Every time, Mr. Shanbourne just nodded.

(17) Mr. Shanbourne asked me to stay in during recess. (18) *This is it*, I thought. I was going to get in trouble, get the detention my ten-year-old self had practically been begging for. (19) After all of the other kids ran outside, I walked up to Mr. Shanbourne's desk.

(20) "How are you doing, Alberto," he said.

(21) I mumbled something.

(22) He told me he was disappointed in my behavior over the last two weeks. (23) I had expected this and just took it. (24) The detention was coming any second. (25) Than Mr. Shanbourne took me by surprise. (26) He told me that even though he didn't know me very well, he believed I could be a hard worker and that I could be successful in his class. (27) He asked me how he could help listen better and turn my work in on time.

(28) I told him I had to think about it and rushed out to recess. (29) Even though my answer seemed rude, I was stunned. (30) I hadn't had a teacher in years who seemed to care about me, and said he believed in my abilities.

(31) To be honest, my behavior did not improve right away and I still turned in many of my assignments late. (32) But over the last few months of fourth grade, things changed. (33) Mr. Shanbourne continued to believe in me and encuorage me and help me, and I responded by doing my best. (34) I had a different teacher for fifth grade, but whenever I was struggling I walked down to Mr. Shanbourne's classroom to get his advice. (35) I'll never forget how Mr. Shanbourne helped me, and I hope he'll never forget me either.

1. What change should be made to sentence 1?
    A. Change *teacher* to *teachers*
    B. Change *4ᵗʰ* to *fourth*
    C. Delete the comma after *grades*
    D. Change *years* to *year's*

2. What is the most effective way to revise sentence 7?
    A. I started his class expecting my teacher to hate me back and for me to hate him.
    B. Expecting to hate my teacher, I started his class expecting him to hate me back.
    C. Starting his class expecting to hate my teacher, I also expected to hate him back.
    D. I started his class expecting to hate my teacher and for him to hate me back.

3. What is the most effective way to combine sentences 10 and 11?
    A. I wasn't sure how to take this, and my old teacher forced me to do things and gave me detention if I didn't.
    B. I wasn't sure how to take this, although my old teacher forced me to do things and gave me detention if I didn't.
    C. I wasn't sure how to take this because my old teacher forced me to do things and gave me detention if I didn't.
    D. I wasn't sure how to take this as a result of my old teacher forced me to do things and gave me detention if I didn't.

4. Which phrase, if any, can be deleted from sentence 15 without changing the meaning of the sentence?
    A. zoned out in class
    B. talked out in class
    C. handed in assignments after the due date
    D. No change

5. What transition should be added to the beginning of sentence 16?
    A. However
    B. Actually
    C. Furthermore
    D. Eventually

6. Which version of sentence 20 is correctly punctuated?
    A. "How are you doing, Alberto?" he said.
    B. "How are you doing, Alberto? he said."
    C. "How are you doing, Alberto." he said.
    D. No change.

7. What change should be made to sentence 25?
    A. Change *Than* to *Then*.
    B. Change *Shanbourne* to *Shanbourne's*.
    C. Add a comma after *Shanbourne*.
    D. Change *by* to *bye*.

8. What change should be made to sentence 30?
    A. Change *hadn't* to *haven't*.
    B. Change *who* to *whom*.
    C. Delete the comma after *me*.
    D. Change *believed* to *believed*.

9. What change should be made to sentence 31?
    A. Delete the comma after *honest*.
    B. Change *did* to *does*.
    C. Add a comma after *away*.
    D. Change *many* to *much*.

10. What change should be made to sentence 33?
    A. Change *continued* to *continues*.
    B. Delete the comma after *in me*.
    C. Change *encuorage* to *encourage*.
    D. Delete the comma after *help me*.

For questions 11-15, select the best option for replacing the underlined portion of the sentence. The first option listed is always the same as the current version of the sentence.

11. Several theories <u>about what caused dinosaurs to have extinction exist</u>, but scientists are still unable to reach a concrete conclusion.
    A. about what caused dinosaurs to have extinction exist
    B. about what caused dinosaurs to become extinct exist
    C. about the causes of the dinosaur extinction exists
    D. regarding the cause of extinction of dinosaurs exist

12. <u>Although most persons</u> prefer traditional pets like cats and dogs, others gravitate towards exotic animals like snakes and lizards.
    A. Although most persons
    B. Because most people
    C. While most people
    D. Maybe some persons

13. It is important that software companies offer tech support <u>to customers who are encountering problems</u>.
    A. to customers who are encountering problems
    B. because not all customers encounter problems
    C. with customers who encounter problems
    D. to customer who is encountering difficulties

14. The fact <u>that children eat high fat diets and watch excessive amount of television are a cause of concern</u> for many parents.
   A. that children eat high fat diets and watch excessive amount of television are a cause of concern
   B. the children eat high fat diets and watches excessive amount of television are a cause of concern
   C. is children eat high fat diets and watch excessive amount of television is a cause for concern
   D. that children eat high fat diets and watch excessive amounts of television is a cause for concern

15. <u>Contrarily to popular beliefs</u>, bats do not actually entangle themselves in the hair of humans on purpose.
   A. Contrarily to popular beliefs
   B. Contrary to popular belief
   C. Contrary to popularity belief
   D. Contrary to popular believing

16. Mitosis is the process of cell division, and if there are errors during this process, it can result in serious complications.
Rewrite, beginning with
<u>Serious complications can result</u>
The next words will be
   A. during the process of cell division
   B. if there are errors during the process
   C. in the process of mitosis
   D. when this process leads to errors

17. It was a very tough decision, but Sharon finally decided after much consideration to study biology at Yale University.
Rewrite, beginning with
<u>After much consideration</u>
The next words will be
   A. Sharon finally decided to study
   B. it was a very tough decision
   C. Sharon studied biology at Yale University
   D. a very tough study was decided.

18. Small business owners must compete with larger stores by providing excellent service, because department store prices are simply too low for owners of small businesses to match them.
Rewrite, beginning with
<u>Prices in department stores are simply too low for owners of small businesses to match them,</u>
The next words will be
   A. so small business owners must
   B. while small business owners must
   C. when small business owners must
   D. because small business owners must

19. Ants are fascinating creatures, and some of their unique characteristics are their strength, organizational skills, and construction talents.

Rewrite, beginning with

<u>Strength, organizational skills, and construction talents</u>

The next words will be

    A. are some of the unique characteristics

    B. are possessed by fascinating creatures

    C. of ants are fascinating characteristics

    D. are unique characteristics of their

20. Many people do not regularly wear their seatbelts, even though law enforcement professionals warn motorists about the dangers of not doing so.

Rewrite, beginning with

<u>Despite warnings by law enforcement professionals</u>

The next words will be

    A. motorists ignore the dangers of not doing so

    B. many people do not regularly wear their seatbelts

    C. about the people who don't wear seatbelts

    D. even though motorists do not wear seatbelts

Essay

In the United States, elections are decided by majority vote with the candidate who receives over 50% of the vote winning the entire seat. However, in many other countries, the election system is proportional, with parties receiving a particular number of seats based on the percentage of the vote they receive. Please write a five-paragraph persuasive essay (approximately 350–500 words) discussing which system you believe to be better and why.

Answers and Explanations

Math

1. A: When graphing an inequality, a solid circle at an endpoint means that the number at that endpoint is included in the range, while a hollow circle means it is not. Since the inequality says that x is strictly greater than 2, the circle at 2 should therefore be hollow; since the inequality says that x is less than *or equal to* 4, the circle at 4 should be solid. $2 < x \leq 4$ indicates that x is between 2 and 4, so the area between the circles should be shaded; the two end rays in choice D would instead represent the pair of inequalities "$x < 2$ or $x \geq 4$".

2. D: To simplify the inequality $3 - 2x < 5$, we can first subtract 3 from both sides: $3 - 2x - 3 < 5 - 3 \Rightarrow -2x < 2$. Now, we can divide both sides of the inequality by -2. When an inequality is multiplied or divided by a negative number, its direction changes ($<$ becomes $>$, $\leq$ becomes $\geq$, and vice versa). So $-2x < 2$ becomes $\frac{-2x}{-2} > \frac{2}{-2}$, or $x > -1$.

3. C: If the exam has 30 questions, and the student answered C questions correctly and left B questions blank, then the number of questions the student answered incorrectly must be $30 - B - C$. He gets one point for each correct question, or $1 \times C = C$ points, and loses $\frac{1}{2}$ point for each incorrect question, or $\frac{1}{2}(30 - B - C)$ points. Therefore, one way to express his total score is $-\frac{1}{2}(30 - B - C)$.

4. B: Call the number of people present at the meeting x. If each person hands out a card to every *other* person (that is, every person besides himself), then each person hands out $x - 1$ cards. The total number of cards handed out is therefore $(x - 1)$. Since we are told there are a total of 30 cards handed out, we have the equation $(x - 1) = 30$, which we can rewrite as the quadratic equation $x^2 - x - 30 = 0$. We can solve this equation by factoring the quadratic expression. One way to do this is to find two numbers that add to the coefficient of x (in this case -1) and that multiply to the constant term (in this case -30). Those two numbers are 5 and -6. Our factored equation is therefore $(x + 5)(x - 6) = 0$. To make the equation true, one or both of the factors must be zero: either $+5 = 0$, in which case $x = -5$, or $x - 6 = 0$, in which case $x = 6$. Obviously the number of people at the meeting cannot be negative, so the second solution, $x = 6$, must be correct.

5. B: First, let's distribute the x and y that are outside the parentheses and then combine like terms: $(y - 2) + y(3 - x) = (xy - 2x) + (3y - xy) = -2x + 3y + xy - xy = -2x + 3y$.

6. B: The average is the total amount spent divided by the number of students. The first three students spend an average of $10, so the total amount they spend is $3 \times \$10 = \$30$. The other six students spend an average of $4, so the total amount they spend is $6 \times \$4 = \$24$. The total amount spent by all nine students is $\$30 + \$24 = \$54$, and the average amount they spend is $\$54 \div 9 = \$6$.

- 179 -

7. B: Dividing both sides of the equation by $\frac{1}{3}\pi h$ gives $r^2 = \frac{V}{\frac{1}{3}\pi h}$. Solving for r gives $r = \sqrt{\frac{V}{\frac{1}{3}\pi h}}$ or $r = \sqrt{\frac{3V}{\pi h}}$.

8. C: The least common denominator of $x(x + 4)$ may be multiplied by both rational expressions. Doing so gives $2x = 3(x + 4)$ or $2x = 3x + 12$. Solving for x gives $x = -12$.

9. D: The radical equation may b0e solved by first subtracting 8 from both sides of the equation. Doing so gives $4\sqrt{x} = 16$. Dividing both sides of the equation by 4 gives $\sqrt{x} = 4$. Squaring both sides gives $x = 16$.

10. C: Using the method of elimination to solve the system of linear equations, each term in the top equation may be multiplied by –2, while each term in the bottom equation may be multiplied by 5. Doing so produces two new equations with x-terms that will add to 0. The sum of $-10x - 18y = 14$ and $10x - 20y = 100$ may be written as $-38y = 114$, where $y = -3$. Substituting the y-value of –3 into the top, original equation gives $5x + 9(-3) = -7$. Solving for x gives $x = 4$. Thus, the solution is $= 4$, $y = -3$.

11. B: Use the Pythagorean Theorem to solve this problem: $a^2 + b^2 = c^2$ where c is the hypotenuse while a and b are the legs of the triangle.
$5^2 + 12^2 = c^2$
$25 + 144 = 169$
$\sqrt{169} = 13$.

12. B: Angles that form a straight line add up to 180 degrees. Such angles are sometimes referred to as being "supplementary."
$60 + 2x = 180$
$2x = 120$
$x = 60$

13. C: Use the formula for circumference:
Circumference = π X diameter (π is approximately equal to 3.14).
To give the best estimate, round to the nearest whole number:
3.14 rounds to 3
12.2, the diameter, rounds to 12
3 x 12 = 36

14. D: As rectangle $ABCD$ is moved from Quadrant I into Quadrant II, it is rotated in a counterclockwise manner. Therefore, rectangle $ABCD$ can be carried onto its image $A'B'C'D'$ by a 90° counterclockwise rotation about the origin.

15. A: If two triangles are similar, then all pairs of corresponding sides are proportional. In order for ΔRST to be similar to ΔXYZ, we need $\frac{RS}{XY} = \frac{RT}{XZ} = \frac{ST}{YZ}$. Substituting in for those values becomes $\frac{24}{8} = \frac{12}{4} = \frac{30}{YZ}$. Simplifying the fractions results in $\frac{3}{1} = \frac{3}{1} = \frac{30}{YZ}$. Therefore, in order for the triangles to be similar, we need $\frac{3}{1} = \frac{30}{YZ}$. After cross-multiplying the terms, it becomes $3(YZ) = 30(1)$, $3(YZ) = 30$. Divide both sides by 3 to get $YZ = 10$. Answer B saw that 30 was 6 more than 24 and then incorrectly added 6 to 8 to get 14. Answer C incorrectly set up the

scale factor as $\frac{24}{8} = \frac{2}{1}$ and set $\frac{2}{1} = \frac{30}{YZ}$ to get $YZ = 15$. Answer D saw that 30 was 18 more than 12 and then incorrectly added 18 to 4 to get 22.

16. C: Hiking due west at 3 miles/hour, the first hiker will have gone 6 miles after 2 hours. Hiking due north at 4 miles/hour, the second hiker will have gone 8 miles after 2 hours. Since one hiker headed west and the other headed north, their distance from each other can be drawn as:

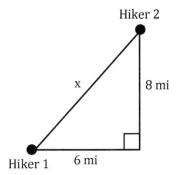

Since the distance between the two hikers is the hypotenuse of a right triangle and we know the lengths of the two legs of the right triangle, the Pythagorean Theorem ($a^2 + b^2 = c^2$) is used to find the value of x. Therefore, $6^2 + 8^2 = x^2, 36 + 64 = x^2, 100 = x^2, 10 = x$. Answer A is the distance between the hikers after only 1 hour of hiking. Answer B incorrectly added the distances hiked after 1 hour. Answer D incorrectly added the distances hiked after 2 hours.

17. A: The frequency table for Choice A correctly shows the frequencies represented by the histogram. The frequencies of values, falling between 1 and 10 is 3, between 11 and 20 is 9, between 21 and 30 is 8, between 31 and 40 is 6, and between 41 and 50 is 4.

18. A: The probability of non-mutually exclusive events, A or B, occurring may be written as $P(A \text{ or } B) = P(A) + P(B) - P(A \text{ and } B)$. Thus, $P(A \text{ or } B) = \frac{3}{6} + \frac{2}{6} - \frac{1}{6}$ or $\frac{2}{3}$.

19. C: The expected value is equal to the sum of the products of the probability of rolling each number and the number's value. Thus, the expected value is $\left(1 \cdot \frac{1}{10}\right) + \left(2 \cdot \frac{1}{10}\right) + \left(3 \cdot \frac{1}{10}\right) + \left(4 \cdot \frac{1}{10}\right) + \left(5 \cdot \frac{1}{10}\right) + \left(6 \cdot \frac{1}{10}\right) + \left(7 \cdot \frac{1}{10}\right) + \left(8 \cdot \frac{1}{10}\right) + \left(9 \cdot \frac{1}{10}\right) + \left(10 \cdot \frac{1}{10}\right)$. The expected value is 5.5.

20. B: The expected value is equal to the sum of the products of the probabilities and the amount she will lose or win. Each probability is equal to $\frac{2}{6}$. Thus, the expected value may be written as $\left(-6 \cdot \frac{2}{6}\right) + \left(3 \cdot \frac{2}{6}\right) + \left(-9 \cdot \frac{2}{6}\right)$. Thus, the expected value is –$4.

Reading

1. A: The passage discusses several problems that can occur with wells. Both of the problems mentioned are associated with wells that are too shallow; no problems associated

with wells that are too deep are mentioned. Therefore, it seems safe to conclude that a deeper well would be more desirable than a shallow one.

2. C: A is mentioned only briefly in the passage. B and C are mentioned, but this information fits into the overall purpose of the passage, which is to discuss the different types of fats, both good and bad.

3. B: C and D are mentioned only briefly. Although the history of satire is discussed, most of the passage focuses on discussing the three major forms of satire that originated in Ancient Greece and Rome, making B the best choice.

4. A: B is incorrect because the passage states that happiness is expressed similarly by people all over the world. C is incorrect because the passage states that there are many emotions felt and expressed by people all over the world. D is incorrect because, although people may express acceptance differently, that is not sufficient to conclude it is not a natural emotion. A is correct. We can conclude that people can't always hide what they are feeling because of the statement in the passage that the facial expressions associated with emotions like fear are largely involuntary.

5. C: C is the correct answer because the passage mainly focuses on discussing the causes of heat island. A, B, and D are touched upon only in passing.

6. C: A and D are incorrect because the passage states that these are characteristics that marsupials and mammals share. B can be eliminated, because it is not mentioned in the passage. C is the correct choice, as "one thing that separates marsupials from mammals is that their young are born when they are not yet fully-developed" is stated in the passage.

7. D: Answer choice (D) best summarizes the main topic discussed here. While choice (C) is a fact given about Tubman in the passage, it is not the main focus. Choices (A) and (B) are not discussed in the passage.

8. A: The author uses phrases like Tubman "was determined to gain her freedom" and "worried that she and the other slaves on the plantation were going to be sold" as he or she describes Tubman's life as a slave. The reader can deduce that author included these descriptions to illustrate why Harriet Tubman wanted to escape slavery, choice (A). The other answer choices are either insignificant details or not explained in the passage.

9. B: Paragraph 3 describes why Harriet Tubman suffered from seizures. An overseer threw a heavy weight and hit her in the head. The weight nearly crushed her skull. She suffered from seizures for the rest of her life. The best answer choice is (B).

10. C: Clue words such as "as a child" and "later," as well as the use of dates, indicates that this passage is arranged in chronological order.

11. A: Paragraph 4 explains how Araminta Ross became known as Harriet Tubman. She married John Tubman and took his last name. She also changed her first name to her mother's name.

12. C: A stanza consists of a grouping of lines, set off by a space, that usually has a set pattern of meter and rhyme. This poem has six stanzas.

13. D: Personification is a metaphor in which a thing or abstraction is represented as a person. Personification is used throughout this poem. However, of the answer choices given, line 11 is the best choice. The author personifies spring as a female.

14. A: The fifth stanza gives clues to whom "we" refers.
"Not one would mind, neither bird nor tree
If mankind perished utterly"
"We" is referencing mankind, choice (A).

15. B: This is an example of a rhymed verse poem. The last two words of each line rhymes in every stanza. A sonnet is a poem of fourteen lines following a set rhyme scheme and logical structure. Often, poets use iambic pentameter when writing sonnets. A free verse poem is written without using strict meter or rhyme. A lyric poem is a short poem that expresses personal feelings, which may or may not be set to music. An epic poem is a long <u>narrative poem</u>, usually about a serious subject. It often contains details of heroic deeds and events significant to a culture or nation.

16. A: Answer choice A gives the best summary of the poem, demonstrated by the phrases about things in nature not caring about war or the extinction of humanity.

17. D: Answer choice (D) best summarizes what this passage is mainly about.

18. C: Answer choice (C) is the best title for the passage because it best summarizes all the topics covered in the passage. The other answer choices are details mentioned in the passage, but are not the main focus of the passage.

19. A: The last paragraph of the passages answers this detail question.

20. C: The third paragraph of the passage answers this detail question.

21. C: The first paragraph states that the main purpose of DST it to make better use of daylight.

22. A: Energy conservation is discussed as a possible benefit of DST, not a negative effect of it.

23. D: The first paragraph states that DST involves setting clocks forward one hour in the spring and one hour backward in the fall.

24. D: The passage gives examples of both good and bad effects extra daylight can have on health.

Writing

1. B: because the word *fourth* should be written out to match the form of *third.* While the word *teacher* could become plural, choice A is incorrect because the second sentence of the passage shows that Alberto is talking about a single teacher. Choice C is incorrect because the comma correctly separates two independent clauses. Choice D is incorrect because

Alberto is talking about several years rather than the possessive of one year. Therefore, the form of *years* should be plural rather than possessive.

2. D: is the correct answer because it uses proper word order to get the point across. Choice D begins with a subject and verb and follows the verb by two objects. Choice A is incorrect because the phrases *my teacher to hate me back* and *for me to hate him* are written in reverse order. It is more logical for *for me to hate him* to be written first. Choice B is incorrect because the subject and verb separate Alberto's two emotions (*expecting to hate my teacher* and *expecting him to hate me back*). This separation makes the sentence more difficult to read and understand. Choice C is incorrect because Alberto states twice that he expected to hate Mr. Shanbourne.

3. C: is the correct answer because the word *because* combines the sentence by showing that the second clause is an explanation for the first clause. Choice A is incorrect because the conjunction *and* doesn't show how the two clauses are connected. Choice B is incorrect because the word *although* doesn't logically connect the two clauses. The word *although* implies that the two clauses contradict each other; instead, the second clause explains the first. Although *as a result of* has a similar meaning to *because* and could be used to effectively combine the sentences, choice D is incorrect because the verbs *forced* and *gave* should be changed to *forcing* and *giving* in order for *as a result of* to be used correctly.

4. C: because the phrase *handed in assignments after the due date* is redundant with the phrase *turned in work late*; only one of those phrases needs to be in the sentence. Choices A and B are incorrect because both phrases add unique information to the sentence. Choice D is incorrect because the sentence has two redundant phrases, and one of them should be deleted.

5. D: because this transition word shows that Mr. Shanbourne waited for a while and then decided to talk to Alberto about his behavior. Choice A is incorrect because the word *however* implies that the following sentence will contradict what came before. Instead, sentence 16 is a culmination of Alberto's behavior. Choice B is incorrect because the word *actually* is also a transition used to show a contrast between the two sentences. *Eventually* is a better transition word because it shows that the sentences are sequentially related. Choice C is incorrect because *furthermore* implies that the following sentence will present additional proof about a point.

6. A: is the correct answer because it correctly punctuates the dialogue with a question mark and with the quotation marks in the correct spot. Choice B is incorrect because the end quotes should be after *Alberto* rather than after *said*. Choices C and D are incorrect because the clause *How are you doing, Alberto* is a question and should be punctuated with a question mark rather than a period or comma.

7. A: is the correct answer because *than* is a comparative word and *then* is a word that shows a sequence of events. Since the sentence shows the next step in a sequence of events, *then* is the correct word to use. Choice B is incorrect because *Shanbourne* is not possessive in this context. Choice D is incorrect because a comma should not separate a subject and verb. Choice D is incorrect because *bye* is the spelling used to say good-bye and *by* is the spelling used for prepositions.

8. C: because a comma should only be used before a conjunction (the word *and* in sentence 29) if the clause following the conjunction is an independent clause, which means it can be written as a complete sentence. Since *said he believed in my abilities* does not have a subject, it is not an independent clause. Choice A is incorrect because this essay is written in the past tense, *hadn't* is a more consistent verb choice. Choice B is incorrect because the word *who* should be used when it refers to a subject. Since one could write a sentence such as "The teacher seemed to care about me."--which replaces *who* with a noun to create a subject)-- *who* is correct. *Whom* would be correct if the word referred to the object of the sentence. Choice D is incorrect because the correct spelling of *believed* has an 'i' before an 'e'.

9. C: because a comma should be added before a conjunction (*and*) that precedes an independent clause. Choice A is incorrect because the comma after *honest* correctly separates a non-essential phrase from the rest of the sentence. Choice B is incorrect because the passage is written in past tense rather than present. Choice D is incorrect because *many* refers to a number of items (such as a number of homework assignments) while *much* refers to an abstract amount.

10. C: because *encourage* is the correct spelling (the 'o' should come before the 'u'). Choice A is incorrect because the word *responded*, used later in the sentence, shows that Alberto is still writing in the past tense. Choice B is incorrect because the comma is needed to separate items in the series. Choice D is incorrect because the comma is needed before *and* because *and* is a conjunction that precedes an independent clause.

11. B: The phrase *to have extinction* in choice A is grammatically incorrect. In choice C, *causes* is plural, and so the word should be *exist* rather than *exists*. D is not the best choice because it is somewhat awkward. B sounds the best and is also grammatically correct.

12. C: C is the best answer because it indicates a contrast and is grammatically correct.

13. A: A is the best answer because it denotes the party to whom companies are offering tech support and because the verb *are* agrees with the noun *customers*.

14. D: D is the best choice. The phrases *high-fat diets* and *excessive amounts of television* agree with each other because they are both plural. The word *is* refers to *the fact that*, so these also agree with each other.

15. B: This is a well-known phrase meaning *despite what most people believe*. The word *contrarily* in choice A makes it incorrect. *Popularity* in choice C is out of place, and *believing* in choice D is incorrect.

16. B: The original sentence states that serious complications can result if there are errors during the process of cell division. A and C refer to the process of cell division only, and not the errors that must be made for complications to occur. D indicates that the process leads to errors, rather than that the errors occur during the process.

17. A: The original sentence states that after much consideration a decision was made, which is why A is the best choice. The decision wasn't still difficult after much consideration, as B indicates, and she didn't immediately attend university, as is indicated by C. D simply doesn't make sense in the context of the statement.

18. A: A is the best choice because it is the only one that indicates a cause/effect relationship. Small business owners must do something *because* prices in department stores are too low for small business owners to match them.

19. A: The rewritten sentence begins with examples of some of the unique characteristics of ants. B does not indicate that they are unique characteristics; C describes them as fascinating rather than unique; and D does not make sense in the context of the sentence because of the phrase *of their* that follows *are unique characteristics*.

20. B: The word *despite* indicates that something is done in spite of warnings by law enforcement professionals, which eliminates choices C and D. A does not indicate precisely what motorists are failing to do, which eliminates that choice. B is the correct answer.

Success Strategies

The most important thing you can do is to ignore your fears and jump into the test immediately- do not be overwhelmed by any strange-sounding terms. You have to jump into the test like jumping into a pool- all at once is the easiest way.

Make Predictions

As you read and understand the question, try to guess what the answer will be. Remember that several of the answer choices are wrong, and once you begin reading them, your mind will immediately become cluttered with answer choices designed to throw you off. Your mind is typically the most focused immediately after you have read the question and digested its contents. If you can, try to predict what the correct answer will be. You may be surprised at what you can predict.

Quickly scan the choices and see if your prediction is in the listed answer choices. If it is, then you can be quite confident that you have the right answer. It still won't hurt to check the other answer choices, but most of the time, you've got it!

Answer the Question

It may seem obvious to only pick answer choices that answer the question, but the test writers can create some excellent answer choices that are wrong. Don't pick an answer just because it sounds right, or you believe it to be true. It MUST answer the question. Once you've made your selection, always go back and check it against the question and make sure that you didn't misread the question, and the answer choice does answer the question posed.

Benchmark

After you read the first answer choice, decide if you think it sounds correct or not. If it doesn't, move on to the next answer choice. If it does, mentally mark that answer choice. This doesn't mean that you've definitely selected it as your answer choice, it just means that it's the best you've seen thus far. Go ahead and read the next choice. If the next choice is worse than the one you've already selected, keep going to the next answer choice. If the next choice is better than the choice you've already selected, mentally mark the new answer choice as your best guess.

The first answer choice that you select becomes your standard. Every other answer choice must be benchmarked against that standard. That choice is correct until proven otherwise by another answer choice beating it out. Once you've decided that no other answer choice seems as good, do one final check to ensure that your answer choice answers the question posed.

Valid Information

Don't discount any of the information provided in the question. Every piece of information may be necessary to determine the correct answer. None of the information in the question is there to throw you off (while the answer choices will certainly have information to throw you off). If two seemingly unrelated topics are discussed, don't ignore either. You can be confident there is a relationship, or it wouldn't be included in the question, and you are probably going to have to determine what is that relationship to find the answer.

Avoid "Fact Traps"

Don't get distracted by a choice that is factually true. Your search is for the answer that answers the question. Stay focused and don't fall for an answer that is true but incorrect. Always go back to the question and make sure you're choosing an answer that actually answers the question and is not just a true statement. An answer can be factually correct, but it MUST answer the question asked. Additionally, two answers can both be seemingly correct, so be sure to read all of the answer choices, and make sure that you get the one that BEST answers the question.

Milk the Question

Some of the questions may throw you completely off. They might deal with a subject you have not been exposed to, or one that you haven't reviewed in years. While your lack of knowledge about the subject will be a hindrance, the question itself can give you many clues that will help you find the correct answer. Read the question carefully and look for clues. Watch particularly for adjectives and nouns describing difficult terms or words that you don't recognize. Regardless of if you completely understand a word or not, replacing it with a synonym either provided or one you more familiar with may help you to understand what the questions are asking. Rather than wracking your mind about specific detailed information concerning a difficult term or word, try to use mental substitutes that are easier to understand.

The Trap of Familiarity

Don't just choose a word because you recognize it. On difficult questions, you may not recognize a number of words in the answer choices. The test writers don't put "make-believe" words on the test; so don't think that just because you only recognize all the words in one answer choice means that answer choice must be correct. If you only recognize words in one answer choice, then focus on that one. Is it correct? Try your best to determine if it is correct. If it is, that is great, but if it doesn't, eliminate it. Each word and answer choice you eliminate increases your chances of getting the question correct, even if you then have to guess among the unfamiliar choices.

Eliminate Answers

Eliminate choices as soon as you realize they are wrong. But be careful! Make sure you consider all of the possible answer choices. Just because one appears right, doesn't mean that the next one won't be even better! The test writers will usually put more than one good answer choice for every question, so read all of them. Don't worry if you are stuck between two that seem right. By getting down to just two remaining possible choices, your odds are now 50/50. Rather than wasting too much time, play the odds. You are guessing, but guessing wisely, because you've been able to knock out some of the answer choices that you know are wrong. If you are eliminating choices and realize that the last answer choice you are left with is also obviously wrong, don't panic. Start over and consider each choice again. There may easily be something that you missed the first time and will realize on the second pass.

Tough Questions

If you are stumped on a problem or it appears too hard or too difficult, don't waste time. Move on! Remember though, if you can quickly check for obviously incorrect answer choices, your chances of guessing correctly are greatly improved. Before you completely give up, at least try to knock out a couple of possible answers. Eliminate what you can and then guess at the remaining answer choices before moving on.

Brainstorm

If you get stuck on a difficult question, spend a few seconds quickly brainstorming. Run through the complete list of possible answer choices. Look at each choice and ask yourself, "Could this answer the question satisfactorily?" Go through each answer choice and consider it independently of the other. By systematically going through all possibilities, you may find something that you would otherwise overlook. Remember that when you get stuck, it's important to try to keep moving.

Read Carefully

Understand the problem. Read the question and answer choices carefully. Don't miss the question because you misread the terms. You have plenty of time to read each question thoroughly and make sure you understand what is being asked. Yet a happy medium must be attained, so don't waste too much time. You must read carefully, but efficiently.

Face Value

When in doubt, use common sense. Always accept the situation in the problem at face value. Don't read too much into it. These problems will not require you to make huge leaps of logic. The test writers aren't trying to throw you off with a cheap trick. If you have to go beyond creativity and make a leap of logic in order to have an answer choice answer the question, then you should look at the other answer choices. Don't overcomplicate the problem by creating theoretical relationships or explanations that will warp time or space. These are normal problems rooted in reality. It's just that the applicable relationship or explanation may not be readily apparent and you have to figure things out. Use your common sense to interpret anything that isn't clear.

Prefixes

If you're having trouble with a word in the question or answer choices, try dissecting it. Take advantage of every clue that the word might include. Prefixes and suffixes can be a huge help. Usually they allow you to determine a basic meaning. Pre- means before, post- means after, pro - is positive, de- is negative. From these prefixes and suffixes, you can get an idea of the general meaning of the word and try to put it into context. Beware though of any traps. Just because con is the opposite of pro, doesn't necessarily mean congress is the opposite of progress!

Hedge Phrases

Watch out for critical "hedge" phrases, such as likely, may, can, will often, sometimes, often, almost, mostly, usually, generally, rarely, sometimes. Question writers insert these hedge phrases to cover every possibility. Often an answer choice will be wrong simply because it leaves no room for exception. Avoid answer choices that have definitive words like "exactly," and "always".

Switchback Words

Stay alert for "switchbacks". These are the words and phrases frequently used to alert you to shifts in thought. The most common switchback word is "but". Others include although, however, nevertheless, on the other hand, even though, while, in spite of, despite, regardless of.

New Information

Correct answer choices will rarely have completely new information included. Answer choices typically are straightforward reflections of the material asked about and will directly relate to the question. If a new piece of information is included in an answer choice that doesn't even seem to relate to the topic being asked about, then that answer choice is likely incorrect. All of the information needed to answer the question is usually provided for you, and so you should not have to make guesses that are unsupported or choose answer choices that require unknown information that cannot be reasoned on its own.

Time Management

On technical questions, don't get lost on the technical terms. Don't spend too much time on any one question. If you don't know what a term means, then since you don't have a dictionary, odds are you aren't going to get much further. You should immediately recognize terms as whether or not you know them. If you don't, work with the other clues that you have, the other answer choices and terms provided, but don't waste too much time trying to figure out a difficult term.

Contextual Clues

Look for contextual clues. An answer can be right but not correct. The contextual clues will help you find the answer that is most right and is correct. Understand the context in which a phrase or statement is made. This will help you make important distinctions.

Don't Panic

Panicking will not answer any questions for you. Therefore, it isn't helpful. When you first see the question, if your mind goes blank, take a deep breath. Force yourself to mechanically go through the steps of solving the problem and using the strategies you've learned.

Pace Yourself

Don't get clock fever. It's easy to be overwhelmed when you're looking at a page full of questions, your mind is full of random thoughts and feeling confused, and the clock is ticking down faster than you would like. Calm down and maintain the pace that you have set for yourself. As long as you are on track by monitoring your pace, you are guaranteed to have enough time for yourself. When you get to the last few minutes of the test, it may seem like you won't have enough time left, but if you only have as many questions as you should have left at that point, then you're right on track!

Answer Selection

The best way to pick an answer choice is to eliminate all of those that are wrong, until only one is left and confirm that is the correct answer. Sometimes though, an answer choice may immediately look right. Be careful! Take a second to make sure that the other choices are not equally obvious. Don't make a hasty mistake. There are only two times that you should stop before checking other answers. First is when you are positive that the answer choice you have selected is correct. Second is when time is almost out and you have to make a quick guess!

Check Your Work

Since you will probably not know every term listed and the answer to every question, it is important that you get credit for the ones that you do know. Don't miss any questions through careless mistakes. If at all possible, try to take a second to look back over your answer selection and make sure you've selected the correct answer choice and haven't made a costly careless mistake (such as marking an answer choice that you didn't mean to mark). This quick double check should more than pay for itself in caught mistakes for the time it costs.

Beware of Directly Quoted Answers

Sometimes an answer choice will repeat word for word a portion of the question or reference section. However, beware of such exact duplication – it may be a trap! More than likely, the correct choice will paraphrase or summarize a point, rather than being exactly the same wording.

Slang

Scientific sounding answers are better than slang ones. An answer choice that begins "To compare the outcomes..." is much more likely to be correct than one that begins "Because some people insisted..."

Extreme Statements

Avoid wild answers that throw out highly controversial ideas that are proclaimed as established fact. An answer choice that states the "process should be used in certain situations, if..." is much more likely to be correct than one that states the "process should be discontinued completely." The first is a calm rational statement and doesn't even make a definitive, uncompromising stance, using a hedge word "if" to provide wiggle room, whereas the second choice is a radical idea and far more extreme.

Answer Choice Families

When you have two or more answer choices that are direct opposites or parallels, one of them is usually the correct answer. For instance, if one answer choice states "x increases" and another answer choice states "x decreases" or "y increases," then those two or three answer choices are very similar in construction and fall into the same family of answer choices. A family of answer choices is when two or three answer choices are very similar in construction, and yet often have a directly opposite meaning. Usually the correct answer choice will be in that family of answer choices. The "odd man out" or answer choice that doesn't seem to fit the parallel construction of the other answer choices is more likely to be incorrect.

How to Overcome Test Anxiety

The very nature of tests caters to some level of anxiety, nervousness or tension, just as we feel for any important event that occurs in our lives. A little bit of anxiety or nervousness can be a good thing. It helps us with motivation, and makes achievement just that much sweeter. However, too much anxiety can be a problem; especially if it hinders our ability to function and perform.

"Test anxiety," is the term that refers to the emotional reactions that some test-takers experience when faced with a test or exam. Having a fear of testing and exams is based upon a rational fear, since the test-taker's performance can shape the course of an academic career. Nevertheless, experiencing excessive fear of examinations will only interfere with the test-takers ability to perform, and his/her chances to be successful.

There are a large variety of causes that can contribute to the development and sensation of test anxiety. These include, but are not limited to lack of performance and worrying about issues surrounding the test.

Lack of Preparation

Lack of preparation can be identified by the following behaviors or situations:

Not scheduling enough time to study, and therefore cramming the night before the test or exam
Managing time poorly, to create the sensation that there is not enough time to do everything
Failing to organize the text information in advance, so that the study material consists of the entire text and not simply the pertinent information
Poor overall studying habits

Worrying, on the other hand, can be related to both the test taker, or many other factors around him/her that will be affected by the results of the test. These include worrying about:

Previous performances on similar exams, or exams in general
How friends and other students are achieving
The negative consequences that will result from a poor grade or failure

There are three primary elements to test anxiety. Physical components, which involve the same typical bodily reactions as those to acute anxiety (to be discussed below). Emotional factors have to do with fear or panic. Mental or cognitive issues concerning attention spans and memory abilities.

Physical Signals

There are many different symptoms of test anxiety, and these are not limited to mental and emotional strain. Frequently there are a range of physical signals that will let a test taker know that he/she is suffering from test anxiety. These bodily changes can include the following:

Perspiring
Sweaty palms
Wet, trembling hands
Nausea
Dry mouth
A knot in the stomach
Headache
Faintness
Muscle tension
Aching shoulders, back and neck
Rapid heart beat
Feeling too hot/cold

To recognize the sensation of test anxiety, a test-taker should monitor him/herself for the following sensations:

The physical distress symptoms as listed above
Emotional sensitivity, expressing emotional feelings such as the need to cry or laugh too much, or a sensation of anger or helplessness
A decreased ability to think, causing the test-taker to blank out or have racing thoughts that are hard to organize or control.

Though most students will feel some level of anxiety when faced with a test or exam, the majority can cope with that anxiety and maintain it at a manageable level. However, those who cannot are faced with a very real and very serious condition, which can and should be controlled for the immeasurable benefit of this sufferer.

Naturally, these sensations lead to negative results for the testing experience. The most common effects of test anxiety have to do with nervousness and mental blocking.

Nervousness

Nervousness can appear in several different levels:

The test-taker's difficulty, or even inability to read and understand the questions on the test
The difficulty or inability to organize thoughts to a coherent form
The difficulty or inability to recall key words and concepts relating to the testing questions (especially essays)
The receipt of poor grades on a test, though the test material was well known by the test taker

Conversely, a person may also experience mental blocking, which involves:

Blanking out on test questions
Only remembering the correct answers to the questions when the test has already finished.

Fortunately for test anxiety sufferers, beating these feelings, to a large degree, has to do with proper preparation. When a test taker has a feeling of preparedness, then anxiety will be dramatically lessened.

The first step to resolving anxiety issues is to distinguish which of the two types of anxiety are being suffered. If the anxiety is a direct result of a lack of preparation, this should be considered a normal reaction, and the anxiety level (as opposed to the test results) shouldn't be anything to worry about. However, if, when adequately prepared, the test-taker still panics, blanks out, or seems to overreact, this is not a fully rational reaction. While this can be considered normal too, there are many ways to combat and overcome these effects.

Remember that anxiety cannot be entirely eliminated, however, there are ways to minimize it, to make the anxiety easier to manage. Preparation is one of the best ways to minimize test anxiety. Therefore the following techniques are wise in order to best fight off any anxiety that may want to build.

To begin with, try to avoid cramming before a test, whenever it is possible. By trying to memorize an entire term's worth of information in one day, you'll be shocking your system, and not giving yourself a very good chance to absorb the information. This is an easy path to anxiety, so for those who suffer from test anxiety, cramming should not even be considered an option.

Instead of cramming, work throughout the semester to combine all of the material which is presented throughout the semester, and work on it gradually as the course goes by, making sure to master the main concepts first, leaving minor details for a week or so before the test.

To study for the upcoming exam, be sure to pose questions that may be on the examination, to gauge the ability to answer them by integrating the ideas from your texts, notes and lectures, as well as any supplementary readings.

If it is truly impossible to cover all of the information that was covered in that particular term, concentrate on the most important portions, that can be covered very well. Learn these concepts as best as possible, so that when the test comes, a goal can be made to use these concepts as presentations of your knowledge.

In addition to study habits, changes in attitude are critical to beating a struggle with test anxiety. In fact, an improvement of the perspective over the entire test-taking experience can actually help a test taker to enjoy studying and therefore improve the overall experience. Be certain not to overemphasize the significance of the grade - know that the result of the test is neither a reflection of self worth, nor is it a measure of intelligence; one grade will not predict a person's future success.

To improve an overall testing outlook, the following steps should be tried:

Keeping in mind that the most reasonable expectation for taking a test is to expect to try to demonstrate as much of what you know as you possibly can.
Reminding ourselves that a test is only one test; this is not the only one, and there will be others.
The thought of thinking of oneself in an irrational, all-or-nothing term should be avoided at all costs.
A reward should be designated for after the test, so there's something to look forward to. Whether it be going to a movie, going out to eat, or simply visiting friends, schedule it in advance, and do it no matter what result is expected on the exam.

Test-takers should also keep in mind that the basics are some of the most important things, even beyond anti-anxiety techniques and studying. Never neglect the basic social, emotional and biological needs, in order to try to absorb information. In order to best achieve, these three factors must be held as just as important as the studying itself.

Study Steps

Remember the following important steps for studying:

Maintain healthy nutrition and exercise habits. Continue both your recreational activities and social pass times. These both contribute to your physical and emotional well being.
Be certain to get a good amount of sleep, especially the night before the test, because when you're overtired you are not able to perform to the best of your best ability.
Keep the studying pace to a moderate level by taking breaks when they are needed, and varying the work whenever possible, to keep the mind fresh instead of getting bored. When enough studying has been done that all the material that can be learned has been learned, and the test taker is prepared for the test, stop studying and do something relaxing such as listening to music, watching a movie, or taking a warm bubble bath.

There are also many other techniques to minimize the uneasiness or apprehension that is experienced along with test anxiety before, during, or even after the examination. In fact, there are a great deal of things that can be done to stop anxiety from interfering with lifestyle and performance. Again, remember that anxiety will not be eliminated entirely, and it shouldn't be. Otherwise that "up" feeling for exams would not exist, and most of us depend on that sensation to perform better than usual. However, this anxiety has to be at a level that is manageable.

Of course, as we have just discussed, being prepared for the exam is half the battle right away. Attending all classes, finding out what knowledge will be expected on the exam, and knowing the exam schedules are easy steps to lowering anxiety. Keeping up with work will remove the need to cram, and efficient study habits will eliminate wasted time. Studying should be done in an ideal location for concentration, so that it is simple to become interested in the material and give it complete attention. A method such as SQ3R (Survey, Question, Read, Recite, Review) is a wonderful key to follow to make sure that the study habits are as effective as possible, especially in the case of learning from a textbook. Flashcards are great techniques for memorization. Learning to take good notes will mean that notes will be full of useful information, so that less sifting will need to be done to seek out what is pertinent for studying. Reviewing notes after class and then again on occasion will keep the information fresh in the mind. From notes that have been taken summary sheets and outlines can be made for simpler reviewing.

A study group can also be a very motivational and helpful place to study, as there will be a sharing of ideas, all of the minds can work together, to make sure that everyone understands, and the studying will be made more interesting because it will be a social occasion.

Basically, though, as long as the test-taker remains organized and self confident, with efficient study habits, less time will need to be spent studying, and higher grades will be achieved.

To become self confident, there are many useful steps. The first of these is "self talk." It has been shown through extensive research, that self-talk for students who suffer from test anxiety, should be well monitored, in order to make sure that it contributes to self confidence as opposed to sinking the student. Frequently the self talk of test-anxious students is negative or self-defeating, thinking that everyone else is smarter and faster, that they always mess up, and that if they don't do well, they'll fail the entire course. It is important to decreasing anxiety that awareness is made of self talk. Try writing any negative self thoughts and then disputing them with a positive statement instead. Begin self-encouragement as though it was a friend speaking. Repeat positive statements to help reprogram the mind to believing in successes instead of failures.

Helpful Techniques

Other extremely helpful techniques include:

Self-visualization of doing well and reaching goals
While aiming for an "A" level of understanding, don't try to "overprotect" by setting your expectations lower. This will only convince the mind to stop studying in order to meet the lower expectations.
Don't make comparisons with the results or habits of other students. These are individual factors, and different things work for different people, causing different results.
Strive to become an expert in learning what works well, and what can be done in order to improve. Consider collecting this data in a journal.
Create rewards for after studying instead of doing things before studying that will only turn into avoidance behaviors.
Make a practice of relaxing - by using methods such as progressive relaxation, self-hypnosis, guided imagery, etc - in order to make relaxation an automatic sensation.
Work on creating a state of relaxed concentration so that concentrating will take on the focus of the mind, so that none will be wasted on worrying.
Take good care of the physical self by eating well and getting enough sleep.
Plan in time for exercise and stick to this plan.

Beyond these techniques, there are other methods to be used before, during and after the test that will help the test-taker perform well in addition to overcoming anxiety.

Before the exam comes the academic preparation. This involves establishing a study schedule and beginning at least one week before the actual date of the test. By doing this, the anxiety of not having enough time to study for the test will be automatically eliminated. Moreover, this will make the studying a much more effective experience, ensuring that the learning will be an easier process. This relieves much undue pressure on the test-taker.

Summary sheets, note cards, and flash cards with the main concepts and examples of these main concepts should be prepared in advance of the actual studying time. A topic should never be eliminated from this process. By omitting a topic because it isn't expected to be on the test is only setting up the test-taker for anxiety should it actually appear on the exam. Utilize the course syllabus for laying out the topics that should be studied. Carefully go over the notes that were made in class, paying special attention to any of the issues that the professor took special care to emphasize while lecturing in class. In the textbooks, use the chapter review, or if possible, the chapter tests, to begin your review.

It may even be possible to ask the instructor what information will be covered on the exam, or what the format of the exam will be (for example, multiple choice, essay, free form, true-false). Additionally, see if it is possible to find out how many questions will be on the test. If a review sheet or sample test has been offered by the professor, make good use of it, above anything else, for the preparation for the test. Another great resource for getting to know the examination is reviewing tests from previous semesters. Use these tests to review, and aim to achieve a 100% score on each of the possible topics. With a few exceptions, the goal that you set for yourself is the highest one that you will reach.

Take all of the questions that were assigned as homework, and rework them to any other possible course material. The more problems reworked, the more skill and confidence will form as a result. When forming the solution to a problem, write out each of the steps. Don't simply do head work. By doing as many steps on paper as possible, much clarification and therefore confidence will be formed. Do this with as many homework problems as possible, before checking the answers. By checking the answer after each problem, a reinforcement will exist, that will not be on the exam. Study situations should be as exam-like as possible, to prime the test-taker's system for the experience. By waiting to check the answers at the end, a psychological advantage will be formed, to decrease the stress factor.

Another fantastic reason for not cramming is the avoidance of confusion in concepts, especially when it comes to mathematics. 8-10 hours of study will become one hundred percent more effective if it is spread out over a week or at least several days, instead of doing it all in one sitting. Recognize that the human brain requires time in order to assimilate new material, so frequent breaks and a span of study time over several days will be much more beneficial.

Additionally, don't study right up until the point of the exam. Studying should stop a minimum of one hour before the exam begins. This allows the brain to rest and put things in their proper order. This will also provide the time to become as relaxed as possible when going into the examination room. The test-taker will also have time to eat well and eat sensibly. Know that the brain needs food as much as the rest of the body. With enough food and enough sleep, as well as a relaxed attitude, the body and the mind are primed for success.

Avoid any anxious classmates who are talking about the exam. These students only spread anxiety, and are not worth sharing the anxious sentimentalities.

Before the test also involves creating a positive attitude, so mental preparation should also be a point of concentration. There are many keys to creating a positive attitude. Should fears become rushing in, make a visualization of taking the exam, doing well, and seeing an A written on the paper. Write out a list of affirmations that will bring a feeling of confidence, such as "I am doing well in my English class," "I studied well and know my material," "I enjoy this class." Even if the affirmations aren't believed at first, it sends a positive message to the subconscious which will result in an alteration of the overall belief system, which is the system that creates reality.

If a sensation of panic begins, work with the fear and imagine the very worst! Work through the entire scenario of not passing the test, failing the entire course, and dropping out of school, followed by not getting a job, and pushing a shopping cart through the dark alley where you'll live. This will place things into perspective! Then, practice deep breathing and create a visualization of the opposite situation - achieving an "A" on the exam, passing the entire course, receiving the degree at a graduation ceremony.

On the day of the test, there are many things to be done to ensure the best results, as well as the most calm outlook. The following stages are suggested in order to maximize test-taking potential:

Begin the examination day with a moderate breakfast, and avoid any coffee or beverages with caffeine if the test taker is prone to jitters. Even people who are used to managing caffeine can feel jittery or light-headed when it is taken on a test day. Attempt to do something that is relaxing before the examination begins. As last minute cramming clouds the mastering of overall concepts, it is better to use this time to create a calming outlook.
Be certain to arrive at the test location well in advance, in order to provide time to select a location that is away from doors, windows and other distractions, as well as giving enough time to relax before the test begins.
Keep away from anxiety generating classmates who will upset the sensation of stability and relaxation that is being attempted before the exam.
Should the waiting period before the exam begins cause anxiety, create a self-distraction by reading a light magazine or something else that is relaxing and simple.

During the exam itself, read the entire exam from beginning to end, and find out how much time should be allotted to each individual problem. Once writing the exam, should more time be taken for a problem, it should be abandoned, in order to begin another problem. If there is time at the end, the unfinished problem can always be returned to and completed.

Read the instructions very carefully - twice - so that unpleasant surprises won't follow during or after the exam has ended.

When writing the exam, pretend that the situation is actually simply the completion of homework within a library, or at home. This will assist in forming a relaxed atmosphere, and will allow the brain extra focus for the complex thinking function.

Begin the exam with all of the questions with which the most confidence is felt. This will build the confidence level regarding the entire exam and will begin a quality momentum. This will also create encouragement for trying the problems where uncertainty resides.

Going with the "gut instinct" is always the way to go when solving a problem. Second guessing should be avoided at all costs. Have confidence in the ability to do well.

For essay questions, create an outline in advance that will keep the mind organized and make certain that all of the points are remembered. For multiple choice, read every answer, even if the correct one has been spotted - a better one may exist.

Continue at a pace that is reasonable and not rushed, in order to be able to work carefully. Provide enough time to go over the answers at the end, to check for small errors that can be corrected.

Should a feeling of panic begin, breathe deeply, and think of the feeling of the body releasing sand through its pores. Visualize a calm, peaceful place, and include all of the sights, sounds and sensations of this image. Continue the deep breathing, and take a few minutes to continue this with closed eyes. When all is well again, return to the test.

If a "blanking" occurs for a certain question, skip it and move on to the next question. There will be time to return to the other question later. Get everything done that can be done, first, to guarantee all the grades that can be compiled, and to build all of the confidence possible. Then return to the weaker questions to build the marks from there.

Remember, one's own reality can be created, so as long as the belief is there, success will follow. And remember: anxiety can happen later, right now, there's an exam to be written!

After the examination is complete, whether there is a feeling for a good grade or a bad grade, don't dwell on the exam, and be certain to follow through on the reward that was promised...and enjoy it! Don't dwell on any mistakes that have been made, as there is nothing that can be done at this point anyway.

Additionally, don't begin to study for the next test right away. Do something relaxing for a while, and let the mind relax and prepare itself to begin absorbing information again.

From the results of the exam - both the grade and the entire experience, be certain to learn from what has gone on. Perfect studying habits and work some more on confidence in order to make the next examination experience even better than the last one.

Learn to avoid places where openings occurred for laziness, procrastination and day dreaming.

Use the time between this exam and the next one to better learn to relax, even learning to relax on cue, so that any anxiety can be controlled during the next exam. Learn how to relax the body. Slouch in your chair if that helps. Tighten and then relax all of the different muscle groups, one group at a time, beginning with the feet and then working all the way up to the neck and face. This will ultimately relax the muscles more than they were to begin with. Learn how to breathe deeply and comfortably, and focus on this breathing going in and out as a relaxing thought. With every exhale, repeat the word "relax."

As common as test anxiety is, it is very possible to overcome it. Make yourself one of the test-takers who overcome this frustrating hindrance.

How to Overcome Your Fear of Math

If this article started by saying "Math," many of us would feel a shiver crawl up our spines, just by reading that simple word. Images of torturous years in those crippling desks of the math classes can become so vivid to our consciousness that we can almost smell those musty textbooks, and see the smudges of the #2 pencils on our fingers.

If you are still a student, feeling the impact of these sometimes overwhelming classroom sensations, you are not alone if you get anxious at just the thought of taking that compulsory math course. Does your heart beat just that much faster when you have to split the bill for lunch among your friends with a group of your friends? Do you truly believe that you simply don't have the brain for math? Certainly you're good at other things, but math just simply isn't one of them? Have you ever avoided activities, or other school courses because they appear to involve mathematics, with which you're simply not comfortable?

If any one or more of these "symptoms" can be applied to you, you could very well be suffering from a very real condition called "Math Anxiety."

It's not at all uncommon for people to think that they have some sort of math disability or allergy, when in actuality, their block is a direct result of the way in which they were taught math!

In the late 1950's with the dawning of the space age, New Math - a new "fuzzy math" reform that focuses on higher-order thinking, conceptual understanding and solving problems - took the country by storm. It's now becoming ever more clear that teachers were not supplied with the correct, practical and effective way in which they should be teaching new math so that students will understand the methods comfortably. So is it any wonder that so many students struggled so deeply, when their teachers were required to change their entire math systems without the foundation of proper training? Even if you have not been personally, directly affected by that precise event, its impact is still as rampant as ever.

Basically, the math teachers of today are either the teachers who began teaching the new math in the first place (without proper training) or they are the students of the math teachers who taught new math without proper training. Therefore, unless they had a unique, exceptional teacher, their primary, consistent examples of teaching math have been teachers using methods that are not conducive to the general understanding of the entire class. This explains why your discomfort (or fear) of math is not at all rare.

It is very clear why being called up to the chalk board to solve a math problem is such a common example of a terrifying situation for students - and it has very little to do with a fear of being in front of the class. Most of us have had a minimum of one humiliating experience while standing with chalk dusted fingers, with the eyes of every math student piercing through us. These are the images that haunt us all the way through adulthood. But it does not mean that we cannot learn math. It just means that we could be developing a solid case of math anxiety.

But what exactly is math anxiety? It's an very strong emotional sensation of anxiety, panic, or fear that people feel when they think about or must apply their ability to understand mathematics. Sufferers of math anxiety frequently believe that they are incapable of doing activities or taking classes that involve math skills. In fact, some people with math anxiety have developed such a fear that it has become a phobia; aptly named math phobia.

The incidence of math anxiety, especially among college students, but also among high school students, has risen considerably over the last 10 years, and currently this increase shows no signs of slowing down. Frequently students will even chose their college majors and programs based specifically on how little math will be compulsory for the completion of the degree.

The prevalence of math anxiety has become so dramatic on college campuses that many of these schools have special counseling programs that are designed to assist math anxious students to deal with their discomfort and their math problems.

Math anxiety itself is not an intellectual problem, as many people have been lead to believe; it is, in fact, an emotional problem that stems from improper math teaching techniques that have slowly built and reinforced these feelings. However, math anxiety can result in an intellectual problem when its symptoms interfere with a person's ability to learn and understand math.

The fear of math can cause a sort of "glitch" in the brain that can cause an otherwise clever person to stumble over even the simplest of math problems. A study by Dr. Mark H. Ashcraft of Cleveland State University in Ohio showed that college students who usually perform well, but who suffer from math anxiety, will suffer from fleeting lapses in their working memory when they are asked to perform even the most basic mental arithmetic. These same issues regarding memory were not present in the same students when they were required to answer questions that did not involve numbers. This very clearly demonstrated that the memory phenomenon is quite specific to only math.

So what exactly is it that causes this inhibiting math anxiety? Unfortunately it is not as simple as one answer, since math anxiety doesn't have one specific cause. Frequently math anxiety can result of a student's either negative experience or embarrassment with math or a math teacher in previous years.

These circumstances can prompt the student to believe that he or she is somehow deficient in his or her math abilities. This belief will consistently lead to a poor performance in math tests and courses in general, leading only to confirm the beliefs of the student's inability. This particular phenomenon is referred to as the "self-fulfilling prophecy" by the psychological community. Math anxiety will result in poor performance, rather than it being the other way around.

Dr. Ashcraft stated that math anxiety is a "It's a learned, almost phobic, reaction to math," and that it is not only people prone to anxiety, fear, or panic who can develop math anxiety. The image alone of doing math problems can send the blood pressure and heart rate to race, even in the calmest person.

The study by Dr. Ashcraft and his colleague Elizabeth P. Kirk, discovered that students who suffered from math anxiety were frequently stumped by issues of even the most basic math rules, such as "carrying over" a number, when performing a sum, or "borrowing" from a number when doing a subtraction. Lapses such as this occurred only on working memory questions involving numbers.

To explain the problem with memory, Ashcraft states that when math anxiety begins to take its effect, the sufferer experiences a rush of thoughts, leaving little room for the focus required to perform even the simplest of math problems. He stated that "you're draining away the energy you need for solving the problem by worrying about it."

The outcome is a "vicious cycle," for students who are sufferers of math anxiety. As math anxiety is developed, the fear it promotes stands in the way of learning, leading to a decrease in self-confidence in the ability to perform even simple arithmetic.

A large portion of the problem lies in the ways in which math is taught to students today. In the US, students are frequently taught the rules of math, but rarely will they learn why a specific approach to a math problems work. Should students be provided with a foundation of "deeper understanding" of math, it may prevent the development of phobias.

Another study that was published in the Journal of Experimental Psychology by Dr. Jamie Campbell and Dr. Qilin Xue of the University of Saskatchewan in Saskatoon, Canada, reflected the same concepts. The researchers in this study looked at university students who were educated in Canada and China, discovering that the Chinese students could generally outperform the Canadian-educated students when it came to solving complex math problems involving procedural knowledge - the ability to know how to solve a math problem, instead of simply having ideas memorized.

A portion of this result seemed to be due to the use of calculators within both elementary and secondary schools; while Canadians frequently used them, the Chinese students did not.

However, calculators were not the only issue. Since Chinese-educated students also outperformed Canadian-educated students in complex math, it is suggested that cultural factors may also have an impact. However, the short-cut of using the calculator may hinder the development of the problem solving skills that are key to performing well in math.

Though it is critical that students develop such fine math skills, it is easier said than done. It would involve an overhaul of the training among all elementary and secondary educators, changing the education major in every college.

Math Myths

One problem that contributes to the progression of math anxiety, is the belief of many math myths. These erroneous math beliefs include the following:
- Men are better in math than women - however, research has failed to demonstrate that there is any difference in math ability between the sexes.

- There is a single best way to solve a math problem - however, the majority of math problems can be solved in a number of different ways. By saying that there is only one way to solve a math problem, the thinking and creative skills of the student are held back.
- Some people have a math mind, and others do not - in truth, the majority of people have much more potential for their math capabilities than they believe of themselves.
- It is a bad thing to count by using your fingers - counting by using fingers has actually shown that an understanding of arithmetic has been established.
- People who are skilled in math can do problems quickly in their heads - in actuality, even math professors will review their example problems before they teach them in their classes.

The anxieties formed by these myths can frequently be perpetuated by a range of mind games that students seem to play with themselves. These math mind games include the following beliefs:
- I don't perform math fast enough - actually everyone has a different rate at which he or she can learn. The speed of the solving of math problems is not important as long as the student can solve it.
- I don't have the mind for math - this belief can inhibit a student's belief in him or herself, and will therefore interfere with the student's real ability to learn math.
- I got the correct answer, but it was done the wrong way - there is no single best way to complete a math problem. By believing this, a student's creativity and overall understanding of math is hindered.
- If I can get the correct answer, then it is too simple - students who suffer from math anxiety frequently belittle their own abilities when it comes to their math capabilities.
- Math is unrelated to my "real" life - math anxiety sufferers are only limiting their choices and freedoms for the rest of their life.

Fortunately, there are many ways to help those who suffer from math anxiety. Since math anxiety is a learned, psychological response to doing or thinking about math, that interferes with the sufferer's ability to understand and perform math, it is not at all a reflection of the sufferer's true math skills and abilities.

Helpful Strategies

Many strategies and therapies have been developed to help students to overcome their math anxious responses. Some of these helpful strategies include the following:

- Reviewing and learning basic arithmetic principles, techniques and methods. Frequently math anxiety is a result of the experience of many students with early negative situations, and these students have never truly developed a strong base in basic arithmetic, especially in the case of multiplication and fractions. Since math is a discipline that is built on an accumulative foundation, where the concepts are built upon gradually from simpler concepts, a student who has not achieved a solid basis in arithmetic will experience difficulty in learning higher order math. Taking a remedial math course, or a short math course that focuses on arithmetic can often make a considerable difference in reducing the anxious response that math anxiety sufferers have with math.

- Becoming aware of any thoughts, actions and feelings that are related to math and responses to math. Math anxiety has a different effect on different students. Therefore it is very important to become familiar with any reactions that the math anxiety sufferer may have about him/herself and the situation when math has been encountered. If the sufferer becomes aware of any irrational or unrealistic thoughts, it's possible to better concentrate on replacing these thoughts with more positive and realistic ones.

- Find help! Math anxiety, as we've mentioned, is a learned response, that is reinforced repeatedly over a period of time, and is therefore not something that can be eliminated instantaneously. Students can more effectively reduce their anxious responses with the help of many different services that are readily available. Seeking the assistance of a psychologist or counselor, especially one with a specialty in math anxiety, can assist the sufferer in performing an analysis of his/her psychological response to math, as well as learning anxiety management skills, and developing effective coping strategies. Other great tools are tutors, classes that teach better abilities to take better notes in math class, and other math learning aids.

- Learning the mathematic vocabulary will instantly provide a better chance for understanding new concepts. One major issue among students is the lack of understanding of the terms and vocabulary that are common jargon within math classes. Typically math classes will utilize words in a completely different way from the way in which they are utilized in all other subjects. Students easily mistake their lack of understanding the math terms with their mathematical abilities.

- Learning anxiety reducing techniques and methods for anxiety management. Anxiety greatly interferes with a student's ability to concentrate, think clearly, pay attention, and remember new concepts. When these same students can learn to relax, using anxiety management techniques, the student can regain his or her ability to control his or her emotional and physical symptoms of anxiety that interfere with the capabilities of mental processing.

- Working on creating a positive overall attitude about mathematics. Looking at math with a positive attitude will reduce anxiety through the building of a positive attitude.

- Learning to self-talk in a positive way. Pep talking oneself through a positive self talk can greatly assist in overcoming beliefs in math myths or the mind games that may be played. Positive self-talking is an effective way to replace the negative thoughts - the ones that create the anxiety. Even if the sufferer doesn't believe the statements at first, it plants a positive seed in the subconscious, and allows a positive outlook to grow.

Beyond this, students should learn effective math class, note taking and studying techniques. Typically, the math anxious students will avoid asking questions to save themselves from embarrassment. They will sit in the back of classrooms, and refrain from seeking assistance from the professor. Moreover, they will put off studying for math until the very last moment, since it causes them such substantial discomfort. Alone, or a combination of these negative behaviors work only to reduce the anxiety of the students, but in reality, they are actually building a substantially more intense anxiety.

There are many different positive behaviors that can be adopted by math anxious students, so that they can learn to better perform within their math classes:

- Sit near the front of the class. This way, there will be fewer distractions, and there will be more of a sensation of being a part of the topic of discussion.
- If any questions arise, ASK! If one student has a question, then there are certain to be others who have the same question but are too nervous to ask - perhaps because they have not yet learned how to deal with their own math anxiety.
- Seek extra help from the professor after class or during office hours.
- Prepare, prepare, prepare - read textbook material before the class, do the homework and work out any problems available within the textbook. Math skills are developed through practice and repetition, so the more practice and repetition, the better the math skills.
- Review the material once again after class, to repeat it another time, and to reinforce the new concepts that were learned.

Beyond these tactics that can be taken by the students themselves, teachers and parents need to know that they can also have a large impact on the reduction of math anxiety within students.

As parents and teachers, there is a natural desire to help students to learn and understand how they will one day utilize different math techniques within their everyday lives. But when the student or teacher displays the symptoms of a person who has had nightmarish memories regarding math, where hesitations then develop in the instruction of students, these fears are automatically picked up by the students and commonly adopted as their own.

However, it is possible for teachers and parents to move beyond their own fears to better educate students by overcoming their own hesitations and learning to enjoy math.

Begin by adopting the outlook that math is a beautiful, imaginative or living thing. Of course, we normally think of mathematics as numbers that can be added or subtracted, multiplied or divided, but that is simply the beginning of it.

By thinking of math as something fun and imaginative, parents and teachers can teach children different ways to manipulate numbers, for example in balancing a checkbook. Parents rarely tell their children that math is everywhere around us; in nature, art, and even architecture. Usually, this is because they were never shown these relatively simple connections. But that pattern can break very simply through the participation of parents and teachers.

The beauty and hidden wonders of mathematics can easily be emphasized through a focus that can open the eyes of students to the incredible mathematical patterns that arise everywhere within the natural world. Observations and discussions can be made into things as fascinating as spider webs, leaf patterns, sunflowers and even coastlines. This makes math not only beautiful, but also inspiring and (dare we say) fun!

Pappas Method

For parents and teachers to assist their students in discovering the true wonders of mathematics, the techniques of Theoni Pappas can easily be applied, as per her popular and celebrated book "Fractals, Googols and Other Mathematical Tales." Pappas used to be a math phobia sufferer and created a fascinating step-by-step program for parents and teachers to use in order to teach students the joy of math.

Her simple, constructive step-by-step program goes as follows:

Don't let your fear of math come across to your kids - Parents must be careful not to perpetuate the mathematical myth - that math is only for specially talented "math types." Strive not to make comments like; "they don't like math" or "I have never been good at math." When children overhear comments like these from their primary role models they begin to dread math before even considering a chance of experiencing its wonders. It is important to encourage your children to read and explore the rich world of mathematics, and to practice mathematics without imparting negative biases.

Don't immediately associate math with computation (counting) - It is very important to realize that math is not just numbers and computations, but a realm of exciting ideas that touch every part of our lives -from making a telephone call to how the hair grows on someone's head. Take your children outside and point out real objects that display math concepts. For example, show them the symmetry of a leaf or angles on a building. Take a close look at the spirals in a spider web or intricate patterns of a snowflake.

Help your child understand why math is important - Math improves problem solving, increases competency and should be applied in different ways. It's the same as reading. You can learn the basics of reading without ever enjoying a novel. But, where's the excitement in that? With math, you could stop with the basics. But why when there is so much more to be gained by a fuller understanding? Life is so much more enriching when we go beyond the basics. Stretch your children's minds to become involved in mathematics in ways that will not only be practical but also enhance their lives.
Make math as "hands on" as possible - Mathematicians participate in mathematics. To really experience math encourage your child to dig in and tackle problems in creative ways. Help them learn how to manipulate numbers using concrete references they understand as well as things they can see or touch. Look for patterns everywhere, explore shapes and symmetries. How many octagons do you see each day on the way to the grocery store? Play math puzzles and games and then encourage your child to try to invent their own. And, whenever possible, help your child realize a mathematical conclusion with real and tangible results. For example, measure out a full glass of juice with a measuring cup and then ask your child to drink half. Measure what is left. Does it measure half of a cup?

Read books that make math exciting:
Fractals, Googols and Other Mathematical Tales introduces an animated cat who explains fractals, tangrams and other mathematical concepts you've probably never heard of to children in terms they can understand. This book can double as a great text book by using one story per lesson.
A Wrinkle in Time is a well-loved classic, combining fantasy and science.

The Joy of Mathematics helps adults explore the beauty of mathematics that is all around.

The Math Curse is an amusing book for 4-8 year olds.

The Gnarly Gnews is a free, humorous bi-monthly newsletter on mathematics.

The Phantom Tollbooth is an Alice in Wonderland-style adventure into the worlds of words and numbers.

Use the internet to help your child explore the fascinating world of mathematics.

Web Math provides a powerful set of math-solvers that gives you instant answers to the stickiest problems.

Math League has challenging math materials and contests for fourth grade and above.

Silver Burdett Ginn Mathematics offers Internet-based math activities for grades K-6.

The Gallery of Interactive Geometry is full of fascinating, interactive geometry activities.

Math is very much like a language of its own. And like any second language, it will get rusty if it is not practiced enough. For that reason, students should always be looking into new ways to keep understanding and brushing up on their math skills, to be certain that foundations do not crumble, inhibiting the learning of new levels of math.

There are many different books, services and websites that have been developed to take the fear out of math, and to help even the most uncertain student develop self confidence in his or her math capabilities.

There is no reason for math or math classes to be a frightening experience, nor should it drive a student crazy, making them believe that they simply don't have the "math brain" that is needed to solve certain problems.

There are friendly ways to tackle such problems and it's all a matter of dispelling myths and creating a solid math foundation.

Concentrate on re-learning the basics and feeling better about yourself in math, and you'll find that the math brain you've always wanted was there all along.

Additional Bonus Material

Due to our efforts to try to keep this book to a manageable length, we've created a link that will give you access to all of your additional bonus material.

Please visit http://www.mometrix.com/bonus948/tsi to access the information.

CPSIA information can be obtained
at www.ICGtesting.com
Printed in the USA
LVOW04*1730060318
568845LV00019B/333/P

9 781516 705399